A Ray of Darkness

ROWAN WILLIAMS

A Ray of Darkness

Sermons and Reflections

COWLEY PUBLICATIONS
Cambridge, Massachusetts

Published in the United States of America by Cowley Publications, a division of the Society of Saint John the Evangelist. No portion of this book may be reproduced, stored in or introduced into a retrieval system, or transmitted, in any form or by any means-including photocopying-without the prior written permission of Cowley Publications, except in the case of brief quotations embedded in critical articles and reviews.

Published in England in 1994 by Darton Longman & Todd under the title *Open to Judgement*.

Dedication
To Canon James Edmund Crowden Hughes
Vicar of All Saints, Oystermouth, 1954-80
in homage

Acknowledgments
Bellew Publishing, London, for permission to reprint "The Touch of God," originally included in *Tradition and Unity: Sermons Published in Honour of Robert Runcie*, ed. Dan Cohn-Sherbok, 1991.
Pan Books (Pan Macmillan) for permission to use the passage from Annie Dillard, *Teaching a Stone to Talk: Expeditions and Encounters* (London, 1984), quoted on p. 98.

Library of Congress Cataloging-in-Publication Data:
Williams, Rowan, 1950-
    A ray of darkness : sermons and reflections / Rowan Williams.
        p. cm.
    Includes bibliographical references.
    ISBN 1-56101-112-6
    1. Sermons, English. 2. Anglican Communion—Sermons. 3. Church of England—Sermons. I. Title.
BV4254.2.W55   1995
252' .03—dc20
                                            95-4253
                                            CIP

Cover design: Gary Ragaglia

This book was printed in the United States of America on acid-free paper.

THIRD PRINTING

Cowley Publications
907 Massachusetts Avenue
Cambridge, Massachusetts 02139
800-225-1534 • www.cowley.org

Contents

Testing Questions

Callings

Celebrating People

Celebrating Occasions

Mission and Spirituality

Introduction

There is always something a bit odd about a collection of sermons. Apart from the echoes of Victorian self-importance that "Collected Sermons" tend to rouse, every preacher knows that a sermon is a particular *event*, far more than a text. It is a moment when you try to make a connection between a specific group of people in a specific time and place and the resources of the Christian vision in its historic wholeness. You try to bring to bear a vast range of words, pictures, doctrines on the problems of the here and now, and you also allow your perception of the needs of the here and now to shape your view of the tradition you draw on, to direct you to *this* rather than *that* in the Bible or the creed. The situation may bring to life a text or doctrine that had seemed abstract and remote: *this*, you say to yourself, is what I need to help me, help us, think and pray our way through the challenges before us. Next week, it may look different. The priorities will have changed, different things will be coming alive and pressing to be spoken.

So the best sermons are, I strongly suspect, those "written in water" (or on the backs of envelopes): the ones that arise out of a deep and patient knowledge of the people you're talking to, and a freedom to let their lives and their questions invade your continuing meditation on the Bible and the history of Christian thinking so as to pinpoint, for this moment only, what in these resources God might want to be heard *today*. A sermon is not a lecture, not a vehicle for instruction and nothing else, certainly not a vehicle for bright ideas and speculations. Good sermons happen when the twofold listening—to tradition and to the present—really becomes a listening to and for God, so that something emerges almost begging to be put into words. As Walter Brueggemann has wonderfully put it in a recent book on preaching, a true sermon discloses not simply truth but life, "life unclosed, life made open." He continues,

The preacher renders a world not known in advance. It requires no great cleverness to speak such a world, but it requires closeness to those texts that know secrets that mediate life....The preaching moment is a moment for the gift of God's life in the midst of our tired alienation.[1]

So the written sermon becomes something rather different from the moment of preaching. If there is a justification for it, I suppose it is that it might suggest a *method*, a worked example of doing theology in a particular way: reflecting on God in that strange "in betweenness" of trying to listen to text and tradition and trying to listen to a particular situation. The pieces included in this book are, in fact, rather untypical, as I normally prefer to preach without a full text; but for one reason or another, certain occasions have required something a bit more formal and organized, and I have managed to write a full script. The result is that most of these are more "literary" than I suspect a good sermon should be, certainly in these days. But I hope they will still show at least a little of the workings that make up the moment of preaching. A few of them have actually been transcribed from tape recordings and edited slightly for coherence, and therefore stand much closer to the spoken word than most of the rest. One sermon has been reconstructed from notes; having been more than once invited to preach to student congregations on the nature of Christian sexual ethics, I adapted in several different ways a single basic outline, and the sermon on this subject here is a conflation from a number of occasions. Apart from this, however, and a few corrections and tidyings-up, the texts are pretty much as delivered.

Many of them were originally written for students; some were given as homilies to the Sisters of the Love of God at Fairacres; several began life at matins in the cathedral at Oxford; and a number were delivered in parishes. I have added two lectures on "Mission and Spirituality" that formed the Pitt Lectures at the Berkeley Divinity School in Yale during October, 1991. I happily acknowledge my debt of gratitude to a large number of people who helped, over the years, with typing and otherwise preserving

---

[1] Walter Brueggemann, *Finally Comes the Poet: Daring Speech for Proclamation* (Minneapolis: Fortress Press, 1989), pp. 10, 41.

many of these pieces, and to all those who said, "I'd like to read that," though I'm realistically aware that this probably meant, "I didn't understand a word of that...."

Penny Green at Westcott House offered to type some of the addresses given to ordinands there. Sally-Ann Ford did the same for several sermons given in Christ Church Cathedral, and Sister Martha Reeves most generously volunteered to tackle others delivered there and also produced a miraculously tidy and accurate copy of the Pitt Lectures from my manuscript. The sisters at Fairacres have helped with transcribing tapes, as have others whose names I don't know in various churches. And Hazel Paling, my present secretary in Newport, has dealt with a large number of texts, with a patience and care that I have found entirely characteristic. Many friends and critics in the congregations also deserve my thanks, and I feel a special gratitude to the communities in Oxford where I preached most regularly in the cathedral and in St. Alban's Church, Cowley. I must mention too all those who helped to make me so welcome at Yale in 1991, especially the Rev. Gail Freeman and the Rev. Dr. Philip Turner, Dean of the Berkeley Divinity School.

Every married preacher knows that his or her spouse is their most candid critic; so my love and thanks as always to Jane, and to Rhiannon, who has sat through her father's effusions with not-quite-detached resignation so many times. The dedication of this collection expresses my abiding love and admiration for the priest who first showed me what preaching might be; who taught me by example what a Christian pastor should be; and who made it clear to me and many others that the gospel can enlarge both mind and imagination. *Hwyl a thangnefedd iddo fe.*

Rowan Williams
Newport, November 1993

The Word Was Made Flesh

1

Advent

A university sermon

Advent pulls the imagination in two directions. We turn our minds to the universal longing for God that is given voice in the Jewish scriptures, the yearning toward the "desire of all nations." In the cycle of the great Advent antiphons that begin with *O Sapientia* on 16 December, the phrase comes twice, in the sixth and seventh texts: *O Rex gentium,* "O King of nations and their desire"; *O Emmanuel,* "desire of all nations and their salvation." Christmas is the moment of recognition, the moment when what we have always secretly known is set out in plain and fleshly terms. And at the same time, "Woe unto you who desire the day of the Lord" and "Who may abide the day of his coming? For he is like a refiner's fire." This morning's Old Testament lesson reinforces this:

> The loftiness of man shall be bowed down...and the Lord alone shall be exalted in that day....And they shall go into the holes of the rocks, and into the caves of the earth, for fear of the Lord, and for the glory of his majesty, when he ariseth to shake terribly the earth.

Christmas is a beauty that is the beginning of terror: the Burning Babe, who has come to cast fire upon the earth. Before his presence, the idols fall and shatter.

In other words, Advent is about the essential ambiguity of our religiousness. We live, as human beings, in an enormous hunger to be spoken to, to be touched, to be judged and loved and absolved. We live—at some level—in the awareness that there are things we cannot do for ourselves. No human being alone can teach herself language; no human being alone can know himself loved. And the whole human race alone cannot assure itself of its worth or interest, its dignity and lovableness, its responsibility. When no reality over against us pronounces a word of judgment or a word of affirmation, how do we know we are *worth* judging? The twentieth century has been in full flight from certain conceptions of personal morality, but what age has ever suffered from so acute an awareness of collective responsibility? Who shall absolve us from the guilt of the Holocaust? Colonialism? The Enlightenment? The failure of the Enlightenment? Who could absolve us from the guilt of a nuclear catastrophe? The appalling moral anxiousness of our age is an oblique recognition that the human being as such waits to hear something; and when we have collectively denied the possibility of hearing something from beyond our corporate culture, we expose ourselves to deep worries about our humanness.

> Man did not lose his self in the modern age but rather became incommunicado, being able neither to speak for himself nor to be spoken to...he becomes invisible. That is why people in the modern age took photographs by the million: to prove despite their deepest suspicions to the contrary that they were not invisible.[1]

It is the same writer who wryly observes that we are obsessed with the idea of being contacted by extraterrestrial beings, and that we have a deep and yearning credulity about this beneath all our skepticism. We long to know that we are addressed. And this is where the ambiguity comes in: we fantasize about what such an address might be; we project onto the empty space before us the voices we need to hear. *Close Encounters of the Third Kind* remains a haunting fiction—a story of extra-terrestrial visitation in which the "aliens" turn out to have the ghostly shapes and faces of a lost childhood. The menacing stranger is, after all, only our own forgotten innocence. It is a striking secular parody of the Christian story, and one that points up the questionableness of our desire. What if our longing to hear a word spoken to us from beyond simply generates a loud echo of our need to be told we are all right, we have never fundamentally gone astray, we have never *really* left an undifferentiated Paradise? But our longing to hear from outside our frontiers is likely to be mixed with appre-

---

1 Walker Percy, *The Message in the Bottle* (New York, 1986), p. 26.

hension about what is completely different. The voice from beyond may assure us that we are not invisible; can it assure us that *we* are heard, taken seriously, valued and understood? Best to be on the safe side and prescribe what we shall hear. Even the language of the grand impersonal beauty of the cosmic void—so dear to a certain kind of semi-popular scientist and the metaphysics of Mr. Don Cupitt—is just as much a projection, a fiction, a noble and unmoved classical countenance outfacing the misery of human affairs, somehow consoling by being indestructible.

Our longings remind us of the essential human fact that we are talked and touched into life, and that a human race struggling to do all its talking and touching for itself faces a paralyzing unhappiness and anxiety. And these longings are also fraught with the danger of illusion, the making of idols to meet our needs. The Israelites pour their treasures into a mold and out comes the Golden Calf; as if surprised, they cry, "Here is God," as if they had not themselves determined the shape of the outcome.

"In that day a man shall cast his idols of silver, and his idols of gold, which they made each one for himself to worship, to the moles and to the bats." For the people of God in Jewish scripture, loyalty to the covenant meant above all the forsaking of idols: the task is not to make sense of the world, beginning from unaided human resource, but to let ourselves be *given* sense purely by the summons of God. This was Israel's own story: being led out of slavery and given shape and solidity by the unexpected presence and pressure of God. Israel's hostility to idols is a measure of the recognition that what I make to meet my needs cannot set me free, cannot give me a new and assured reality. The eyes of the idol are my own, looking back at me; I am still incommunicado.

And in Advent, in that day, we all become—as it has been said—Jews once more. We relearn the lessons of the first covenant: that we cannot make God, however we long for him; that we must be surprised, ambushed, and carried off by God if we are to be kept from idols. The loyalty of the Jewish people to God is the fierce preservation of such a story: there is no sense to be made by thinking or imagining, only the violent upheaval by which Israel became a single community of obedience and praise. That loyalty remains in the Jewish people: in the refusal to "make sense" of, to explain and domesticate the nightmare upheaval of this century, the Holocaust; refusing comfort, refusing reconciliation with the memory—this can be the most potent of witnesses to the faith of the Mosaic covenant. No idols, no images to mirror back to us what we long to hear.

The Christian in Advent needs to listen to that, listen to such a degree that this season becomes *both* a season of joyful expectancy *and* a season of poverty—the knowledge that we cannot talk and touch ourselves into life, the deep poverty of the imagination which can only stand helplessly before the outrages and miseries of our world, utterly at a loss for a word of meaning or hope to speak. We are here at all, celebrating Advent (as the Jew celebrates the Passover) because there *has been* a word spoken, a word of unexpected interruption, a word that establishes for good the difference between the God we expect and the God who comes, a word that shows us once and for all what an idol looks like in the face of truth. We are here because those acts we call liberation and absolution have turned our history into new and strange courses—the history of Israel (up to the present time), the history of a church struggling to keep open its doors to all people. Yet we cannot imagine how tomorrow and the day after that form of liberation and absolution will renew itself, how the word will go on making itself heard to renew the world. We are perpetually looking to and giving thanks for an uncovenanted event, a transforming newness, the history of Israel and Jesus; we are perpetually "on the eve" of God's coming, knowing and not knowing what it will be. Advent insists that we stay for a while in this tension of being "on the eve," if only in order that the new thing we celebrate at Christmas may have a chance of being truly new for us, not a stale and pious cliché.

There is a risk for any religion that looks to accomplished events as its foundation. The word once unexpectedly spoken becomes *ours,* is absorbed more and more into our needs and fancies and preferences. Once it was strange, now it is familiar and idolatrous. The Advent tension is a way of learning again that God is God: that between even our deepest and holiest longing and the reality of God is a gap which only grace can cross; otherwise we are alone again, incommunicado, our signals and symbols bounced back to us off the glassy walls of the universe.

"The idea of God remains uncompletable for humanity," wrote Hans Urs von Balthasar. We begin building a bridge from two ends—philosophical questing for unity and meaning, and mythological interest in a divine life that is personal and *engage;* but "the idea cannot complete the bridge spar." Historical action alone closes the gap, the *discovery* all at once of a unity existing not as a theory but as a community of love and worship held together in response to the unexpected moment when history turns and there is disclosed "a total and presuppositionless love."[2]

If we keep Advent faithfully, we shall know a little of how the word of this love can be freely heard only when we *recognize* the power of our urge to idolatry. Advent, we have said, sets out before us the richness of religious *eros*. It is a season of beautiful, elegiac hymns, voicing our longing to be spoken to, judged, and absolved. But in its deeper aspect, its pushing of us back into the experience of Israel and Israel's unconsoled rejection of idols, it shows us also the danger of religious *eros*, its capacity to become another vehicle for human self-reflection. The Christian, in the Advent season above all, must learn something of God's own simultaneous "yes" and "no" to all religious aspiration and expectation. God, say the mystics, is *innominabile* and *omninominabile*, the one for whom no name is adequate, the one of whom all true words speak.

Only the newness of a new turn of history, the specific newness of new words, acts, and relations, can show the God who will not allow himself to be caught in the circle of ideas alone, and so can show the God who exceeds both the fiercest longing and the profoundest speculation of creatures. Because Advent tells us to look for mystery, absolute grace, and freedom in a fleshly human face, within the mobile form of our shared history, it brings our idolatry—philosophical and mythological alike—to judgment. Our hunger *is* met, we *are* talked and touched into new and everlasting life, our desire *is* answered—but only insofar as we have lived in an Advent of the religious imagination, struggling to let God be God, casting our idols of silver and gold to the moles and bats, "for fear of the Lord and for the glory of his majesty," longing simply for our God to show himself as God in the "total and presuppositionless love" of his incarnate speech to us.

---

2 *The Von Balthasar Reader*, ed. Medard Kehl and Werner Löser (New York and Edinburgh, 1982), pp. 101-102.

2

Knowing and Loving

Knowledge is power, we are told. And perhaps the place we realize this most clearly and acutely is where knowledge of other people is concerned. If we know something of the secret of another person's heart, we are often aware of enormous power in our hands—weapons to hurt, even destroy. Something very vulnerable and fragile has been put into our grasp—because most people's hearts are pretty fragile—and there is sometimes the fearsomely strong urge to *use* it to turn against someone, to lay them under obligation to us, to exert a kind of blackmail. Weakness invites crushing: that is one of the terrible things about it. (I suspect I am not the only one who has to suppress the urge to break eggs or drop cut-glass vases just because I *know* they're fragile.) And we know this too from the other side. I have shared something very private, perhaps very humiliating or embarrassing, with my friends. And as soon as they've left, I'm in an anguish of fear and regret: should I have done that? Am I safe? There is a sensation of having "signed over" something, put myself at the mercy of others: I have put a knife into their hands and bared my breast, and there's only myself to blame if they stab me with it.

And it isn't even true, alas, that it's somehow better if the other person has had comparable experience to yours. It's quite possible for someone to say, "I know exactly what you mean; I had the same experience, but I came to an opposite conclusion." That is, I've wrestled with this problem and conquered it; why the hell can't you? The sheer, dreadful, irreducible difference between person and person, never solved, never healed. I may feel I want to talk—for example—about my sexual temptations to someone I know has experienced that particular little Calvary, but I'm quite likely to find the chilling, utterly humiliating and devaluing reply, "I don't see the problem. Yes. I experience all this, but I come to terms with it" in this way or that. That doesn't help, and it intensifies my sense that I can't even trust my judgment of my own situation. There's no such thing as automatic empathy.

All this really comes to one thing: the terrible threat of knowledge without love. Is anything in human relations more frightening than that? And how often has the Christian picture of God concentrated on God's *knowledge* in a way that is totally oppressive? "O Lord, thou hast searched me out and known me. Whither shall I go then from Thy presence?" That can be a cry of despair; we have no privacy before the terrible omnipresent eye of God. And our fear of exposing ourselves to any other—in therapy, in the confessional, or simply in ordinary friendship—has a lot to do with that primitive dread of knowledge without love. There are no guarantees that what we show won't produce revulsion or worse, perhaps contempt or amusement. In Dostoyevsky's novel *The Possessed*, the central figure, Stavrogin, determines to make a public confession of a particularly appalling episode in his earlier years and goes to read this confession to a local monk with a reputation for sanctity, Bishop Tikhon. Tikhon listens without a word of condemnation, then shocks Stavrogin by asking if he can bear not the hostility but the *mockery* of the world. Stavrogin leaves in disgust and fear, unable to publish his confession. He cannot face that ultimate rejection, laughter.

We can see all this clearly if we think about our own knowledge of ourselves as well. To know about ourselves, our histories and motivations, can be a cause of self-hatred, self-despising. Thomas Merton has a passage somewhere about the "humility of hell": the damned *know* their sins absolutely thoroughly and loathe themselves all the more for it. It is an added refinement of self-torture. St. Bernard in his sermons on the Song of Songs says something similar when he refers to two kinds of humility: one that is "without warmth," just naked self-knowledge, the vision of our miserable selfish motives and deeds, that is worlds away from the other kind, the "warm" humility of willing self-denial. To know ourselves doesn't make us love ourselves—often quite the contrary. And if we're afraid of being known by others, so too we're afraid of knowing ourselves, because we don't and can't know whether we'll be able to love what we find and live with what we find.

Iris Murdoch, in her novel *The Black Prince,* makes one of her characters say, "Curiosity is a kind of charity." The falsity of that is as apparent in the book as it is in our experience. It is an unscrupulous rationalization of the lust for power which can be hidden in curiosity, the diabolical thirst to know without loving, to *substitute* knowing for loving. Anyone entering on a way of life that will involve hearing other people's secrets must become aware of the deeply ambivalent element present in his or her motivation: the desire for power over other people that priests, teachers, psychiatrists, and many others are so often afraid to admit to themselves. People *are* going to put their hearts in your hands again and again, and unless you face the massive dangers at work here—recognize that you are probably the sort of person who *needs* to see the hearts of others—the consequences will be destructive. You won't know how much damage you can do.

But don't think of this as an exclusively negative thing. People open their hearts because they have to, and people ask others to open their hearts because they have to. All of them, on both sides, are compelled by the magnetism of *truth.* I may dread the rejection of the person to whom I confess, but can I live with lies, fantasies, and public roles? I may fear the damage my probing may do, but can I be content if my friend offers me only a superficial mask? In any case, these things cannot and will not be forced; it's only by long, careful practice in both speaking and listening that we shall recognize "right moments" and respond with *accurate* sensitivity to the needs of someone else. And one of the things that is required from the "counselor" is a kind of pastoral imagination—the ability not to see others in terms of me, but me in terms of others; not just relating their experiences to my similar ones, but trying to sense the experience as they are experiencing it, seeing with their eyes, feeling with their nerves. This is the "ecstasy" of love, the ability (as St. Thomas Aquinas said) to "go out" from yourself and to understand others as they are in themselves and for their own sake.

And it is of course God who teaches us this imagination. For God's knowledge of us is not the dreadful, stifling omnipresence I spoke of earlier, the all-seeing eye in the middle of heaven. When St. John tells us that our Lord "knew what was in us," he is pointing to something very different, what Langland in *Piers Plowman* called "kind" knowing—knowing by kinship—and what scholastic philosophers called (unpromisingly) "knowledge by connaturality": feeling with our nerves, seeing with our eyes, "made like us in every respect except sin." This is the complete ecstasy of God, entering into the morass of human subjectivity and human motivation. Whatever we may want to say in detail about the doctrine of the Incarnation, it seems to me an indispensable part of our gospel to be able to say that God has been, and *is*, "inside" human motivation. "He knoweth whereof we are made." He is capable of this unparalleled act of imagination, of knowing what it is to be a creature as well as creator, knowing what it is to be in doubt, in agony, in temptation, in darkness and abandonment, in hell. There is the lesson of ecstasy, understanding the other in the other's own terms.

Yet perhaps the doubt remains. W. H. Auden, in his "oratorio" *For the Time Being*, makes Herod say that if God has lived as a human being, he will now expect everyone to live a perfect life because it's been shown to be possible—a very alarming doctrine indeed, and a not unfamiliar one in some kinds of Christianity. God can say to us, "I've had this experience but it didn't defeat *me*," which will be a very depressing thing to hear on the day of judgment. But surely we have our corrective in the gospels themselves. Not only do we have the grand schematic doctrinal story of the God who identifies with humanity, we have also the particular local history of Jesus of Nazareth, whose compassion was such that he could be represented by St. John as saying, "I judge no one." It is usually frivolous, if not blasphemous, to speculate about Jesus' state of mind, but it is hard not to feel in our Lord's responses to the sinful an element of sheer visceral pity. "Where are your accusers? Is there no one who condemns you? Neither do I condemn you." Jesus was tempted as we are: if Gethsemane gives us any insight, he was tried in ways from which most of us would shrink. And what his struggles seem to have produced was a sense of the *precariousness* of goodness, love, and fidelity so profound and strong that no failure or error could provoke his condemnation, except the error of those legalists who could not understand that very precariousness. To Christ, the sinner is a victim more than a criminal. He knows what is in us. He is within human motivation and understands just how free and how unfree we are. He knows the measure of our own responsibility better than we ever can ourselves. He is a high priest who knows our weakness and whom, then, we can approach without fear.

That sense of precariousness ("there but for the grace of God...") is perhaps the only thing that can be relied on to lead our knowledge into love, into true sympathy, true identification, into weeping with those who weep. Knowledge gives power, leverage, advantage; only the sense of *our* frailty can save it from destroying. Even where love of ourselves is concerned, it is, ultimately, the grace and acceptance of God that lets us know we are lovable, that saves us from self-condemnation ("God is greater than our conscience").

> Why all the souls that were were forfeit once
> And He that might the vantage best have took
> Found out the remedy.

Three of Shakespeare's most beautiful lines, summing up unforgettably the essential character of God's saving work. God has the advantage in his Godhead, and he lays that aside. He has the advantage—so we believe—in the sinlessness of his humanity, and he lays that aside in the humility and compassion that refuse to judge and only love and serve. So he indeed finds out the remedy. In him we see what is almost unimaginable in our bitter and tangled relationships—perfect knowledge united with perfect acceptance. He knows what is in us, he has searched us out and knows us and understands our thoughts; in the cross he shows us the very depths of our destructive refusal of health and life, our violence and fear. And through everything he accepts us still.

Knowledge is power. But God does not deal with us in power of that sort. Where we are vulnerable and fragile, it is *he* who is wounded and broken. He will not break the bruised reed or quench the smoldering flax, but carries all our hurt in himself. So we may take to him our whole selves, in the sure trust that nothing will be thrown back at us to wound or destroy. And that is the gospel whose ministers we are. That is the measure of clear-eyed love and loving knowledge for us to pray for—praying that if others come and give us their secret we may by God's grace merit their trust, soften their fear, feel their trouble as they do, and bring it *from* them, *in* us, *to* God. "Forgive one another as God in Christ has forgiven you." Understand one another as God in Christ has understood you. *Know* one another as God in Christ has known you, and in no other way.

3

Waiting on God

A sermon for Lady Day 1992, preached to members and friends of the Movement for the Ordination of Women

When she first sensed the urgency of God's Word inside her, the longing of God to be here, in this body, "in my acts and words," the first feeling was a mixture of fear and exhilaration. God had begun to exist in her belly, not through the work of any man, but out of a kind of meeting of her longing and God's. How can anyone carry God, bring God to birth in the world? How can you carry the cup without spilling it? But what if the cup is no fragile container but a deep well that can never run dry? Then you know it isn't just your resource, your decision, but God's insistent generosity, carrying you as you carry God.

Her body changed, her face changed. She was no longer on the edge of things, a mere extra in the spiritual drama. As she went around, her body spoke to other women: others with unlikely pregnancies, early and late, recognized her, and what was in them leapt up in greeting. Conspiracies of hope.

Her body changed. Men and some women stared and began to ask about legitimacy; some friends slipped away. Her partner, even, was for a while wretched and embarrassed. She began to think: Why does God ask this when it makes me so exposed to their doubt and cynicism? Things were no longer simple. Was God's longing bound up with her humiliations? Was God another male working out his fancy through her flesh?

Her body changed and rebelled. She was sick with her new lodger, her new intruder, the alien growth of God within her. At times her body itself seemed a humiliation, a nauseating burden; as if all the old words about earthy uncleanliness were right after all, as if a woman's body really were a compound of disgusting things. Sometimes she would wash her clothes obsessively, over and over, to get the smell of nausea off them. What did it mean that women could evoke such shame and fear and disgust in men? For a while some of that shame made sense, and her body with its heavy burdens seemed an awful stranger, and she could cry, "Why did you make me thus?"

The first real movements inside were like waking from a bad dream. Feet and hands pushing, a whole life suddenly there like a lover's footstep on the stairs, bringing you back from terrors and suspicions to what you know and trust. It is life after all: not just something about me but something with authority, something more than me, that will make a difference to more than me. "But," she thought, "that means I don't know what will happen when this does come into the world: here is something that is most profoundly me, my flesh and blood, the sheer stuff of me, depending on me and vulnerable to me; and yet it is not me and will be strange and impenetrable to me." And sometimes, then, she felt afraid again, and sometimes the old anger came back: "Why give me a task so full of contradictions, a path of knives to tread?" Too much hope for comfort; too much restlessness for comfort; and at the same time too much solid reality, too much vigor and promise, for the anger and the fear to fill the whole sky.

Some births are terrible. There are miscarriages and still births. Sometimes she wondered if this would end in death, not birth; and sometimes, looking around, she thought that was what the staring faces wanted. Not a birth, a beginning, but a great bloody wound, with life running out like blood. And she wondered how to live with that, with the whole thing ending in loss and diminution, all the risks for nothing. All she could think of was that there was something that couldn't be lost: knowing that once her flesh had been what God wanted so as to make God's Word present, and that perhaps the fear of terrible loss could also be God speaking. She didn't let herself think a great deal about that, because she didn't know—and no one else could tell her—how to live through a wound like that so as to make even the loss speak of God. And if it could speak of God, it would not be a God familiar to those who speak most easily of God.

What manner of child might this be? She thought a lot about the stranger she would bring into the world, hers and not hers. She thought about how the new life she had mothered would put hers in question: she wouldn't stop changing when she had given birth, the relation would always be with a presence both utterly strange and utterly intimate. When the waiting was over, the world wouldn't just end—easy to think that, perhaps, when the time came, problems would be solved and tears wiped away and the kingdom would begin. Well, she knew in some part of herself that that couldn't be so: the world would go on and tears would still be shed. Still, something would be different. A connection would have been made, between God and the bodies of women, God and the desires of women, that would change for ever what was said about God and the bodies and desires of men—wouldn't it? Though it would not be at once. The whole process of bringing the Word to birth, with all its strangeness, the tearing and distancing, was all moving toward some moment when, with the pain of truthfulness and respect, God and men and women might be able to look at and speak with each other without the fear of violence and disgust she had felt so harshly. That, she thought, *that* is why the Word is given, that is the desire of God: that is the difference.

As the time got closer, nothing became easier. It was as if there was some kind of a test ahead and no way of guessing if the body was strong enough to bear it. What had been inner and in a way secret was going to become public. People would see what she had brought to birth; she would be judged in a new way, she would have a new place, a new name because of what was coming to be. Her body changed; her identity would change. Even if the worst terrors were not realized, she would change. She would be vindicated, or she would mourn as never before. But she had been touched, she had been inhabited by grace, by a summons, a gift, a being wholly trusted. She could look back into the eyes of her staring neighbors and say, "The Almighty has done great things for me; the Almighty has done great things in me. He has not abhorred this flesh as you do."

When the Word was brought forth it would be to her what it would be to all—judgment, promise, food and drink, absolution, communion. But the long waiting, the containing, the holding inside herself the dangerous difference that God's Word would make, the building up the living presence of the Word by her history, her patience, her anger, and her trust, by the fluids of her soul and her body—about that there was something distinctive. Not a privileged access, not an exclusive intimacy, but a unique coloring of the love that would be open to all. For the Word is never for human beings in general, but is always colored by a secret connection special to each. And this would be hers, that she had waited with the Word, her patience and her impatience bound up in and with the Word's; as if God in her, bringing the divine purpose to reality, was learning the patience of flesh and the risks and hurts that make up the world.

Whose story is this? It is the story of the woman we celebrate today, the story of the women we celebrate here tonight. We shall celebrate better though, if for *all* of us there is a spark of recognition here. Some at least of this is the story of every Christian, called and gifted, hopeful and frightened by the Word they must learn to give into the world. We shall learn more about celebrating Mary and her sisters if we can see that they are living out in the immediacy of their flesh and blood what we all face something of: God's desire.

We must all discover how to say to it the "yes" that acknowledges how it is bound up with our own desire. And we must press insistently on whatever it is in us and in our church that pushes back divine and human longing, praying that the Word will go on being flesh and speech and bread in the lives of women.

4

Born of the Virgin Mary

For us and for our salvation he came down from heaven: by the power of the Holy Spirit he became incarnate from the Virgin Mary, and was made man.

Few people would deny that this is a central, pivotal, moment in our creed; few would deny that, when we start reflecting on it, it's also one of the most difficult and tantalizing. The writers of the creed knew perfectly well that the incarnation, or "humanization," as they sometimes called it, of the Word of God wasn't a matter of somebody who lives in heaven moving to live somewhere else (earth); nor did they think the Word of God had come down from the sky to the human level. They knew they were using a metaphor, because they were convinced that God was timeless and bodiless, and that you couldn't tell any stories of God's life "in itself," but only stories of his action and manifestation in the world.

Yet they spoke of a "coming down," as so many of our Christian prayers and carols do. Perhaps they were afraid—and rightly—of being too abstract. They wanted to say clearly that the whole life of Jesus is God's gift to us, that God's own everlasting Word *did* something, *does* something, in Jesus; that what seemed far off has become unbearably close, what seemed secure and strong meets us in the form of weakness (a baby, a suffering man, a dead man). It is as if God *had* left heaven to be with us:

He left his Father's throne above,
So free, so infinite his grace.
Emptied himself of all but love,
And bled for Adam's helpless race.
'Tis mercy all, immense and free;
For, O my God, it found out me!

The love that would, *in human terms,* be involved in someone utterly giving up safety and status to join and support and rescue a helpless fellow human being provides a hint about the kind of love that is God's and is God. Not that God the Word suddenly and literally—in 4 or 5 B.C.—makes a heroic self-sacrifice, squeezing into the narrow confines of humanity, but that a human being comes into existence who so transforms what we mean by "God" that we can boldly and almost playfully say that God has moved, or changed places.

But the creed has already made it clear that what is shown in Jesus is an eternal fact in God, the unchanging God. God is "Father": from God all things take their origin. God is the final generating power in everything, a completely free initiative. But God is not only a *generating* power: that power forms an image of a response to itself so full and perfect that it is no less ultimate, comprehensive, and creative than the first moment of power and gift. God is also "Son" or "Word." God's being is both a free and endless giving of life, and the result or effect of that gift in perfectly real and active life, reflecting and returning to its source. God is gift and God is responding, active life, and the gift works through the life, the response, to give itself still further. All things are made by the Father through the Word, the Son: "In him was life; and the life was the light of all people." Father and Son create together, but more than that. Their power is a power not only to give life, but also to bring it to perfection, working within the world so as to draw it closer to that first inexpressible moment of gift and response—to perfect or sanctify life *in* the creation, *in* our history. And that perfecting dimension of creative power is what we call "Spirit."

What the writers of the creed wished above all to say was that Jesus embodied that second moment of divine life—the perfect, active response to the divine gift—in the whole of his existence. *In him was life,* a life which transmitted, translated, God's creative life in and to a human world trapped in its destructive past, unable to believe in or experience newness of life. What Jesus in every moment expresses is a power for renewal and response entirely continuous with the power on which all things depend.

But for all this he is a human being, he stands inside human—and specifically Jewish—history. In the history of the Jews, God's sanctifying power, God's Spirit, has been for centuries pressing this people toward a complete openness, receptivity, and vulnerability that will "clear a space" for renewing grace to flow freely. Luke's gospel brings this theme to a dramatic climax: a daughter of Israel finally realizes Israel's destiny by putting herself utterly at God's disposal, so that the new human life beginning in her body is a life in which God's Word is indeed set free, given space to work in the world and make it new. The Holy Spirit "overshadows" Mary so that the child she brings forth is an embodiment of creative holiness, the Word made flesh.

So Mary, along with John the Baptist's parents and Simeon and Anna in the Temple, stands for all the saints of the old covenant who have, bit by bit, made it possible for God's Word to be manifest in flesh. And Mary, as the immediate source of Jesus' human existence, has, for Luke, a unique importance. The language of his story deliberately echoes that of the Old Testament story (in 2 Samuel 6) of how the Ark of the Covenant was brought back to Israel; Mary is the new Ark, carrying within herself the sign and seal of the new covenant, so God's presence is, through her, returning to his people.

Luke and Matthew both relate the story of Jesus' birth so as to make it plain that Jesus' existence depends on God's initiative: it is the climax of Israel's story, yet it is not in the order of nature, not a predictable part of the world's process. Jesus is a "miracle," an unpredictable surprise. For the evangelists, not even the physical initiative of a human father can be thought of as complementing or accompanying the divine act that brings Jesus into being. In Jesus' birth, God works through someone of no legal or tribal importance, someone who normally would be significant only as a potential bargaining piece in the dynastic game—not the father of the family, but an unnamed woman, someone on the edge of society. "He hath put down the mighty from their seat, and hath exalted the humble and meek." The startling newness of God's saving work begins in this choice of an insignificant person for dignity and greatness. This is the new world of grace that Luke's Mary celebrates in the Magnificat. The savior is the "adopted" son of David, but his human flesh derives from God's act in a person of no importance.

It is possible, then, to see in the theological views of the two evangelists—Luke especially—why the story of a virginal conception makes powerful sense. It is certainly not being recorded as an interesting and unusual bit of information. Luke and Matthew obviously believed they were recording real events, yet that is not how they would have seen their main job. Now, the fact that we can see how useful the story of the virginal conception was to them doesn't mean that it *can't* be true (unless we have a prejudice against miracles as such). But the more we become aware of the storytelling conventions by which such narratives grew in the first century, the harder it becomes to reach a firm judgment on the historical ground of all this. Jesus is like the Old Testament "children of promise," Isaac, Samson, and Samuel; and he is like Abraham and Melchizedek—they too had stories told of their miraculous conception and birth by Jews of the New Testament period. But Jesus is greater than Isaac or even Isaac's father. He is *pure* grace, *pure* promise, and so the story of his birth develops accordingly. The core of it may be literally true, or there may have been an oddity or mystery about Jesus' birth that sparked off legend and speculation. (Some scholars point out that "virgin" in the Hebrew of the rabbis can mean a girl who has not yet had her first period; did Mary conceive at an exceptionally young age?) The difficulty of the virginal conception isn't so much a problem about miracles, as the fact that we can see too clearly for comfort what *job* the story is meant to do and the means by which it might have been built up.

I don't think certainty on this is available on purely historical or literary grounds. But this would be worrying or disastrous *only* if these were the sole grounds on which we could be certain of God's freedom to make new beginnings, or if the story expressed a truth vital to the gospel which could be grasped in no other way. It tells us, with great vividness, that the *real* miracle is *the fact of Jesus himself*. But if the miraculous newness of Jesus and his embodying of the perfect responding love of God as "Son" could *only* be spoken of by insisting that no human father had a part in bringing Jesus into being, then it's odd that Mark, Paul, and John, who are all so eloquent on the creative newness of Jesus and on his showing to us God's Word and Wisdom, should not use the language that Matthew and Luke do. Mark, Paul, and John don't suppose that a virginal conception is *necessary* to make it possible for the Word to become flesh. It can't be a "mechanism" by which a heavenly person turns into an earthly one (we've already seen that this isn't what the writers of the creed were saying anyway). They may or may not have known the story, but in any case they were able to preach the good news without it—the good news of God's creative power set free in the world, of our being called and drawn into a full and fulfilling intimacy with the generosity from which all things flow.

We should be cautious about making this story—however appropriate, however vivid and haunting—a necessary condition for believing in or speaking of God in our midst in Jesus. If we can have some freedom in interpreting the vividly mythological language of "he came down from heaven," we can claim equal flexibility in our understanding of "incarnate by the Holy Ghost of the Virgin Mary." Such flexibility may even give us more space to reflect on the heart of the wonderful event these words encapsulate for us, the mystery of God's coming to be among us, and the mystery in which that itself is rooted: God's own life as gift and love. "'Tis mercy all, immense and free."

5

Christmas Gifts

It sometimes seems these days as though the Christian faith and the Christian tradition are going to survive not in the church but in the theater. While we are busy wasting our time emptying out various bits of our heritage and tradition, vast audiences pack the theaters of London to see and hear Alec McCowen reciting the gospel of St. Mark and to watch Tony Harrison's version of the medieval mystery plays. For those people the message of the gospel, the imaginative riches of the Christian doctrine, comes with the freshness of a genuinely new revelation. Those people are in some sense luckier than we are: for many of them it really is a revelation.

Some of you may have seen on television recently the first part of Tony Harrison's adaptation of the medieval mystery plays. The nativity scene is particularly memorable and moving, adapted from the Wakefield play of the fifteenth century, the *Second Shepherds' Play*. The three shepherds, unmistakably West Riding workmen, come to the cradle and give their gifts. The verses the men speak to the Christ Child are perhaps among the most beautiful in the English language.

First Shepherd
Hail, comely and clean! Hail, young child!
Hail, maker, of all I mean, of a maiden so mild!
Thou hast confounded, I ween, the Warlock so wild:
The false guiler of men, now goes he beguiled.
  Lo, he merries!
Lo, he laughs, my sweeting!
Ah! A well fair meeting!
I have holden my telling:
  Have a bob of cherries.

Second Shepherd

Hail, sovereign saviour, for thou hast us sought!
Hail, fresh root and flower, that all things hast wrought!
Hail, full of favour, that made all of nought! ·
Hail! I kneel and I cower. A bird have I brought
   To my bairn.
Hail, little tiny mop!
Of our creed thou art crop:
I would drink on thy cup,
   Little day-star.

Third Shepherd

Hail, darling dear, full of Godhead!
I pray thee be near when that I have need.
Hail, sweet of thy cheer! My heart would bleed
To see thee sit here in so poor weed,
   With no pennies.
Hail! Put forth thy hand.
I bring thee but a ball:
Have and play thee withall,
   And go to the tennis.

Three gifts: a bob of cherries, a pet bird, and a tennis ball. Much more difficult, aren't they, to allegorize and make theological mysteries out of than the gifts of the wise men. And so infinitely more touching: pointless, useless presents, and so more eloquent than almost anything could be.

What can I give him, poor as I am? What indeed! For God today has recreated the world and refashioned you and me in his own image. God today has burst open the frontiers of all possible and imaginable experience and come among us. The Maker of all reaches out his hand and touches the bob of cherries that a West Riding workman offers him. And for that reaching out there is no exchange, there is no fit return we can make. God's pure, causeless, gratuitous love can have no answer, except some faint fumbling echo of that very gratuity and pointlessness itself: the gift too great to make sense of. All we can do, like the shepherds, is offer our meaningless little presents. All we can give to God is the equivalent of what the shepherds here give: a packet of sweets, a budgie in a cage, a tennis ball.

That is what it all comes down to: all the useless, pointless beauty of our music and our ritual, our words and our acts, our struggles in prayer, corporately and privately, all the great achievements of Christendom, every cathedral, the *B-Minor Mass* and Rembrandt and all the rest of it; a packet of sweets and a tennis ball. All we can do is offer God playful gifts, the gift of our celebration, our playing. He does not need it but he wants the hearts that will and can rejoice, gratuitously, uselessly, pointlessly, and beautifully, in what he has done.

What pleases God is himself, his own glory and his own loveliness, and the gift that he gives himself is himself, his own beloved Son. What can we add to that to please God? Budgies and tennis balls. Jesus himself has something to say about it, when the woman comes to anoint his body for burial. "She has done a beautiful thing for me," he says. "For that reason, wherever in the world the gospel is preached, this will be told for her memorial." She did a beautiful and pointless thing, and he accepted that gift, as in the *Second Shepherds' Play* he accepts these silly, infinitely moving presents.

It is only when we learn to give, not from a sense of debt but from an overflowing of joy, that we can have some share in the action of his redeeming and recreating love. The useless gifts of art and beauty, of ritual and music, are there to liberate our joy. And when our joy is liberated, so will our generosity and compassion be. That, too, may wake some echoes in the experience of recent months. Why is it that a marathon rock concert could raise more money for the starving than any amount of moral exhortation from pulpit or press? It is because (whether you like marathon rock concerts or not) there is an overflowing of joy, and out of that overflowing of joy is an overflowing of compassion and generosity. We are such bad creatures at loving that we need the shock of joy, just as we need the shock of pain, to set our love free. And that is why we need to come again and again to this sacrament to have our shells—our selfish habits and our self-obsession—broken open in the remembrance of the horror of Jesus' betrayal and the glory of Jesus' resurrection. Our love needs to be set free, to be pierced and shocked into action.

Now, of course, if you start cultivating joy for moral purposes—let's have a good time so that we can be better people—then both the joy and the morals will dry up pretty promptly. Likewise, if you cultivate joy for the sake of nice feelings, the same sort of thing happens. The point is not, in a sense, about joy; it is about what *causes* joy. We don't go out looking for joy. We are, in the immortal phrase of C. S. Lewis, "surprised by joy" constantly, and we must yield ourselves to the wonder of God's great gift. When we have made that basic surrender, then the joy and the beauty, the transfiguring compassion and charity, will flow. As we make these helpless, childlike gestures of love and celebration, then indeed we are truly brought into and immersed in the Father's gift to himself of his Son.

The beauty of worship, the beauty of holy lives, the beauty of lovely objects—none of these, as is so often said, is an end in itself. But that does not then mean they are a means to something else. They simply *are*, the overflowing of response, the superabundance of love, and that is what is Godlike about them. Today, as we celebrate the Father's gift to himself of his everlasting Word and the Father's gift to us of that same Word in Jesus Christ, as we celebrate that unimaginable flowing forth of joy, generosity, and compassion, all we can do in response is expose ourselves to the shock of it, allow ourselves to be opened by it, and, stumblingly, make such gestures as we can of generous, joyful love.

> Hail, sovereign saviour, for thou hast us sought!
> Hail, fresh root and flower, that all thing hast wrought!
> Hail, full of favour, that made all of nought!
> Hail! I kneel and I cower. A bird have I brought
>   To my bairn.
> Hail, little tiny mop!
> Of our creed thou art crop:
> I would drink on thy cup,
>   Little day-star.

6

Not to Condemn
the World

At first sight, these seem easy words to say at Christmas, easy and comforting. God comes among us as a child, vulnerable, wordless, dependent; and he calls forth from us a love that is the most natural and unforced in the world—that tender sympathy, even protectiveness, that so many of our carols speak of. We declare our intention of rocking and cuddling him, of letting him sleep. We tiptoe round his cradle, hushing each other and smiling at each other in the great and universal conspiracy of baby-worship. That God did not send his only Son into the world to condemn the world seems obvious to us at the manger. What has condemnation to do with this?

Well, in fact, when we *think* about what we're doing, the threat of condemnation and the ways we invent of avoiding it are a disturbingly large part of our agenda. It is, remember, *God* that we are talking about, God the maker and the goal of all, the source of all value and—so we are often told—of all power. As such, he is often for us the source also of *anxiety:* are we in the right before him, can we count on his approval and support? If God is the source of all value, we need to find our own value in aligning ourselves with him—or aligning him with us. So we get involved in quite complicated strategies to make things all right with him. We devise systems of religious law and observance, saying to God, "This *is* it, isn't it? That *is* what you want? Aren't I right? And this is what I can do, watch me!" We recruit God on our side as the supreme moralist, saying to him, "You don't like this sort of behavior any more than I do, do you? So if I don't do this (whatever "this" is, from drunkenness to rape), it's all right, isn't it? You approve?"

We use God to bless crusades for this or that, for sexual liberation or sexual repression, for the free market or social ownership. If God is value and power, in short, we need him badly. To allay the anxiety that we might not have the kind of value and power that matters, we invent all sorts of ways in which we can be sure of having him with us, echoing what we say. And the God we thus capture and display as our ally is most emphatically a God who is there to condemn: thank goodness I, or my particular group, have avoided condemnation by getting on the right side of him, and now he can turn his wrath elsewhere, on my behalf.

For this to work, we must never ask certain questions about how value and power work, or what they really mean. We *know* they are about strength and security and we *know* that strength and security mean the ability to threaten or dominate others. God becomes our last and best alibi for not being disturbed. And at the most superficial level, Christmas seems to give us an excuse for going on with this. The tightly swaddled baby is a gift-wrapped object, passive and docile for use in *our* business, *our* transactions; a lucky mascot; the sleeping partner in the firm (the little Lord Jesus asleep on the hay); God at last made functional and quiet, wordless and dependent, while we do the talking and the acting and brandish this beautiful little idol to menace others; little Lord Jesus, like Little Lord Fauntleroy, who generates in us such good and warm feelings that we *know* we can't be wrong.

But there is something very peculiar about this—the passive child-God, his power swallowed up in us so that we boost our strength and confidence by invoking his name and delighting in our warm feelings about him. There is something odd about this neat diverting of God's possible judgment away from us onto the outsiders, the ones not included in our warm circle of religion, morality, or ideology. And the oddity has something to do with the often forgotten fact that this is a real human child we are speaking of. "The cattle are lowing, the baby awakes, But little Lord Jesus, no crying he makes." Every parent in Christendom must have blinked with incredulous envy at this miracle: never mind the angels and the star, a baby who doesn't cry when surrounded by a herd of hungry cows is something of a prodigy! Babies, in fact, may be wordless and dependent, but they are not as a rule silent, nor are they passive. They make their presence felt, they alter lives. Their dependence is a matter of fingers clutching at ours when we'd like to be getting on with something; broken nights, hungry mouths at the breast; the need to be taught and watched and entertained, brought into the world of human speech and relation. If God is with us as a child—a real child—he is not after all so tidily gift-wrapped, so functional. If God is with us as a child, he is certainly with us as one who calls out our tenderness and compassion, but he does so by an insistent presence without shame or restraint, crying and clutching. He is the God who, in St. Augustine's unforgettable words, penetrates my deafness by his violent, loud crying.

And all that crying, as every parent knows, can be alarming precisely because we don't understand what the baby wants. What is the matter? Pain? Hunger? Loneliness? The child can tell us only by crying and we have to wait, attending patiently, till it becomes clearer. We have to wait much longer before we can find how to speak together. At first, looking into the little scarlet face and screaming mouth, we are confronted with something strange and uncontrollable. So far from the divine child being a cipher, the tool of our schemes and systems, he confronts us with the alarming, mysterious, shattering strangeness of God.

Ask a baby about the ordination of women, about divorce legislation, violence on television, who will win the election: it is not a fruitful experience. It will take a long time to forge the common language in which we can talk about such things. Meanwhile, we face something that is disconcertingly like the master's answer to the disciple in the Zen Buddhist tradition: when the disciple raises a speculative question—a question not connected with enlightenment, not coming from the person's heart and guts—the master simply replies *"Mu!"*, "No." And so with us, if we bring to the divine child our questions of theory and policy, we have the same answer—*"Mu!"*—in the baby's crying and the baby's equally incomprehensible laughter and the silent clutching of a finger or sucking of a breast. Our questions and, with them, our desperate and fearful need to be right, are relativized. They are not foolish or trivial questions, but before we ask in our eagerness to get it tidily wrapped up, our longing to have God's endorsement, we need to put aside the whole world of our perceptions and our transactions, recognizing in silent attention the

God who will not let himself be captured and turned into a staring wax doll, a totem or fetish for our tribal passions.

One of the great English historical novels of this century is Hilda Prescott's *The Man on a Donkey*, in which the events of Henry VIII's reign, especially the dissolution of the monasteries, are seen through the eyes of five people in North Yorkshire whose loyalties in this great period of conflict are widely different. Beside them all stands the figure of Malle, the inarticulate, half-witted servant at Marrick Priory, who is said to have visions of Jesus, the man on a donkey. Each of the five main characters interrogates her at crucial points in the story, struggling to get her to say something that will prove that God is on one side of the conflict or the other. Will God protect the priory? Will he support the reformers? Will he promise victory to the Catholic rebels? To them all, Malle replies with dumbness or with strange words that seem irrelevant to these intense concerns: "There was a great wind of light blowing, and sore pain"; "Darkness, and God moving nigh-hand in the darkness." The man on a donkey does not stay to be questioned. He moves, in all the events of the story, into the heart of suffering and defeat, and gives no answer but his indestructible presence.

Malle is the spokeswoman for the inarticulate crying of God in the stable, for the wordless cry from the cross. She speaks for a God who gives no answer short of his own life and presence. A God who could be relied on to guarantee our judgments or our prejudices would be a passive, imprisoned God, but the God of the stable and the cross is free. His weakness, his wordlessness, *is* his power. And it passes annihilating judgment on our efforts to be right and secure, defended by God against others. Here there *is* condemnation, and we must hear sentence pronounced in the child's crying upon all our silencing and domesticating of God. If we are to act well, to do God's will, it can only be by hearing this sentence daily. We shall then know at least that the acts we do and the choices we make (have no choice but to make) are *human* acts, offered to God in humility, hope, and trust, acts that are themselves part of our learning to be creatures, not dazzling epiphanies of God's righteousness dwelling in us. We shall, God willing, forge a language in which we and Christ may speak to each other, as we wait patiently with him; and there is a wisdom and learning in our church that spells out the first steps in this language. There will be unobtrusive growth in insight and in hopefulness, and so in authority, in our choices and deeds. But the judgment of God's final mysteriousness remains. All we know is that his condemnation is uttered against all the ways in which he is manipulated as a weapon against others.

And in *that* condemnation, paradoxically, we see what the gospel means when it says that the Son is *not* sent to condemn. For only in the utter freedom of God can we see hope for the *whole* world. The free God of the stable and the cross, the wordless stranger, because he is no part of the policy and program of *me* and those who think like me, can be known as the God who is there for all—for the enemy and the outcast and all who are not just "like me" or "like us." "God so loved the *world*"—not the church, not the Moral Majority, not the Ministry of Defense or the Campaign for Nuclear Disarmament, not Iran or Iraq, but the world. He condemns not the world, but the fantasies of absolute rightness that torture and disfigure the world. In the minds of some, there is a God who blesses the atrocities of an anticommunist crusade in Nicaragua, or a God who supports the violence of Palestinians and black Africans but not that of their enemies, or a God who declares his wrath at male homosexual promiscuity by striking dead children and hemophiliacs and heterosexual Africans with AIDS. Such a God is the silent, passive, swaddled doll, glass-eyed and wax-limbed, of our anxious fantasy—a tribal fetish. God save us from such a god!

But he has. On this happy morning, we give thanks that the *true* God is with us, sweeping away our tribalism, our moral smugness, our religious fuss. The idols fall and perish. The inarticulate crying and the incomprehensible laughter of a real, fleshly child wake us out of our deathlike sleep and life begins: the life of patient and loving attention to our great lover, the slow learning of a new language and a new world we can share with him.

7

The Covenant
in Our Flesh

For the Feast of the Circumcision

Both he that is born in your house and he that is bought with
your money shall be circumcised. So shall my covenant be in
your flesh an everlasting covenant. *(Genesis 17:13)*

When we read in Genesis of the first institution of circumcision
we find there the phrase *this shall be a covenant in your flesh.* The
Feast of the Circumcision of Christ is very important as a feast of
the covenant—the covenant in our flesh in a very strong sense
indeed. But what *is* the covenant? In the Hebrew scriptures the
covenant is the fusion of the faithful promise of God with the
faithful obedience of God's people. This is obedience not just to
a set of rules, not to laws but to *the law,* the law of God's being,
the consistency and coherence of everything in the mind and
wisdom of God. The obedience of God's people is above all else a
glad response to that great consistency in the being of God, the
law of God's own life.

So covenant is the promise of God's faithfulness, and covenant
is our response to that faithfulness. Without the provision of the
law of God's being—the self-consistency, the eternal faithfulness
of God to his own being—we could not begin to be obedient, we
would not know what it was we had to attend to. So if this is a
feast of covenant, it is thereby also a feast of obedience.

"Obedient to the law for our sake," says this morning's collect
about Jesus, because Jesus' obedience shows us what the word
most fully means.

Almighty God, whose blessed Son was circumcised in obedience to the law for our sake and given the Name that is above every name: give us grace faithfully to bear his Name, to worship him in the freedom of the Spirit, and to proclaim him as the Savior of all.

The life of Jesus is not a series of acts of jumping to attention to commands issued by a holy despot. The obedience of Jesus is the readiness to see the Father's will in every circumstance, every situation, and every person presented to him, and to respond to it with wholeness of heart at once. The obedience of Jesus lies in *seeing* the need of the leper or the blind man or the Syrophoenician mother *and* saying "yes." That is obedience: it is seeing the situation, seeing the drawing of God's will in it, and being drawn into response.

As we celebrate today the covenant in our flesh, the new and everlasting covenant made in Christ, in the flesh and blood he shares with us, we may usefully think about the obedience involved in covenant. We are able to obey, to give ourselves in glad response to God in person after person, in situation after situation, because we know God has promised to be there for us, that God's great self-consistency underlies all these. With that revelation, in that confidence, we know whom we must obey. We begin to learn how to give ourselves obediently to God as we search expectantly, hopefully, for God in people and in situations, knowing that God is promised to us there.

The promise of God means the promise of every person and every situation. The promise of God and the obedience of human beings also mean that we are committed to the promise of human beings. The world is a "promising" place, though not in the trivial sense in which we say of some apparently cheerful situation, "That looks promising." No one but a fool would say that of the world. The world is promising, people are promising, because God has promised to be there; through the difficulty, through the risk, through the tragedy, God is committed to that world and no other.

Is there also a final way in which we can turn that original definition of covenant on its head? The promise of God, the obedience of human beings, the promise of human beings—and, surely, the *obedience of God.* Can we dare to say that as well? The faithfulness, the self-consistency of God is nothing other than loving attention and responsiveness to the world he has made—a kind of obedience.

God looks at the world and in it sees his own promise. He responds to the needs of the world, knowing that the world can be brought into his light, can be healed and transfigured. The promise of God, the obedience of human beings: the promise of human beings, the obedience of God. All these focus very obviously today in the One who was born of a woman, born under the law, the One in whom there is a covenant in our flesh. He is born under the law and obedient to the law so that we may know what the law truly is. He is obedient to the law because he is unceasingly responding to God's everlasting consistency, God's wisdom which is his own deepest identity. Obeying the Father by obeying the need and the cry of those suffering around him, he is himself a sign of God's promise to the world and the world's promise to God, of the world's obedience to God and of God's obedience to the world.

That is the mystery in which we live, striving to find ourselves daily more and more deeply in that promise and that obedience. That life in which we live is the life which today and for ever is named Jesus, whose name is called upon us, in whom we stand, upon whom God the Father looks when he looks upon us. To him be glory for ever and ever.

8

Hearts of Flesh

I will give them a heart of flesh. *(Ezekiel 36:26)*

Flesh is what we live in—warm, mobile and frail. Flesh is how we learn—through the bits of flesh called eyes and ears and vocal chords. Flesh is how we communicate—with hands and eyes, lips and tongues. We are always ready to be persuaded that learning and sharing are really about some other realm than flesh. But whether or not people can communicate by telepathy, the primary way in which we are connected to each other is by flesh. Even—or perhaps especially—our apprehension of beauty has to do with flesh, with the sense of an *embodied* gift or grace. Our "hearts of flesh" are all pretty obvious, so why the fuss about a divine promise to give us what we've already got?

It's because we are afraid and suspicious of our flesh. "Frail children of dust and feeble as frail": "flesh" has come to stand above all for our family ("*only* flesh and blood"), and we don't very much like it. We have some apparent encouragement from St. Paul, who almost always speaks of flesh as bad, as a source of deception, a downward drag. We want to be more than flesh. Yet Ezekiel assumes that if we refuse to be flesh, we become less, not more, than human: we acquire a heart of stone, a heart that is unteachable by God and devoted to idolatry. There is no learning or sharing here and so the heart has no object but itself, no speech but what it says to itself, no prayer but what it prays to itself—idolatry. The opposite of flesh is not spirit, but stone: "A rock feels no pain, And an island never cries."

Frail children of flesh? Yes, because flesh is what hurts. Not only is it simply and literally fragile, the hurts inflicted on what we think of as our spirits are the hurts we have in relations with other fleshly beings, absorbed through our ears and eyes. And

God promises us hearts of flesh! He promises that at the very center of ourselves will be something essentially fragile. What kind of a promise is that?

It is the promise that God will make us members of the human race—no more and no less; able to listen, speak, and share with the imprisoned and ill-treated; belonging in the same world as the poor, the despised, the people without hope or legal redress. It is a promise that we shall be given the strength to open our hearts in welcome. All this is what the letter to the Hebrews describes as the life of the community that lives by God's gift, the church. Why should we want to live thus? Because the alternative is having no object but ourselves, no world but what we can imagine: the hell to which the heart's idolatry leads.

To be a friend of God is to learn to be a friend of my own frailty, accepting and affirming it, entrusting it to God. It is recognizing that the self God deals with is not some mysterious inner core, but my body. I am that body, whether young or old, fit or diseased. Who I am is to be seen and known in my flesh. I may be ashamed of or hostile to it. People with chronic disabilities or disorders will often feel they are strangers or enemies to a body that seems to betray them. People dying of AIDS, of motor-neurone disease, of cancer, may feel passionately that they are more than the wasting flesh. And they are right, of course, but the Christian is bound to say that this "more" is found only in first meeting and loving that fragile flesh. When St. Francis embraced the leper and put his lips to kiss his sores, he loved a man whose very selfhood was to be met *in*—not behind or above—that material wretchedness. He did not search for a distant and intact soul or personality to love, to avoid the shaming flesh. "Love's mysteries in soules do growe, But yet the bodie is his booke," wrote Donne. He—a vigorous, lecherous man—had a particular kind of love in mind, but as so often in his erotic poems, he is already the great theologian he would become in his maturity. Bodies are where we read love, and where we write it. Bodies are where we learn and where we speak and share. If we cannot love our mortal vulnerability, our own frail flesh, we shall love nothing and nobody. The more we seek—individually, socially, and nationally—to protect ourselves at all cost from intrusion, injury, and loss, the more we tolerate a public rhetoric incapable of affirming our mortal uncertainties, errors, and insecurities, the more we stand under Ezekiel's judgment for "abominable deeds"—the offering of fleshly persons on the altar of stone.

"*We* have an altar," says the writer to the Hebrews: it is wherever Jesus is to be found. Our God has met us in the flesh, and we have learned God in the flesh of Christ: "in thy *wounds* hide me," because there is our security. The rock is struck and shattered, the waters flow. "Flesh hath purged what flesh had stained, And God, the flesh of God, hath reigned." God's way is to be incarnate, fleshed out, in Jesus and in the friends of Jesus. Our way too is toward and into the flesh, not away from it: the love of bodies is the condition for learning, sharing, and growing—for becoming "spirit" in St. Paul's sense. For what Paul means by "flesh" is what Ezekiel meant by stone: the self turned on itself, unteachable and unloving, the body itself turned into a self-serving, self-defending machine, instead of being (in a fine phrase of Professor Peter Brown) "the means of our connection with the world."

So we ask our incarnate God to give us the gift of incarnation, the heart of flesh, to keep us so in touch with our mortality and our own special pains that we are free for welcome and for compassion, friends with our vulnerability and so friends with the vulnerable, bearing the reproach Jesus bore—the reproach of a world often much readier to understand stone than flesh.

May God make of us what he would have us be through Jesus Christ, to whom be glory for ever and ever. Amen.

Toward Easter

9

God's Time

My time has not yet come, but your time is always here.

(John 7:6)

John's gospel is haunted by the idea of the "time" or the "hour" for which Jesus waits. There is a moment at which the purpose of the Father will be fulfilled, the glory of the Son made manifest, and that moment is signalled in the nineteenth chapter as Jesus dies with the cry, "It is accomplished." The "hour" is the time of his humiliation, betrayal, and murder: as John puts it, this is the time at which the world is judged, when its fears and its lies are dragged into the open. In the betrayal and slaughter of Jesus, we are shown what it is we do to one another and ourselves in our self-justifying, self-defending terror, our refusal to penetrate to and face our inner divisions and their destructive effects.

Jesus says to his brothers, "My time has not yet come," because this drama has still to be enacted in its bloody final form. It is still possible for Jesus to *debate* with his opponents. Only slowly is it becoming plain that he is so total a stranger that he must be killed, although in our reading today, Jesus already sees through the surface opposition and hesitation to the murderous conclusion. It is in the eighth chapter that, for the first time, stones are picked up to stone him to death, only a page or two from the indignant protest of the Judeans in today's lesson, "You have a demon! Who is seeking to kill you?"

The judgment is beginning, then: the painful glory of the mercy that can only be uncovered after the ultimate darkness of the human heart has begun to break through. If we understand that it is the time of *judgment*, discovery, and conversion that Jesus speaks of here, we may see why he says to his skeptical brothers, "Your time is always here," a very odd remark at first sight. For his brothers, history—their history and their world's history—does not move to judgment and mercy, to events that crush and test and force decision. They are not conscious of *waiting* for the moment of God's truth; their "time" is simply whatever happens to be going on, and what is going on is not pregnant with the possibilities of heaven and damnation. In this world, the truth of God's Word never appears, to be feared and hated and cast out. No one is called on to recognize a time that is God's time, when true decision and true witness are forced into the light.

Now we are rightly suspicious of easy rhetoric about decision and witness, of apocalyptic accounts of the implications of our present situation. When a left-wing South London councillor announced that we were on the path toward the gas chambers, she was greeted by a chorus of mockery and contempt in most of the news media. Or—to take another example, which the same councillor might herself greet with hostility—when we are told that our practices regarding abortion are moving fast toward abortion on demand and that the implications for the rights of children born deformed or disabled are disturbing, we are inclined to be skeptical. Or we write off anxieties about the safety of nuclear energy reactors as idle scaremongering. The great and good of our society still have a fair amount of confidence in our collective reasonableness.

If we have that confidence, John's gospel should make us uncomfortable. It *may* be that there is no likelihood of any real and dramatic escalation in racial violence, or of any increase in legal discrimination against non-white immigrants, or in illegal but perfectly manifest discrimination against ethnic minorities. It *may* be that it is a ludicrous overstatement to say that some form of euthanasia for the disabled infant is a logical next step from our abortion practices. It *may* be that nuclear energy is still the least environmentally worrying future we can imagine for satisfying our fuel needs. These are real, not rhetorical, "maybes." And yet, those who worry us with what look like ridiculous or misplaced warnings are more than deluded pessimists. We must learn to hear behind such words something of the warning of this gospel: "Your time is always *here*," here and now.

How far does our "reasonableness" mean that we refuse to ask about the initially incomprehensible anger of our South London councillor? How far does it mean that we refuse to ask why we tolerate or ignore the unprecedented severity with which black citizens are treated by our immigration officials and the unprecedented scale of violence against Asian school children in some of our cities? How far does it mean that we refuse to feel the necessary *tragedy* in abortion and the real questions it poses about how we evaluate the worth of human lives? How far does it mean that we never question the assumption that we shall go on consuming ever greater quantities of energy because the economy will go on expanding and our standard of living will go on rising? You may not be moved to go out of this cathedral and join Greenpeace or become a subscriber to the Runnymede Trust, but you may at least ask certain questions about signs of the times, questions that go below the surface of our reasonableness.

For the gospel soberly reminds us that the human heart is not reasonable at its center: without *knowing* it, the human heart may slowly give more and more place, more and more tolerance, to the unreasonable, the destructive. Or it may grow the kind of hard skin that blocks off questions of moral imagination, of conceiving and hoping for a certain kind of humanity. "Your time is always here" means that we refuse to know in ourselves that which unleashes hell on ourselves and on others. "You have a demon! Who is seeking to kill you?" we say to those whose fears are—however confusedly, even hysterically—voiced to us, just short of picking up stones. It is because the Christian is mindful of the Father's hour, the breaking-in of a terrible light upon the human heart, that he or she can never hear the voice of real pain, anxiety, honest questioning, or powerless indignation without taking to heart the question, "Have I, have we, allowed ourselves to become people whose time is always here, who do not hope for—and *fear*—God's judgment, a moment when we are called to true decision?"

When the church is living in the truth, it is a place where we are becoming people capable of *bearing* such a question and capable of decision and witness, of coming into the light so that it may be seen that what we do, we do in God. I've just finished reading a moving and disturbing book, H. P. Ehrenberg's *Autobiography of a German Pastor*, written in England in 1943. Ehrenberg was a German refugee, a Jew converted to Christianity, who had become a pastor and who suffered in the 1930s as a result of the Third Reich's attempt to enforce anti-Jewish legislation on the church. He had been instrumental in establishing the "Confessing Church," the network of congregations that refused to accept this legislation. He spent time in a concentration camp, where he was tortured and interrogated, and detailed to help in the disposal of corpses.

In this book, Ehrenberg describes how both he and his congregation discovered what the church was and why it was the center of the Christian enterprise. They met each Thursday evening to test their experience of their society, their problems and crises, against the Word of God and the great Reformation confessions of faith. He speaks of this as a "rehearsal" for whatever decision and witness may be demanded:

> We came to realize that instruction itself already contains the seeds of fellowship, of true community. In our case it was as important as the final rehearsal of the orchestra: a sort of "performance before the performance."

He describes how ordinary and uneducated people learned for themselves the discernment of spirits:

> It was only *within* the Church, if I may put it this way, that individual witnesses of the Confessional Church [he has just described the reaction of a railwayman in his parish to the teachings of a pro-Nazi pastor in the neighborhood] learned to resist the enemy, to attack, to condemn, to exorcise, to overcome in actual places, such as the concentration camp.

And he describes a dramatic incident that occurred at a summer camp for teenage girls, where a "united service" for Catholics and Protestants was held in a room dominated by a large picture of Hitler set up on a table. A recently confirmed Lutheran girl grabbed the picture and threw it against the wall, with the words, "Thou shalt have no other gods but me." "The remarkable thing," says the pastor, "was not that she smashed Hitler's picture, nor even that she had the courage to confess the First Commandment, but that she was *prepared beforehand* to do both."[1]

---

1 H. P. Ehrenberg, *Autobiography of a German Pastor* (London, 1943), pp. 48, 50, 64.

Hans Ehrenberg puts to all of us the question of how we can be "prepared beforehand" for such moments. With such a record behind us in our century, we should know now that the church must be a place where the voices of anger or fear can be heard and not mocked, and where we have the freedom to go beyond the surface of things and face the dangers in our "reasonable" society—whose reasonableness has no root in anything beyond itself; no attunement, except by chance, to the reason, the Word, of God. And as we look into the darkness that is *our* humanity (not a fiction, and not someone else's), we shall, the gospel tells us, meet that compassion that takes us through this darkness into the life of Christ, the forgiveness that establishes us in love and freedom, and creates in us the capacity for witness. Is the church such a place? Are we free to learn from one another what it is to be obedient to the Word of God, what it might mean to come to judgment? And is our own prayer a sufficient exposing of ourselves in silence and expectation to God, a bringing to him of ourselves in all our hesitation and shrinking, all our potential destructiveness? Will it "prepare us beforehand" for times of violent trial?

Only if the church makes such claims on our honesty and courage will it be a place where we can hear the word of grace and be remade and equipped for witness, whether or not it will ever be the dramatic resistance of an Ehrenberg. Only if the church ministers to us (which means, of course, us ministering to each other) in this way can we be brought to the "time" of Christ in his agony and glory, the consummation of a grace that breaks into the time that is "always here."

10

Palm Sunday

Archaeologists seem to think that under the Temple in Jerusalem was a huge storage area, a vault, like an underground car park, and that this was almost certainly the area where the booths of the money-changers and the pens of the animal vendors stood. It's quite a powerful image: a vast echoing chamber, with a few slits for light right at the top, perhaps some flares or oil lamps, deafeningly noisy, smelly, airless, overcrowded. It's easy to imagine the panic and uproar in this crowded space when a dusty and unkempt northerner pushes over a few stalls and sets the pigeons loose, and begins to shout incomprehensible biblical quotations about "prayer" and "all nations" and the evils of commerce in the holy place.

As has often been pointed out, we've no reason to suppose there was anything *wicked* going on in that dark and noisy vault. Traders of (no doubt) average honesty were doing what such people do the world over, providing a necessary service as efficiently as they could. The noise and the smell and the crowding were doubtless unfortunate in some ways, though we shouldn't apply western bourgeois standards too rapidly, even here. Anyone who's been to a great shrine like the Lakshmi Narayan Temple in Delhi will realize that the idea that silence and solemnity are necessary for reverence is a new and strange one to a good part of the human race. We can't assume that what was going on was exceptionally squalid or exploitative. So what exactly is wrong?

The traders could reasonably say that they *had* to be there: they weren't an agreeable but optional extra, a cathedral shop, but part of the very business of the Temple. To go in, you had to empty your pockets of foreign, idolatrous coinage and acquire approved Temple currency. And, of course, you had to have animals or birds for sacrifice, pleasing things to offer to the Lord. The trade was essential to the system, a *condition* of the Temple worship continuing as usual. If the authorities chose to see an attack on the traders as an attack on the sacrificial system, perhaps they weren't so far wrong; and when St. John associates Jesus' action in the Temple with the words "Destroy this temple and in three days I will raise it up," he was not wrong. There is more at stake here than a Chestertonian attack on wicked grocers.

The Temple attacked by Jesus was once a sign of grace—the spot where God *chooses* to make his name to dwell, as in Deuteronomy, where he makes himself "public" and accessible. You go up to Jerusalem to *see* the God of gods in Zion (Psalm 84), to his gracious presence, from which it is pain and humiliation to be cut off by exile or sickness (Psalms 42 and 43). In the last days, the prophet said, the Temple hill would tower above all hills and draw all people to it like a beacon. But what has it become? A place with rigorous and complex conditions of entry, conditions that generate a whole cottage industry around the Temple: the right coinage, the ritually pure animals, and so on have to be supplied. Religious activity, seeing God and serving God, has become a busy, satisfying, and distinctive area of human action and experience.

Jesus, in his acts and parables, is a strikingly secular figure, unconcerned to ask questions about the status or purity of those who come to him. In the light of his proclamation, the Temple makes perfect sense as a sign of promise, a space consecrated to the openness of God's invitation to the world. It does not and cannot make sense as the center of a bustling religious subculture, devoted to satisfying the demands of God and God's purity. But the story we tell this week presses this further still: Jesus "consecrates" himself, makes himself holy, as he goes outside the city to a godless and cursed death in an unhallowed public place, a rag-and-bone heap beside the road, where he is stripped naked and nailed up like a scarecrow. And as he dies, says the evangelist, the partition between the Holy of Holies and its forecourt is torn in half. In this week, the holy is redefined and recreated for us. The Temple is rebuilt as the body of the crucified Christ, not a place of exclusions, a house of merchandise where we must barter to be allowed in, trading our daily lives, our secular joys and pains for the sacred currency of ritual and the acceptable pure gifts that will placate God, but the cross by the roadside, unfenced, unadorned, the public and defenseless place where God gives us room.

And these words are spoken in a holy place, in the context of an archaically strange liturgy, by a priest wearing ritual garments; the irony shouldn't escape us. This cathedral is a long way from the rubbish dump outside Jerusalem. We are caught. We can only remember and celebrate and expose ourselves to that dangling scarecrow, it seems, by gathering all the resources of beauty and solemnity to force us *out* of our unthinking worldliness; we need annually to hear the Allegri *Miserere* or the *St. Matthew Passion* so as to be reacquainted with our own solitude and pain, with what in us is hidden from us by "the world." We need to see and taste the ritually broken bread, so as to remember the breakage of sacrificial death that creates our freedom day by day. We need this to understand the secret of God in the heart of everything, to live as secular men and women in the secular world without letting that secularity distort itself into self-serving complacency, consumerist greed, and hunger for control. This liturgy tells us that behind and beneath the smooth wheels of the socially constructed world are two abiding facts: unreconciled pain and unexhausted compassion, the history of men and women and the history of God with them (with us). Some who live daily with those two facts may not need this solemn reminder, as you and I do. But that is what our holy performances are *for:* so that we may live before God anchored both in our history and his, anchored in the cross, the divine scarecrow on the rubbish dump.

And so we must tell ourselves, again and again. Beneath *this* shrine, beneath the words we say and hear today, as beneath the old Temple, is a lightless, deafening, choking, and smelly vault, a place we're constantly in danger of slipping away to without noticing. Down there, we haven't yet really noticed the public nakedness of God, the open space of his love. We brush aside the rumor of the cross and stick with the God we can do business with. This God is pleased with our bustle, our willingness to make him an absorbing, even an expensive, hobby. He is pleased that we treat our worship as something isolated and special, pleased by our religious professionalism. He is delighted that we so successfully manage the conditions under which he may be approached, saying "yes" to this one, and "no" to that one, and "possibly, if you do the following things" to another. The scribes sit and discuss who is pure enough to come to the altar, and the anxious crowds mill around to find where they can acquire the right coinage to come into the sacred precinct. Religion and morality become religiosity and moralism. The wholeness of persons—their sin and their need and their thanksgiving—is broken down, as bits are exchanged for the acceptable equipment of the cult.

Of course the crowds *aren't* that much in evidence these days. To most people, the hectic activity of that vault is both comical and alarming. The tragedy is that they suppose that it *is* the holy place, the Temple of God. And for all of us who are religious, who dutifully perform the rites of our faith—and especially for those of us who are "professionally religious," clergy and so on—there is enough of that hot and crowded vault somewhere not too far from the surface to give plausibility to that error. We live down there a good deal of the time without even noticing, with the God who needs both pleasing and managing—occupations that substantially eat into the time we have for the concerns of the world.

This isn't a plea for sixties-style relevance and worldly holiness, but a plea that our work and worship in places like this should not fail to lead us back to the central fact of grace, God's gift shown in the depth of human pain. Then the vault can be emptied, because the service of the holy is set free from the setting of boundaries and conditions. It can call forth the riches of imagination, the discipline of our singers, the quiet dedication of all those here who help to welcome and serve people, and even the long-winded labors of us theologians. There can still be life, thought, vitality, and beauty in the service of holiness, perhaps even more when we are set free from the manic and obsessive God and the hectic, airless religion of the subterranean vault. But what will matter is the patterning of all this toward the truth at the center of the world, God's cross, in all its openness, all its secularity and unprotectedness.

John's Jesus reproaches his people for making the Father's house a place of merchandise: God is not served with bargaining and managing. The Jesus of the other gospels says that the traders have made the holy place a den of thieves: the honor given to the God of the traders' vault is taken from the true God. The real Lord of the real creation, God with us, is robbed of love and trust and service by the fantasies of our religious busyness, robbed of those who are his scattered children by the way we men and women "of faith" so readily make it into a defended fortress.

Holy Week, with all its intensity of ritual and imaginative elaboration, comes paradoxically to break down the walls of self-contained religion and morality and to gather us around the one true holy place of the Christian religion, Jesus himself, displayed to the world as the public language of our God, placarded on the history of human suffering that stretches along the roadside. This is a week for learning—not management, bargaining, and rule-keeping, but naked trust in that naked gift.

11

The Forgiveness of Sins

Hosea 11:1-9; Matthew 18:23-35

Belief in forgiveness is just as much a matter of *faith* as anything else in the creed. It is no more obvious and demonstrable than the existence of God or the divinity of Jesus Christ. This is perfectly clear if we think a little about the meaning of forgiveness and the realities of human existence and relationship. I am what I am because of what I have been and done, good and bad. My self is woven out of a great web of complicated motivation, reflections, intentions, and actions, some of which have turned out to be creative, while others have been destructive for myself and for other people. And mature persons need to be able to see and accept all this, to take responsibility for some things and to accept the inevitability of others—to *own* the whole of ourselves, to acknowledge realities both past and present, to destroy all the crippling illusions about ourselves that lock us up in selfish fantasies about our power or independence. I depend on the past, and it is part of me; to deny it is to deny myself. I *am* my history.

People will often talk about forgiveness in a way that suggests this is not true. "Forgive and *forget*," we say; we'll say no more about it. We look at forgiveness as if it were the same as acquittal—leaving the court without a stain on our character, as if it simply obliterated the past. If that is how we think of forgiveness, it really *does* become incredible—an arbitrary fiat which unties all the knots we are bound in by simply pretending certain things haven't happened. It is rather like the attitude of those who seem to think that the resurrection cancels out the crucifixion. But we *know* this is not true: if we have been badly hurt by someone, then whatever happens the scars and memories will still be there, even if we "forgive" them. And if we have hurt someone, the same is true: we may be "forgiven," but we can see the effects of what we have done, perhaps for years after. If forgiveness is forgetting, then it isn't only incredible: it is a mockery of the depth and seriousness of the suffering that human beings inflict on each other. The monument at Auschwitz to the Jews killed there has the inscription, "O earth, cover not their blood." There are things that should never, never be forgotten—Auschwitz is one of them—and if forgiveness means forgetting, then forgiveness is a trivial and profoundly offensive idea, as that monument indeed suggests.

Well, though, isn't forgiveness still a possible idea even if we agree that the past can't be changed? Can't we say that forgiveness is an agreement not to forget, but at least to suspend judgment on the past? In other words, I deserve your anger, I deserve punishment, but you kindly excuse me what I owe you. This approach has a good deal of support in the New Testament; it is the basis of a lot of Christian thinking on the subject. I am a sinner, but God graciously treats me as if I weren't. This is important, and it is an advance on the "forgive and forget" idea. But is it enough on its own? Surely not. This is a forgiveness that changes nothing—something that sounds almost cynical if we're not careful. A forgiveness that says only, "I know exactly what you are and what you have done, but I'll say no more about it," can be, in fact, a terrible, negative judgment. I don't take you seriously enough to do anything: do what you like, I won't make any difficulties.

That's a travesty, of course, but it is something to beware of. No, we need something more positive to say about forgiveness. We need to recognize both the reality of the past and the hope of a future forgiveness. Because real forgiveness is something that changes things and so gives hope. The occasions when we feel genuinely forgiven are the moments when we feel, not that someone doesn't care what we do, but that someone *does* care what we do because he or she loves us and that love is strong enough to cope with and survive the hurt we have done. Forgiveness of that sort is creative because it reveals new dimensions to a relationship, new depths, new possibilities. We can find a love richer and more challenging than before. If someone says to me, "Yes, you have hurt me, but that doesn't mean it's all over. I forgive you. I still love you," then that is a moment of enormous liberation. It recognizes the reality of the past, the irreversibility of things, the seriousness of damage done, but then it is all the more joyful and hopeful because of that. Because this kind of love doesn't have illusions, it is also all the more mature and serious. It can look at and fully *feel* my weaknesses, and still say, "I love you."

But what does this say about the unhealed human injuries, about the death and catastrophe that can find no human resolution? Who is to forgive the camp commandant at Auschwitz, the murderer of a child, the tyrant waging genocidal wars? Only the victim has the "right" to forgive: I can't forgive on someone else's behalf. I can't intrude into that dreadful intimate relation between the one who hurts and the one who is hurt. So it seems as if there can be no forgiveness if the victim doesn't forgive—and the dead, you might say, don't forgive. We might find a reason for *pardoning* the murderer, but that is not the same thing. Are there, then, wounds never to be healed, personally as well as globally? After all, our love is *not* very strong. It is hardly surprising if we come to a point where we say, "I can't take that. That is the end of love." Is forgiveness to depend on this, on our hopeless, inept struggles to love?

The reply of the gospel is "no." Christian faith here pushes right against the limits of the credible once again in saying that *God* forgives and has the *right* to forgive. God is the ultimate victim of all human cruelty, says the gospel: God bleeds for every human wound. Inasmuch as we do good or ill to any human person, it is done to God. Forgiveness is not only a matter to be settled among ourselves—or left unsettled because of our inadequacies. It is God's affair too. And the good news of Christianity is that, since God suffers human pain, since God is the victim of human injury, then there is beyond all our sin a love that is inexhaustible. God's love for this creation never comes to a point where it can take no more. In the old Prayer Book epistle for today, we hear Paul reminding us that *agape*, God's love, never comes to an end. So God can always survive the hurt we do him; whenever we turn to him in sorrow and longing, after we have done some injury, this love is still there, waiting for us, a home whose door is always open. *Whatever* we do can never shut that door to his merciful acceptance. The only thing that can keep us out is the refusal to ask for and trust in that mercy.

And the gospel proclaims all this in virtue of the cross of Jesus. Without that, we cannot begin to understand the forgiveness of sins. Jesus crucified is God crucified, so we believe. Jesus is the total and final embodiment in history of God's loving mercy; and so this cross is a unique, terrible, extreme act of violence—a summary of all sin. It represents the human rejection of love. And not even *that* can destroy God: with the wounds of the cross still disfiguring his body, he returns out of hell to his disciples and wishes them peace. Because Jesus as preacher and teacher had proclaimed and enacted God's identification with the world of human beings, Jesus the condemned criminal speaks of God's presence in the extremity of suffering, in abandonment and death—God as victim. And thus he proclaims God as the one who, above all others, has the right to forgive. "In all their affliction he was afflicted." The prophet in the Old Testament saw a little of that, but here in Jesus it is spelled out in the detail of a human life and death. There is our hope—the infinite *resource* of God's love, the relationship with his creatures that no sin can finally unmake. He cares what we do because he suffers what we do. He is forever wounded, but forever loving. The possibilities of our relationship with him are indeed "new every morning."

So our sins become not stopping points, but starting points. They can be the occasions of constantly fresh, constantly *wider* visions of the grace of God. It's often been said, boldly, that the saints in heaven rejoice over their sins, because through them they have been brought to greater and greater understanding of the endless endurance of God's love, to the knowledge that beyond every failure God's creative mercy still waits. We have a future because of this grace.

A matter of *faith*: yes, indeed, not of clear knowledge or vision. To see God in Christ crucified is a matter of faith; to believe in the unyielding and inexhaustible love of God is a matter of faith; and to believe there is a future for us despite the reality of our sins is a matter of faith. Still more difficult to imagine is how God can forgive in the name of those most desperately and terribly hurt. How can God forgive the tyrant and the murderer? We can't talk too glibly about reconciliation and resolution here. It is hard to see how some people might ever let themselves be forgiven, even if forgiveness is offered. But it's not our business to work that out. All we can be sure of is that whatever the deficiency and the drying-up of human capacity to love, the killing of love by pain, there is still, at the heart of everything, a love that cannot be killed by pain. That is a warning against regarding or treating *any* human being as unforgivable; that is the positive side of this problem, this brick wall for the imagination. We don't know how some situations can issue in forgiveness, and we have to bear their dreadfulness without pious evasion, but it would be worse to deny the possibility of grace, however unthinkable. That possibility is our only hope, and it is the only clue to what "grace" can mean in our relations with each other—the refusal to set the limits to our love.

As Jesus' parable forcibly reminds us, the man who forgets how much and in what way he has been loved and forgiven, how much hurt he has inflicted on the eternal heart of God, and who clings to his "rights" and nurses his unforgiven injuries—that man is in mortal danger. He has understood nothing and sees forgiveness as a thing canceling the past. And of course he duly finds out that the past is not canceled. But we who profess belief in the forgiveness of sins must see forgiveness as something creative of the future, the future of our own love. It is never a possession, it is not something finished; it is a gift and a hope, and also a call.

The gift is itself a task. We can pray in gratitude to God for being forgiven, but we must pray too for help to live with forgiveness, and to *live* it in our own future.

12

I Do Not Know
the Man

Peter...began to invoke a curse on himself and to swear, "I do not know the man." *(Matthew 26:74)*

For years I shared his life; I listened to him, I ate at his table. In a small way I took risks with him and for him, giving up some comforts and securities. I began to let my life be shaped by him. But I do not know him, and I never did. How could I know that it was all leading to this place? The cold dawn and the glare of torches and the grinning faces that might laugh it off, or turn you over to the military, or lynch you themselves? I never knew that healing a leper or sharing a meal with a prostitute might cost you a life.

I do not know the man.

It's one thing to be where you can give, where you can be generous and even a little daring in your generosity, and think quite well of yourself. And then that generosity you've played at makes a claim you can't meet, and things become serious. How can I be loyal to promises I never really understood? How can I forgive myself for the foolishness of a commitment whose scale I couldn't know? How can I forgive him for bringing me face to face with my fear and my impotence here in the glare of the torches? I do not know him, and I do not want to know him; I do not want to know the self he makes me see, its comfort and its untruthfulness.

I do not know the man.

I am more comfortable with the God. The man speaks to me not in solemn commands, in law and majesty, but in the touch of a hand, a baby crying, a death, and expects me to hear and obey these voices of need and friendship as if they were the voice of God. The man says "follow me," come with me in a journey along the roads of the flesh, its sufferings and limits, so that God will speak there.

I want to know God; I want to be lifted away from uncertainty and dread, and see things calmly from the height of his eyes, my frailty left behind. I do not want to know the human, the provisional and ironic, tears and laughter, the future still to make, steps in trust to be taken, even over deep and stormy waters. Show us the Father and it is enough. Take us away from all this; like the ultimate romantic hero, sweep us into the world of distant panoramas, magical controls, solved problems. I do not want to be forced back to the earth where I must choose and travel and be hurt.

I do not know the man.

I have tried to be generous and tolerant to the unfortunate: to the whores and collaborators, the Jews and the blacks, the homosexuals and the pacifists and the handicapped, the great mass of people who don't have my liberty. I am nice to them, and I deplore prejudice and discrimination. So don't embarrass me; remember I'm not one of them, and I can't be held responsible for the bad taste of their suffering or their protest. You must remember that they haven't had our advantages, and so they're bound to be a little shrill. But you and I can disagree in a civilized way. I'm one of you really; please believe me. The torchlight is making me sweat. I do not really know them.

I do not know the man.

I do not know myself. I don't know what I want or where I am. I thought I knew the paths I wanted, but look where they've led. Here in the unforgiving hour before dawn, I watch my desires stripped down to the one great longing to stay alive the way I am, to hold on to *me*. I'd rather *I* lived than anyone else. "All that a man has he will give in exchange for his life."

And is that all? Did I deceive myself when I thought I wanted something more, really wanted to be part of a love that would make all the difference in the world? I do not know. I can't believe that was just illusion. Perhaps I wanted to want that; but I never saw how deeply I'd want to escape, how I would clutch my life, my ego, here in the dawn under the torches and grinning faces. If I do not know him, I do not understand myself. I shall not know who I am until I know whether I dare be with him or not.

I do not know the man.

I shall never know him. There is always more than I can say or think, and when I believe I have understood him, he will turn and look out of such silence that I'll know I have still known nothing. Of course, he goes alone to his death, because we shall not know what it is for him to accept and live his way into that great breach with the source of his life, which he calls "Father." I do not know him; all I have known is the stirring of a knowledge that in his silence and his death all men and women will find themselves free. I do not need to know him, tó master him and categorize and theologize him, only to know that my life is to be found there. I do not know the man; I want to be where he is; I want to escape; I want his love; I want his absolution. I want to live, and I am afraid when he tells me I must learn to be mortal. I want the questions to stop.

And he went out and wept bitterly.

Erbarme dich, mein Gott...
Have mercy, Lord, on me,
For my tears' sake, forgive;
See, here, my heart and eyes
Grieve bitterly before thee.
Have mercy.

13

Risen Indeed

He laid his right hand upon me, saying, "Fear not, I am the first and the last, and the living one; I died, and behold I am alive for evermore, and I have the keys of Death and Hades."

(Revelation 1:17-18)

In the calendar of the Eastern Orthodox Church today is Easter Sunday, and in the *very* small hours of this morning a rather bleary-eyed little group from Westcott House was standing in a Russian Orthodox church in London, sharing in one of the most unforgettable of Christian experiences, a Russian Easter. Hugging and kissing all round, and again and again the great cry from the altar steps, *Christos voskrese*, "Christ is risen," and the shouted reply from hundreds of voices, *Voistinu voskrese*, "He is risen indeed." And again and again the Easter hymn, "Christ is risen from the dead, trampling down death by death."

Conquering death by death. It is here that we must start in thinking about Christ as *Lord*. As St. John saw in his vision, Jesus holds the keys of hell *because* he has died and yet is alive. And in the gospels it is the risen Christ who says, "All authority in heaven and earth has been given to me." The earliest Christians thought of the resurrection as the event in which God invested Jesus, the carpenter of Nazareth, with authority, brought Jesus to sit on his right hand in heaven to share his kingship. Why? First and foremost, because Jesus raised from the dead "dies no more," as Paul says. The risen Jesus is set free from all the constraints and limits that keep men and women at a distance from God and from each other—from the "principalities and powers" of the New Testament. The resurrection is not a resuscitation; it is the gift of a new *kind* of life, the life that exists on the far side of death and hell, of destruction and disintegration. He will not die again; "death has no more dominion" over him. He is no longer the prisoner of the past; he is not an historical memory, whose life is neatly tied up and put away. No, from now on he belongs to all people and all times, he is *available* to all. He is free.

What this means in effect is that what Jesus preached to a limited group in his lifetime is now offered to all. And this preaching is the assurance of God's absolute acceptance of all who trust him. But how is the depth and seriousness of this acceptance demonstrated? Jesus does not simply *talk* about it, but enacts it; in his own compassion, service, and openness to all who turn to him, he "fleshes out" the mercy of God. He continues to do so in the very depths of costliness and pain, realizing—it seems—with greater and greater clarity what it will mean for him to give himself as a living sign of God's compassion. It will be death, the total emptying out of life and self. And so his expected death too becomes invested with this character of "fleshing-out" the mercy of God. Jesus went to his death, we are told, in horror and loneliness, and, as far as we can see, inner turmoil and darkness. There was no stoic resignation, no Socratic dignity, nothing to make it easy or natural: Jesus looked at his coming death and saw it as monstrous and dreadful.

What compelled the imagination of the early believers was precisely this—that he was obedient *in spite of all*, that he endured the nightmare for the sake of God's mercy. He has given himself up to the task of embodying compassion; if it leads to death, death must be accepted, and to turn from it is to stand in the way of God's mercy, to obscure its light. And so Jesus in his agony in Gethsemane says "yes" to the death he dreads, so that he will not obscure God's mercy. His gift is total; there is nothing in him that intervenes between God and suffering humanity. Here is a man who has given the entirety of his life and death to be a token, a pledge, and a taste of God's outpouring, costly, unconditional compassion for alienated men and women. The author of the fourth gospel puts it with characteristically blunt and shocking imagery: Jesus has made himself our food. His flesh is the bread of God's goodness: eat him and live.

Jesus empties himself to the point of death and *therefore*, says Paul, God has highly exalted him. Jesus has made himself translucent, the burning glass through which God's light comes to set the world on fire; he has made an empty space in the world for God to come in. And so he does not any longer belong just to the world of human beings: he is a space in the world, a silence in human speech, the place where God is free to act and to suffer. He has made room for God. That is why Jesus' death is not the end of a story, but the last point in his great struggle to *free* God into the world. The cross is the final liberation of God's healing love; and the Father seals Jesus' work by setting him on his right hand in glory. Now he belongs with God, not only with us: risen and ascended, he is the one who gives us "holy Spirit," the breathing of God in our hearts, the life of God that unites us with the Father.

All authority in heaven and on earth: Jesus has decisively "made space" for God in the world of human beings, so that from now on God is found in the world definitively in the history of Jesus. This is what God's mercy is: an unconditional gift of incalculable cost. It can only be embodied in history in human shape, in the shape of a life and a death seen and accepted as something *entirely* defined as God's gift to all; a life which is a total offering both to God and to men and women, so total that human limitation becomes irrelevant. A human life like this is not just a matter of history, it is the abiding sign of God's presence in the world. The empty grave, that strange and ambivalent sign, stands as our reminder that the life of Jesus is not "over," not limited and defined and tidied up. He is "with us." In every extremity, every horror and pain, Jesus is accessible as the one who continued to make God's loving presence wholly present in the depth of his own anguish and abandonment. There is place for God now in all suffering, at the heart of suffering and even of death, because we have seen the glory of God abiding in the squalor and humiliation of Jesus' execution. Jesus has "authority" in that he has the right to be there and to be called on in suffering and death. He holds the keys of hell, because he has dwelt there and still lives.

Death and the hells of dereliction and abandonment eat people up, exhaust them, scrape them out, and bring them to nothing. Jesus is already empty, already poor, already nothing, for God is everything in him; and so the inexhaustible life of God meets death and eats it up and exhausts it. "Death and life have contended," says the Easter hymn. And Jesus by death, the death of obedience, of self-emptying, of gift and grace and mercy, has trampled death underfoot and shown us the way to life by union with the pattern of his death—his mercy, his self-emptying, his self-offering. By this we can, with him, pass from death to life and die for the life of all the world. By service and the gift of our whole being to God and to his suffering world, we may stand with Jesus, live the life of God, and share the lordly freedom of God, the lordship uncovered for us in humiliation and death.

Jesus is Lord. Jesus of Nazareth is the face of God turned toward us in history, decisively and definitively. All this life is God's act. The church did not invent the doctrine of the Incarnation: slowly and stumblingly, Christians *discovered* it. If Jesus is translucent to God in all he does and is, if he is empty so as to pour out the riches of God, if he is the wellspring of life and grace, what then? He *is* God: in infancy, in death, in eating and drinking, in healing and preaching. This is not simply a man witnessing to a vision, or transmitting a word from the Lord. This is the Lord, God in flesh, God made known in history; this is God fearing, struggling, and suffering, the only God we know or can know, the glory of God in the face of Christ, love and healing in human hands and eyes—how else could we grasp it? God dying, meeting us at our last pain and our greatest fear and taking all death, all wounds and tears, to his endless resource of life and compassion.

Jesus is for us the Alpha and the Omega, the beginning and the end of all things, because there is no place where the icon of that suffering face cannot be unveiled and worshiped. For him there are no divisions, no parties, no exclusivities of race or sex or achievement or power: he is there for all, because he has made himself God's "space," God's room in the world, and in him there are no longer the boundaries and limits of human self-regard and self-protection. He is *unprotected;* no walls, no gravestone even, can seal him in. In God he is free for all humanity; in him *God* is free. God and humanity are knotted together there in that space of history, those short years in Palestine, so that *that* history is the sign that interprets all history. And by that death all death is conquered.

14

My Dancing Day

Tomorrow shall be my dancing day;
I would my true love did so chance
To see the legend of my play
To call my true love to my dance.
Sing 0, my love, my love, my love—
this have I done for my true love.

Many of us had the joy of watching BBC2's "Stepping Out" program recently, dealing with the world of a lovely young Chilean teacher in Australia who is developing dance and drama with the mentally handicapped. We were treated to scenes showing the very first stages, as these young people in their twenties and thirties gradually learned controlled breathing, coordinated movement, learned to relax into their bodies and *live* in them. Then costumes and masks were tried on, the music became more adventurous, the dancing more subtle, until Chris—the thirty-one-year-old natural soloist of the group—emerged, dancing to Villa-Lobos and Puccini, portraying the death of Madame Butterfly with total conviction and a kind of ritual pathos few professionals could manage. We watched the awkward, superficially lumpy and vacant face of a "retarded" man turn into a tragic mask: every inch, every corner of the body answering the music with discipline, accuracy, complete engagement. And the climax, a breathtaking performance in the Sydney Opera House, no less, was greeted with a standing ovation, as well it might be.

You might have started out (I did) prepared to feel a little moved in a rather patronizing way—how touching, how pathetic, how cute—but the only final response worth making was humble, awed delight. We had been *watching* grace, in every sense. We had been watching love, the patient, humorous, grave care of the teacher getting these people to value and admire their bodies, giving words and hugs of encouragement to each one as they prepared to perform. Love, too, in the relationship between Chris and the "handicapped" girl who spoke the commentary, the easy, respectful happiness they shared. And then the overpowering grace of Chris on stage, which it is useless to try to describe.

"This have I done for my true love...To call my true love to my dance." I don't want to moralize this experience: it is quite enough to be made to feel delighted and proud to be a human being (rare enough, too). But many things of wider import emerged from the Laura Hodgkinson Sunshine Home in Sydney. "Love to the loveless shown, That they might lovely be." We watched people blossom into unpredictable beauty by being taken seriously. If you're made to feel all the time that your body is graceless, it will indeed be a lump of messy fat. And who, normally, cares to inform the "mongol" or the "spastic" or the "retarded" that they are *physically* alive in any more than an animal sense? Who's going to awaken the "grace of sense" (in Eliot's words) that transforms fat and bone and hair into achieved, assured dignity? Remember that even the transforming grace of sexual love is normally denied or repressed for the "handicapped."

But *put* grace and you will *find* grace. Invite the unlovely partner to sit opposite you, breathing slowly and deeply, and to mirror your gestures: the slow circling of an arm, the opening of a hand. That's how our Chilean teacher began. That's how dancing begins. Sit and watch. I'll give you grace and you can give it back. You can answer me because you are like me. You are alive, too. Here are the signs of my life, the patterns I make, the beauty I create, and so can you. As we sit like this, my life makes yours more alive.

Listen to this invitation. Sit down, all of you handicapped, lumpish, empty, afraid, and start to feel that you too are rooted in a firm, rich earth. Opposite you is someone who, it seems, doesn't need to learn. His roots are very deep, very deep indeed; he knows he is lovely and loved. Dancing is natural to him; he has no paralyzing, self-conscious dread, no self-protection to overcome. So he begins: he stretches out his arms, wide as he can. And so do you. Then he rises up, arms to the sky. And so do you. Then he takes your hand and swings you loose and leaves you to improvise to the music—on your own, then combining with the others, then alone again, then with one or two, then all together, and alone again....

He dances so that you will dance. He shows you what beauty is, his body awakens yours. He's there to be your partner and everyone's; sometimes you'll see him opposite you, sometimes not (beside you, behind you, holding someone else's hands). But he's there, in and out of your dance, always affirming your beauty, fusing together your mind and your imagination and your flesh, so that none of it will be lost. He gives you the fusion of his mind and imagination and flesh—his glorious body. The signs of his life, the patterns he makes, the presence of his beauty—all this is his body, signing to us, inviting us, making us alive. He repeats over and over his central gesture—arms flung wide, then palms carried upward as he stands on the earth, carrying us, embracing us. As we watch, we know; our roots grow deeper downward. We can afford to dance, dance the useless dance of love for its own sake, beauty for its own sake: the dance of Mother Teresa, of Charles de Foucauld, of all who work with the hopeless, the incurable, the dying, the wretched. The dance of a hospice for the terminally ill: work done gratuitously, to celebrate the glory of the human face, even in its last agonies. Dancing on coals or nails in that case, but how can you not do it? Our life now is not for usefulness but for beauty: we can have no other. Dancing is natural to him; bit by bit it becomes natural for us. He can't help himself, and, in due course, neither shall we be able to help ourselves.

But of course, sadly, we're not handicapped. So we switch channels for the "Nine o'Clock News," to reassure ourselves that we live after all in a world of sane and non-retarded adults, where no one, no one will *ever* ask us to sit and watch and learn, and then dance. We look at our partners across a table with dry cynicism. We read in their eyes the mirror image of the dread and hatred in our own: the mirror image of our rejection and contempt across a street in Brixton; the mirror image of our ruthless manipulative violence in a jail in Ulster; the mirror image of our obsessive, hysterical games with apocalyptic weapons in Moscow. Feel hate and you will find hate. Feel contempt and you will find contempt. No dancing day tomorrow or the next day. We can leave the dancing to the handicapped, the wounded, and the inadequate. We sane adults must get on with the serious business of living, or rather, dying—or rather, killing one another.

15

Building Up Ruins

They shall build up the ancient ruins, they shall raise up the former devastations. *(Isaiah 61:4)*

Israel's hope was always and invariably a hope for return, return to the Land. When at various times in the twentieth century suggestions were made about the creation of a "Jewish Homeland," a good number of possibilities were considered in Africa, Asia, and America. But for the Jews there could be only one serious proposal. The Land given to them is the land they must return to. Anything else is a nonsense. Jews are not Jews without their history, and they have no history apart from the memory of the Land and the hope of return. "Next year in Jerusalem."

So the hope of Old Testament prophecy is never abstract or generalized. Arguments will no doubt go on about what degree of "universalism" can be found in the Old Testament, but one thing is clear: the prophets do not think in terms of a general hope for all human beings. They see first the concrete situation (Israel redeemed and restored) *then* the potentially universal (the gathering of the nations). "All who see them shall acknowledge them, that they are a people whom the Lord has blessed," "priests of the Lord...ministers of our God." It has been said with some justice that "humanity" is not a thing we can easily feel for, and that "love of humanity" can be an alibi for not loving the immediate and particular humanity around you in your own situation. This isn't the prophets' problem. Restoration can only begin *here*.

The new age is not a general utopia in which all that has gone before is simply canceled. No, for the prophets it means going back to the ruins of the past, to the devastated and depopulated land of Israel and building there, with the help of God, a city which is new but which still stands on the same earth as the old.

It is going back to the memories of the painful, humiliating past and bringing them to redemption in the present. Israel cannot deny her *memory,* her past, without denying her God, without suggesting that God is not faithful. Land and covenant, earth and history are the stuff of God's speaking to his people. It is (as in Isaiah's next chapter) *Zion* that will be vindicated. It is the city of David that stands at the end of the great highway the Lord will make from Babylon. For Israel, to think of redemption and of the coming reign of God is, inevitably and necessarily, to think of her own particular memory of victory and defeat, her own story now brought to conclusion—not to think of bland universal prosperity, but of the binding up of her own particular wounds and the recreation of her city.

Of course, the memory of *your* particular wounds, the acute consciousness of *your* history, can be one of the most terribly destructive emotions known to human beings. The defeat of 300 or 500 or 1,000 years ago that is still remembered and resented and regularly bewailed is a sure recipe for a pathological society (and we don't have to look very far afield for this). But, in the context of authentic hope and the readiness not to see restoration as something to be won and held at the expense of the rest of humanity, it is a vastly significant awareness. My future will not be *mine* without the concrete memories of all my past. To deny that is to deny that I am one person, one person with one life, a seamless coat, every moment sewn into every other. Individual talk about conversion and political talk about revolution both represent something important, but considered in isolation both are potentially inhuman things. If you have begun to understand yourself at all, you will have to acknowledge the need to bring your memories—individual or collective—with you. It is on that ground or nowhere that restoration begins.

Where does the risen Jesus appear to his disciples? In the upper room, in Galilee, on a hill, on the seashore—all the diverse and rather muddled stories of what happened after the first Easter seem to point us to the same thing. The theme is, again, return. He meets them where he met them before. This morning's gospel sets it out with skill and subtlety: "I am going fishing." Back to the very beginning, back to the first call and response. And there the risen Jesus comes to bind up the broken-hearted and build up the ruins. The disciples with their memories of terror and betrayal and shame come back to their beginnings, back to their "earth" in Galilee, and Christ comes to repair the devastation. Peter's threefold denial is countered with his threefold confession and the Lord's threefold charge to him. And—an unobtrusive but haunting detail—there is a "fire of coals" burning on the shore, just as there was in the High Priest's courtyard (the only two occasions when the expression appears in the gospel). Peter must stand again on the soil of his first vocation, his response, and his failure; he must smell again the sour scent of his betrayal in the drifting smoke of the fire. On that foundation rests his future, his pastoral authority, his martyr's crown: back to the native earth and the memories of defeat, in the presence of the undefeated, ever-faithful Lord.

It is perhaps one reason why the apparition stories, with all their lack of clarity, are so important. In very different ways, they underline the truth that the resurrection is a recapitulation, not a reversal, of the history of Jesus *and* of his disciples. Their failures, his cross, all bound together, are memories never to be obliterated, but now taken up to be healed in the new age. These stories not only tell us something about the continuity of Jesus' risen life with his ministry and passion, they tell us about the continuity of the apostles' experience. There is no shattering conversion that blots out the shame and wretchedness of the past; no, they are led through it again by the hand of Jesus, gentle and relentless. Here I called you, here I broke bread with you, here you betrayed me; and here I still stand with you, calling you and breaking bread with you again and giving you a destiny in my love. Do we not remember all this every time we celebrate the eucharist? "In the same night that he was betrayed, he took bread...." Don't forget that: here it is, made into grace and healing.

So to speak of the resurrection of our bodies is to look for the restoration of all our memories. This is a very hard thing to believe and, in some ways, not an immediately attractive thing to hope for. Some things we should very much prefer to have buried. With some memories, it is unthinkable that the grace of God should be able to do anything with them; they seem irredeemable. All the perfumes of Arabia will not sweeten this little hand? Our temptation is to try to shut them away from the eye of God and from our own consciousness. But Christ continues gentle and relentless. His light must make its way into every corner, and we must be ready to turn to it. Being aware of our memories in God's presence is, of course, part of the prayer of confession.

The hard thing is to make it part of our thanksgiving too, in the sense of being ready always to acknowledge before God what we are and therefore what we have been, and at the same time bless God that his grace makes opportunities out of all our sin and unhappiness. This is what Paul himself does, in joy and amazement, time and again, recollecting that he was a persecutor, with martyrs' blood on his hands, and yet knowing that from that persecutor God made an apostle. For Paul, this is the most extreme and unexpected work of the risen Christ, appearing "as to one untimely born," yet it is a work which is of a piece with all he does.

Our hope, then, is like the prophetic hope, a hope for the past, a hope for our native soil. God will take us back to the place where our cities and temples, our ideals and aspirations, faith and love, were destroyed and defeated. Like Nehemiah's return to old Jerusalem, it begins as a sad nocturnal tour around the relics of defeat. But God belongs to the future, and there is a new city to come down out of heaven. Risen life in and with Christ is *now*, entirely fresh, full of what we could never have foreseen or planned, yet it is built from the bricks and mortar, messy and unlovely, of our past. God is faithful: it is his hand that will uncover in all our experiences the golden thread of his covenant love, and so point us to a future where our memories can be healed and transfigured. *Our* earth, *our* dull and stained lives, these are the living stones of God's new Jerusalem. "So the Lord God will cause righteousness and praise to spring forth before all the nations" when he builds again and again—however often we are defeated—on the devastations of our history, builds the everlasting city where the marriage of earth and heaven is celebrated.

16

Ascension Day

One of the great trials of human life is putting the light on for the first time in the morning. Strange things happen to your eyes; you don't see at all clearly for a bit, and you're liable to go around bumping into things. Usually by the time you've made it to the bathroom the world is settling down a bit. At first you've been so conscious of the light that you can't—as you might say—*use* it to see with; after a bit, though, your attention isn't focused on the light itself any more but on the world that the light *shows* you. It would be odd to see someone going around in broad daylight or in a brightly lit room asking, "Where's the light?" as if the light were something extra to all the things you can see, one more item to count.

The gospel stories of the resurrection are full of the "early morning" sensation: things aren't clear, people aren't recognizable. It would have been more comfortable to stay in the dark. These are stories about surprise and disorientation: a surprise and disorientation brought about as the friends of Jesus discover that he is not dead. He is not a piece of history, a body under a memorial slab; his life, his *earthly* life, body and mind, has become the channel by which God goes on speaking to the world, the way in which God is with us, committed to us whatever we do. The life of Jesus can now be seen as bound up with the life of God. In the forceful phrase of one modern French writer, the resurrection has "tipped Jesus over" into the transcendence of God. But because the risen Jesus is still a recognizable human being, this doesn't mean that Jesus has abandoned the world he belongs to, *our* world. He is the sign and the power of God's freedom at work in and through the limitations, the tragedies, the frustrations of the world of human beings.

The resurrection is about God's commitment to this world of flesh and blood: it tells us that when we look at things and persons in the world, we're looking at the place where God has promised to be. In other words, the resurrection of Jesus really is like a light going on, giving us a way of seeing everything. And just as first thing in the morning it is the *light* you're aware of, dazzling and disorienting, so with the Easter stories: it is *Jesus* that his friends are conscious of—the center, the heart of the bewildering new world. For a bit, the disciples see Jesus, they see the light going on and they experience all the strange, exhilarating, and frightening sensations involved. But after a while there are no more reports of people seeing Jesus, as at first. The light has ceased to be something that draws our attention in its own right. It's something we see by.

This is the transition that Ascension Day marks. As the readings suggest, it is the moment when Jesus "goes away," stops being an object we concentrate on in itself, and yet becomes more deeply and permanently present: "I am with you always, to the end of time." He is with us as the light we see by; we see the world in a new way because we see it *through* him, see it with his eyes. So it's not only that we learn to see that the world is a place where God has promised to be; if we see it in the light of Jesus, because Jesus has become the very sight of our eyes, we see it as a place to which *we* are committed. Jesus raised from the dead is the great sign of God's faithfulness to the world, and, as his presence with us becomes the light by which we see everything, we come to share in the same faithfulness. We, with and through Jesus, are also signs to the world of God's promise.

The transition involved here is one we all need to go through. At every real point of growth in our lives, every point when the world looks new, we're bound at first to be dazzled, thrown off balance by whatever has made the difference. Christians are constantly rediscovering Jesus in their lives. And the temptation is often to try to hold on to the vision of Jesus when we ought to be letting the life of Jesus change our vision of the *world.* We can get fascinated, even obsessed, with the odd and exciting experiences that go along with the upheavals and renewals of faith. But ultimately, to have faith in Jesus is to let your life, your way of relating to the world, be transformed into the pattern of Jesus' life—not to acquire an intriguing new hobby, the study of religious experiences. This doesn't of course mean—any more than it did for Jesus' disciples—that we ignore the figure of Jesus or forget about the story of his life and death. It means that we think about Jesus not as someone completely outside us, but as the power *in us* gradually setting us free to see the world with clarity, hope, and love. Jesus does not greedily demand attention for himself: he points us to the God he calls Father, and enables us to go on our journey toward God the Father as he himself did, by the path of commitment to the world.

In prayer, we seek to be more deeply in touch with this reality that is coming to be within us; from our roots in that prayer, we deepen our own faithfulness to God's world. We don't all that often think of faithfulness or commitment as the central virtue in our relation to the world, but it is worth pausing a minute or two to explore the idea. We understand a bit about being faithful to people in our personal relations; we're perhaps less clear about being faithful to human beings as such, being loyal to the human race. This is hard and risky work: it involves not treating anyone as dispensable, but acting on the assumption that everyone has a future with God and so must be taken completely seriously. There are no surplus people, people whose needs or claims we can safely ignore—the unborn, the handicapped, the dying, or just those who are far away from us. Christian faith can have no room for any notion that the rights of some human beings simply overrule the reality of others; that's why Christians are going to be a nuisance in any imaginable human society. Their loyalty can't be given to anything less than the human race to which *God* has promised commitment.

It involves also a concern for the future of human beings on this planet. Being faithful means thinking and planning for a future that is not clouded by the threat of nuclear destruction and environmental disaster. If we can't rest content with taking the human race less seriously than God has done, we must work for God's promise to be a reality in the whole of our earthly setting. And that means, too, that faithfulness to the human race brings with it faithfulness to the material environment in which we live. We can't be faithful to each other and to our children without a care for the natural world of which we are a part. Our present anxieties about almost irreversible degeneration of the environment—the erosion of the ozone layer, the destruction of rainforests, and so on—take it for granted that the human future is part of the planet's future. And taking this further, our anxiety over the animal world—over the disappearance of species, over unrestricted experimentation on live animals—assumes that even when our practical interests aren't so much engaged, we know quite well that our indifference to the rest of creation corrupts our own *human* morality and imagination.

Perhaps all this is a bit of what the Ascension Day hymns and prayers mean when they speak of the whole of human nature being raised to heaven in the ascension. If Jesus is the presence of God's promise in our world, and if the ascension means that, through the power of the resurrection, we now share the same calling as Jesus, seeing in his light and with his eyes, then two things follow. First, we as Christian believers are "in heaven," but not so as to remove us from earth. Quite the contrary: in the middle of the world's life, we are given some share in God's perspective on things, so that God through us may make his loving faithfulness real and effective here and now. And second, the things and persons of this world are seen in a new way, seen as charged with hope, with a future of glory and of healing. They are seen as if already part of the new heaven and new earth in which God's purposes have been brought to completion.

The ascension celebrates the new creation, the bringing together of heaven and earth that has begun in the life of Jesus. When Jesus is seen no more in the old way, that does not mean he has abandoned the world, so that we must go and look for him outside it—"looking up into the sky" like the disciples. His life is being lived in us: the new world is being brought to birth in us, gradually and sometimes painfully. We are caught up in the eternal movement of God's commitment to his creation. In and through Jesus we, too, have become a sign of promise. The light is on; the morning has come. The daystar from on high has dawned upon us.

The Unknown God

17

An Enemy Hath
Done This

Now there was a day when the sons of God came to present
themselves before the Lord, and Satan came also among them.

(Job 2:1)

There are moments for all of us when the liberal, rational, humane categories we normally operate with suddenly collapse;
sooner or later, we must all drive into the extermination camp
and confront without illusion the most unbearable truth about
what it is to be human, the truth that benevolence and rationality are not at the heart of people's actions. There is a "horror of
great darkness" in our dealings with each other. Nor do we have
to go to the camps to learn this, though they are the most appalling sacrament of it that we have seen for centuries: the record in
our own lives is likely to be bleak enough. And when we see how
swiftly and easily the edge of gratuitous cruelty slips into our
well-intentioned, even our loving, transactions, we may echo William Golding: "People don't seem to be able to move without killing each other." Faced with the destructive fruits of what we have
done as individuals—or as a whole civilization—it is not surprising
that the cry springs to our lips, "An enemy hath done this."

"An enemy hath done this." Not I or we. How could we? This
is not what we meant. How can I be responsible for what I did
not mean? Yes, it is a child's cry, and it sounds so painfully like
the child's evasion of responsibility—the refusal to be adult and
accept the consequences of our actions. But perhaps there is
more to it—another kind of maturity that understands that "responsibility" is not the last word about human behavior. This is a

difficult thing to say convincingly, yet the Christian, with his or her perennial problem of understanding the relation of grace to freedom, is apparently stuck with the task of trying to say it. For human activity is misunderstood if it is seen as a sequence of "responsible" decisions taken by conscious and self-aware persons in control of their lives. More often it is a confused, partly conscious, partly instinctive response to the givenness of a world we do not dominate, a world of histories and ideas, languages and societies, structures we have not built. More perhaps than we ever realize or accept with our minds, we are being acted upon as much as acting. If our assumption of "responsibility" rests on a belief that we can construct the patterns of our own lives, it is an illusion—not the child's evasiveness this time, but the infant's assumption of omnipotence. It is a hard lesson, this; we should all like to believe otherwise, but intentions are not enough. Reality is stronger. Our uncertainty about the degree of our responsibility need not be cowardly or self-deceiving; it can be an honest acknowledgment of the way in which reality, even human and personal reality, resists the mind's desperate attempt to organize it reasonably.

The mind's *desperate* attempt: there's the rub. It is not at all comforting to recognize that we are not "in control," that incomprehensible forces are at work in and through us, involving us willy-nilly in a bewildering and horrifying chain of events. It seems to place us in that familiar situation of nightmares where everything is developing at great speed with a logic we cannot quite grasp and certainly cannot modify. Pushing these thoughts to their most extreme point: if we do not fully know what we have done, what we are doing, or what (worst of all) we may do—what is this but the condition we commonly call madness? If our reason is not "at the wheel" to unify and direct what we are and do, have we any unity at all in ourselves? Where is my soul? One of the worst threats one can feel is the sense that one's identity, one's particular and single being, is menaced; there is an unfamiliar presence in the home, a contradiction and a frustration, to trip us up, to catch us out, to twist our words, to bewilder and encircle us. "He has a devil": a *diabolos*, a maker of discord, an accusing presence because it mocks the mind's failure to bring the world—inner and outer—into order and meaning. And madness is the accuser's triumph, his coming into possession of the house, when the mind at last finds the contradictions insupportable.

The devil is not a convenient metaphor for extreme wickedness or even for the acute sense of meaninglessness. It may even be less of a mistake to think of him as a kind of person than to think of him as a kind of symbol. There is more than a "projection" here, more than an "externalization of inner conflicts"; in some sense, we really do meet another, a stranger, not a symbol from our conscious imaginings, but something that waits for us. As Ivan Karamazov discovers in his terrifying encounter with an amiable middle-class, nineteenth-century liberal Satan, his most refined torture is the refusal to tell us clearly whether he is us or not; that is the torture which drives Ivan insane. As soon as the question, "Inside or outside?" "I or not I?" is put, we have capitulated to the enemy's terms. We have entered a game of spiritual tail-chasing, the conscious mind frantically trying to close its teeth on a mockingly elusive shadow. We cannot rationalize it away by saying either, "I am the victim of a totally independent superhuman power," or "I am discovering the untapped resources of my individual psyche." The intolerable fact is that we meet the really alien in what is really human: if that is not so, the scriptural "mystery of iniquity" ceases to be mysterious.

How then shall we be saved? How are our lives to be preserved from disintegration and senselessness? There will be no answer to such questions as long as we persist in looking for a unified picture of our lives that our consciousness can take in without any difficulty, as long as we think of our relationship to God primarily or actively as a matter of individual self-awareness coming to fulfillment and integration. As Augustine might have said, the only integration we can achieve in this life is the knowledge that we cannot achieve integration, and the fullest maturity is to know our immaturity. Forget this, and you are proposing another kind of justification by works, a righteousness of intelligibility, a situation in which the judging and forgiving Word of God must wait on the divided consciousness and the troubled conscience of men and women, and can enter only to solve the problems dictated by us. No: "I cannot of my own understanding...come to Jesus Christ my Lord" (Luther's *Small Catechism*). God "is found by those who do not put him to the test and manifests himself to those who do not distrust him" (Wisdom of Solomon 1:2). Faith is the spirit that confronts the divider, the maker of discord, and rejects the invitation to put the Lord to the test by seeking the rational, the unified, the intelligible pattern. To believe is to hear and accept the proclaiming of God's victorious compassion, the mercy that is more than our conscience and our consciousness; it is to be able to say, "Whatever is in me and in the human world, God has seen, known, and taken to himself in Jesus who descended into hell." Christ has conquered.

The language of the Christus Victor tradition is, in many ways, a better model for us than any theory that sees the atonement as bringing order and control into the world. It takes with full seriousness the uncontrolled and uncontrollable, the alien and the menacing in the world, and says not that Christ has obliterated them, but that Christ has overcome them. They are there still, but their horror is seen in a new perspective: the wounds they inflict are the prints of the nails in the body of the Lord. He has battled with the unintelligible dark, the *surd* of evil, and still lives. He contains evil, he has shown that evil cannot contain him: the darkness comprehended it not. He has looked into the "heart of darkness": he has held the burning world to himself, and holds it always, at the cost of a pain we cannot begin to conceive. "The Lord is King...be the earth never so unquiet."

"This have I done for my true love." Faith rests on a victory that has been won; it is not a task or work that must be achieved by us, however much it demands the daily struggle to renew and mature a response in every corner of our lives. And in this context, does it matter where the devil dwells? The questions, "Inside or outside?"; "I or not I?" begin to seem insignificant, because the glorious victory of our Lord teaches us at once both the enormity, violence, and reality of Satan's power, and the truth that it is not final. Satan is the prince of this world; chaos and menace are the texture of our lives—yet the compassion of God encircles the whole. "It lasteth and ever shall because God loveth it." Can we now understand that our unity, integrity, wholeness, *salus, shalom* is not in us but in God-in-Christ, who is our peace? Any interest in the diabolical, any so-called expertise in demonology and the analysis of the dark and the absurd, is a failure in faith. If "exorcism" is ever anything more than the proclamation of God's victory and God's acceptance, if ever it becomes a matter of clinical technique, it has entered the conflict on the devil's terms, attempting to fight again the battle that Christ has won. No one will finally remove for us the risk of darkness, the influx of "black grace"—in Iris Murdoch's memorable phrase—that inflates our hatreds and pushes even our loves into cruelty. All that can be done is, again and again, to refuse the temptation to rationalize, and turn to the compassionate Word of God. To dramatize and objectify the world's senseless evil is to yield to its undeniable magnetism and to swell its potential power; and it is destructive enough without that. But to know it as the wounds of Christ is to see without illusion: not the pain but the threat can be healed.

So Satan is among the children of God; he is not outside of the company of God's beloved, and his unpredictable working and uncontrollable power cannot break the bond by which the love of God holds us to him. Only we—the conscious and rational and self-determining we—can do that, because we alone can say "no" to God's acceptance; we alone, in our struggle for control and meaning for ourselves, can objectify and eternalize the discord, the horror, the destructiveness of the human world, since that world will never of itself yield the order we look for. We are not wrong to fear hell: it is constantly present as a possibility in what we do and think. We are wrong only if we forget that the one freedom that is assured to us, the only freedom that finally matters, is the capacity to say "yes" to God's great "yes" to us in Christ, and that no powers of darkness and chaos and evil can rob us of that without our consent.

> For I am sure that neither death nor life, nor angels nor principalities, nor things present, nor things to come, nor powers, nor height, nor depth, nor anything else in all creation, will be able to separate us from the love of God in Christ Jesus our Lord.

18

The Dark Night

He has walled up my way, so that I cannot pass, and he has set darkness upon my paths. *(Job 19:8)*

It is very easy to go round and round the paths for a long time. There may be nothing in particular that puts an obstacle in the way. Whether we think of ourselves as "conservative" or "radical" where spirituality is concerned, the same is true. If I am a "conservative," my circular path will be one of conventional sacramental observance and a theological picture, however vague or naive, that sees God as the reliable source of meaning behind it all—God arranging the church and its observances as the best available means for me to get to him. If I am a "radical," my God will be the disturber of the social order, the one who calls me into freedom and into creative action—the God of the future, of the new and liberated humanity.

Both of these pictures as they stand are delusional. They are, equally, religious games designed to comfort and justify us in the style of religious life we have found congenial. As they stand, they are projections and wish-fulfillments, and all the unkind things psychologists have always tended to accuse religion of. "God" is a word or a concept that has a well-defined function in the way I order my life, and when you have explained that function, you have explained God. Something else might do just as well.

The only defense religion ever has or ever will have against the charge of cozy fantasy is the kind of experience or reflection normally referred to by Christian writers—at least since the sixteenth century—as the "night of the spirit." The "night of the spirit" or "night of the soul" is often thought of as another kind of religious experience, a very exalted, very painful, very dramatic mystical sharing in the sufferings of Christ, or something of that sort. But the truth is, alas, that it is simpler, and much more alarming. It is the end of religious experience, the very opposite of mysticism. It is a wall in the way, as Job says; it is the evacuation of meaning. We have been going round and round the paths, and suddenly we see that our path goes round a hole, a bottomless black pit. In the middle of all our religious constructs—if we have the honesty to look at it—is an emptiness. It makes nonsense of all religion, conservative or radical, and all piety.

People come to an awareness of this emptiness in different ways. For some, it can be the fruit of a personal growth in prayer leading inexorably to the point where words, books, and techniques will no longer help; then there is only nonsense and darkness, and a sense of utter lostness. For others, it can be some personal crisis in which the pain and senselessness of human experience suddenly rings so true that the cheapness and falsity of glib religious patterns appear for what they really are. Perhaps for the "radical" it can come when human beings prove intractable, when words like "liberation" and "justice" fall to the ground before the incurable destructiveness of men and women, privately as well as socially. It can be the sudden bursting of pent-up frustrations with the church and the liturgy: the very hollowness and banality of a lot of modern liturgy has been for some a revelation that there was never any meaning there at all.

But however it is reached, the experience is the same: the breakdown of order, the breakdown of schemes and maps. There are no guiding lines in the darkness; there is no straightforward religious experience we can hold on to. If we can still pray at all, we talk to an iron heaven, empty of signs. In an "age of faith" this was felt as an experience of God's anger: God had withdrawn from the soul and rejected it. Today, it is much more likely to be felt as the total breakdown of any religious meaning whatsoever. If language about God cannot survive this kind of testing, it is no use; it cannot refer to anything, and reality is God-less, so I can only go on being religious if I turn my back on reality.

There is only one other possible response to this experience. "Let the darkness come upon you," wrote Eliot, "which shall be the darkness of God." The same is said at greater length by John of the Cross, the sixteenth-century saint who analyzes the "dark night" with unparalleled clarity and honesty. The real question, John suggests, is about what you are really after: do you want "spirituality," mystical experience, inner peace, or do you want God? If you want God, then you must be prepared to let go of all—absolutely all—substitute satisfactions, intellectual and emotional. You must recognize that God is so unlike whatever can be thought or pictured that, when you have got beyond the stage of self-indulgent religiosity, there will be nothing you can securely know or feel. You face a blank, and any attempt to avoid that or shy away from it is a return to playing comfortable religious games.

The dark night is God's attack on religion. If you genuinely desire union with the unspeakable love of God, then you must be prepared to have your "religious" world shattered. If you think devotional practices, theological insights, even charitable actions give you some sort of a purchase on God, you are still playing games. On the other hand, if you can face and accept and even rejoice in the experience of darkness, if you can accept that God is more than an idea that keeps your religion or philosophy or politics tidy—then you may find a way back to religion, philosophy, or politics, to an engagement with them that is more creative because you are more aware of the oddity, the uncontrollable quality of the truth at the heart of all things. This is what "detachment" means—not being "above the battle," but being involved in such a way that you can honestly confront whatever comes to you without fear of the unknown. It is a kind of readiness for the unexpected, if that is not too much of a paradox.

But why make this response rather than the other? Why interpret it positively and not negatively? Each individual must answer as he or she sees fit, of course. But there is something in Christian faith itself, at its very roots, that gives a clue, something that has enabled serious Christians throughout the ages to interpret the "dark night" as the experience of the strange and elusive reality of God himself. This is, of course, the constant stress in the gospels upon the necessity of losing one's life, taking up the cross, being baptized with Jesus' baptism, and so on. And its climax and focus is in the passion and death of Jesus himself, in Gethsemane and Calvary. Jesus is presented to us as the one human being who enjoys unconditional intimacy with God, who in some sense shares God's own authority, but this intimacy presses him to go to his death, a death of agony and senselessness—"Why hast thou forsaken me?" It is this very closeness to God that sends him into this hell of suffering.

In Gethsemane we see this intimacy—*"Abba,* Father" and the demand it makes. Intimacy with God means refusing all consoling substitutes for God and bearing the consequences. In Gethsemane Jesus says to his Father, in effect, "I accept from your hand whatever happens. Nothing can break our communion, however little I see or feel it. I am ready to give myself to you, whatever the cost." And what happens is Calvary, Calvary where God virtually disappears. Our image and expectations of God are shattered when we see God helpless to save his Son. To take Jesus' cross means to enter into this: a commitment to God for his own sake, whatever happens, a declaration that we are ready to face the cost of truth, to let God be God and not prescribe what he shall and shall not be according to our selfish wants. It is a promise made with Jesus in Gethsemane to go with Jesus into abandonment and hell, so that we may be led away from self-indulgent delusions, from religious games.

To "deny oneself" is a radical matter—not a question of mortifications and acts of self-denial (games again), but a loosening of our hysterical, terrified grip on what we know and are comfortable with. "Denying oneself" amounts to the decision that I am not going to try to shape the truth to my wants and needs, but am determined to accept the truth as it is, not as I want it to be; it is to accept that I am part of reality, not the lord of it. It is the risk of saying "no" to religion in order to come to the truth of God, even if it breaks and kills everything I am familiar and happy with. Christians who claim to find God uniquely and definitively in Jesus, and especially in the cross of Jesus, are claiming that the roots of their faith are in a massive and total negation of false God-images and religious securities. They thus have some ground for interpreting darkness and doubt in their own life in a similar way—as God himself sweeping aside all that is between themselves and him, to give himself to them as he is.

And finally, it is because God is as he is that all this is not just nihilistic and terrifying. God in Christ shows himself as the God whose compassion is without bounds, utterly identified with our pain and working to bring us out of death and bondage into life. It is only when false images of God, the world, and myself have been broken that I can be truly free. When I look on the world as something focusing on me, when I look on God as something functioning usefully in my philosophy, then I am imprisoned in myself, and I cannot give or receive true and compassionate love.

When God breaks through in this terrible darkness, he begins to displace and destroy that dominating and manipulating self; he then sets me free to be loved and to give myself to him and to my brothers and sisters.

So a prayer that is content to stay in and endure the darkness, to come back daily to look into the unmanageable blank mystery of God, can be and should be the true wellspring of love and service, because it is a constant questioning and weakening of the selfish ego. And it is only by living through it, discovering what it can do to our faith and our love, that we shall finally understand the night of the spirit. As Jesus, having given himself over to hell, was raised alive for ever, so must we pray to find, in and through the night, the true and enduring newness of life that God wills to give us. As Jesus, though raised, still carries the marks of the cross, so we cannot hope to escape or avoid the full seriousness and costliness of the night by some final reversal that gives us back our comfort. The light is at the heart of the dark, the dawn breaks when we have entered fully into the night.

When we recognize our God in this experience, we can indeed say with the psalmist, "The darkness is no darkness with thee; the night is as clear as the day" (Psalm 139:12). As for John of the Cross, it is "The night that joins the beloved with her loved one, the night transfiguring the beloved in her loved one's life" *(Canciones del alma,* 5).

19

Holy Space

I saw no temple in the city. *(Revelation 21:22)*

In the old Jerusalem, the heart of the city was the Temple, and the heart of the Temple was the throne, the *kapporeth,* or mercy-seat—the empty space above the Ark of the Covenant, between the two golden cherubim. It was the most potent sign of Israel's repudiation of idols, the great speaking absence between the images. In the middle of the life of the covenant people is the space where God is. To go and see God in Jerusalem is to look at the curtained holy place and know that behind it is the empty space from which mercy and promise come forth, the "help from the sanctuary" and the "answer from heaven" referred to in the psalms.

In our history, the only possibility of knowing God is to face, at least sometimes, the silence, the absence between the cherubim. Only by doing so can we learn to look to a God who is free to forgive and re-create because he is not bound by our imaginings. The mercy-seat is the place of reconciliation, because here we make no claim on God, place no restriction on him by our guilt-conditioned fancies, but only stand before him in trust and expectancy. While we still live in history, our images of God are always shaped by our past, our memory. How then shall we meet the God who is free from all this, free to give us a future, without the silence of the sanctuary, without the moments when we face the emptiness between our words and images?

In the new Jerusalem, however, there is no temple, because its temple is the Lord God and the Lamb. The place of atonement and promise is no longer the hopeful silence between our words; it is the whole space of the city, the whole common life of the redeemed community. The light of presence is not a sanctuary lamp but the light in which the people of God see each other's faces. God is not a thing to be seen, not even a distant sun in the sky. God is the common air we breathe, the very possibility of seeing and moving. Clement of Alexandria spoke of the goal of our life as a coming to be at home with God—a state where there is no gap between knowing ourselves, knowing each other, and knowing God. In this city beyond our history and our imagining, we shall not be the prisoners of our memory; even its pains and traumas will speak to us of God. Our language and our bodies will not be mechanisms for isolating ourselves, but will be the sharing of God with each other, the showing to one another of the divine freedom and creative mercy. "His name shall be on their foreheads." We shall be to each other not idols but icons, effective signs of God's transfiguration of the world; and God will no longer be for us the eruption into our lives of an alien silence.

Meanwhile we live between the old Jerusalem and the new. We cannot be without that alien silence, the emptiness between the cherubim, yet we live in hope of a city where no space need be set aside for a mercy-seat. It is in the life and death of the Lamb of God that the silence culminates; it is in his life and death that we know there is no more need for a mercy-seat, and the veil of the sanctuary is torn down. To stand before Jesus in his action and passion is to stand, as did the ancient Israelites, before something that intrudes between our images and fancies. The merciful freedom of God steps into the world, becomes a physical hand outstretched, a name spoken, a meal shared, something resisting all the categories we wish we could bring to it. A god? No. An angel? No. A virtuous man? No. A prophet? No, but a life whose acts are the acts of the Wisdom of God, the beginning of his ways. And at last, a silence not between the cherubim but between two thieves, and an absence between two white-clad figures in a burial vault.

Here is our altar and our sanctuary. This life and death and empty grave are the mercy-seat, the space of God's freedom. If we pray and wait before God in silence, then, as the greatest Christian mystics have so often said, that is a silence that can never forget or blot out the humanity of Jesus. Our prayer moves between the naked trust of listening for a God whose ways we cannot speak of, and a pondering of the particular history of Jesus' words and deeds and suffering. All our prayer is nourished from these two sources—silence and the reading of the gospel.

Jesus is our holy place, which also means that he is the promise of a new kind of holiness. Here is a life in which the detail, even the triviality, of a human story becomes the word and name of God to us, so that we know that the contours of a human story can be the presence of God. If we are so drawn into the words and acts and passion of Jesus that (as Paul said) his life and death are at work in us, we become sanctuaries to each other, holy places, mercy-seats. And at the last, when we come at last to be at home with God and the Lamb, this process will be complete; we shall speak God's name to each other in the very fact of our being. There will be no temples.

In concluding, there are two things worth remembering about the holy places of the Christian church. First, as our patronal festival has just reminded us, holy places are normally linked by history, dedication, or both to Christian *persons*. They are places that recall to us a life in whose detail and movement Christ has been made visible. Second, they are places whose structure and function cannot be understood apart from the reality of a *community* (which is how they differ from pagan temples, ancient and modern). They are for Christian persons assembled, and in that assembly we are learning the lessons of John's vision, learning to read the name of God on the foreheads of our neighbors, to see each other as signs of God's mercy and liberty. We are learning to see God face to face as we learn to see each other face to face in trust and hope. When we have learned to look to each other for signs of God's promise, then indeed, for the whole human world, "there shall be no more night."

20

Different Christs?

For a theological college

That vision of Christ which thou dost see
Is my vision's greatest enemy.

People who say to one another, "If you think *that*, you shouldn't be here," are, I suppose, implicitly echoing Blake's horrifying couplet. I've heard—and overheard—remarks like this too many times for comfort, and not just in matters of theology either. After all, "visions of Christ" have to do with every aspect of life in Christ, which is what we're supposed to be learning about here, believe it or not. When you have fifty or so people living more or less in each other's pockets, it will be very surprising if you find no conflicts. But what gives conflicts their bitterness? What makes them cut us to the bone so that we bleed and suffer? What gives them their resilience and permanence, their power to cloud our thoughts and prayers for weeks on end?

You know what I mean, I'm sure: the trivial remark someone makes that strikes at the ground of your faith. The surprised "You don't believe *that*, do you?"—whether uttered by conservative or radical—that suddenly devalues all your intellectual struggles and puts your integrity into question. The bright pupil in the seminar—or the bright lecturer or supervisor—who implies that *of course* this or that view is out of court, almost casually pulling away carpets from under people's feet, denying (without even noticing it) any significance to their thoughts, their struggles. I may hold to a belief as a result of long and costly wrestling with its implications; I may hold it desperately in the face of consuming doubt; I may question or abandon a belief after costly engagement, reluctantly yielding before some kind of imperative questioning. And, if so, something very considerable is involved when someone says, "I don't see how any intelligent (or orthodox or contemporary or whatever) person can believe *that.*"

The question answers itself, doesn't it, as to why these things are bitter. It's my life you're threatening, my sense and my judgment, my *meaning*, the way I painfully struggle to understand myself in the light of God and the gospel. We all have heard people say, "How can you deny this when your ancestors shed their blood for it?" Conservative Catholics say it about the theology of the Tridentine Mass, conservative Protestants say it about the rejection of the same theology. And what we are saying when people menace our beliefs in this way is a weaker form of, *"I've shed my blood for this belief."* Not much, and not my life's blood, probably, but it still hurts. "Do you think I *enjoy* believing this?" we sometimes want to say. "Do you think I find this easy or congenial? Do you think I *wanted* to come to this conclusion?" Perhaps you know the terrible story of the old priest who committed suicide after hearing a broadcast in which a fashionable theologian appeared to demolish a particular "traditional" doctrine. The priest felt he had pinned all his hopes on a lie and a delusion. Now I don't use that story to prove a point one way or the other about traditionalism or radicalism, but only to draw attention to the seriousness of these questions of belief. If we are even a little committed to Christ, then however our vision is organized it will have a little of our blood invested in it.

But the answer to all this isn't talk about mere tolerance (though there are, I believe, worse sins). Liberal indifference seeks to draw the sting from bitterness and conflict by suggesting that both sides should stop believing things so *hard*. If you didn't take it so seriously, you wouldn't be in such a stew about it, say the liberals. Yet that is saying even more strongly that my struggles aren't worthwhile, that my life is not at stake here. Theology *is* a matter of life and death, because in it I find my own sense and direction, however vaguely or inarticulately. If we were not hurt by the dismissive remarks of others, we should not be caring enough. At least conflict is a sign of life: dead people don't bleed.

And it won't be settled by argument, by new facts or new perspectives. People don't change their understanding of themselves overnight because one or two new bits of information are provided. ("Good Lord, I never thought of that! So God doesn't exist after all.") In Christian terms, it is especially hard. Visions of Christ: yes, and there is our Christ, the totally enigmatic face on the wall, the cross, the bread and wine. *Silent* signs, as silent as he was before Pilate, consistently refusing a straight and simple answer. We can't feed him questions like a computer and receive tidy, systematic replies. He won't let on: we can shout and wave our arms at that icon, and it stays the same, a dark expressionless face that gives us nothing but itself to think about. We can shout and wave our arms at each other, appealing to Christ, and when we turn to him and say, "There! That's what I mean: *now* do you see?" all we meet is that silence, a kind of annihilating judgment on all we say. Christ can bear all sorts of interpretations, and we can't expect him to tell us which he likes. We can draw little balloons coming out of his mouth as much as we like. What does that tell us? The vulgarity of the analogy underlines the futility of the exercise.

Yet interpret him we must. We're constructive, imaginative beings, after all, and we can't escape from language, so we must talk. As soon as we do, as soon as the balloons are scribbled over, we have visions of Christ at enmity with one another, and conflicts that can't be resolved. The end of it all is that we are so passionately involved in staring at and hating or fearing someone else's vision of Christ that we turn our backs almost permanently on our own. This is horrible, because one of the things visions of Christ have to do with is reconciliation, our reconciliation with ourselves and each other and God. If we are not looking at our own vision, we have stopped thinking about reconciliation; and where is our hope then? Visions of Christ at enmity with one another cease to be visions of Christ at all.

So what do we do about all this? There's no point in trying to take the edge off the reality of the conflict, and I don't propose to try. But there are a few things we might reflect on to help us understand and contain the pain involved. First of all, there's one painfully obvious thought. We worry about other people's visions when we have leisure to take our eyes off our own. If we were really preoccupied with, really in love with our vision, we'd have less time for fussing about someone else's. This is the message in Jesus' reply to Peter in John 21, when Peter sees the beloved disciple and asks what will happen to him. Jesus replies simply, "Mind your own business and follow me."

But that alone can be pretty selfish and individualistic and can lead to a situation where we cease to care about truth at all. Sooner or later, Peter and the beloved disciple will have to come together and compare notes, if only because they are, after all, called to one discipleship in the one body. Then, I think, the question may be this: Can your Christ save me as well as you? Can my Christ save you as well as me? How far are our visions exclusive? How wide is our vision, how big is our God? If Christ can only save me and those who think as I do, God help us all! But if I can conceive, if I can imagine with enough sympathy how the Christ of my brother or sister can be saving and lifegiving, if I can begin to see how and why that vision is loved and trusted—then we shall have moved forward. This needs patience and care, and the refusal to assume that visions are exclusive. If I ask the question, "What is healing or lifegiving in your Christ?", I can at least think it possible that there is Christlike reality in your thought and your life. It's not at all an indifference to truth, but a recognition that the most important truth about Christ is that he is resurrection and life. And if I ask, "Can my Christ save you?", I am asking how far I have distorted Christ's face into my own unlovely shape, how far I have imprisoned Christ in me, in my exclusiveness and unlovingness. This is not mere tolerance, but active, *compassionate* understanding.

The third point relates to the first: if we have two rival visions of one thing or person, at least that thing or person is central to both of us. Somewhere we acknowledge implicitly an authority we both accept. It may be fairly notional and almost empty of content, but it is there and we both look to its "thereness." We are all here to learn one discipleship in one body; that icon of Christ is there in front of all of us, whatever we think or talk about. As long as we're all facing that way, something is preserved, some objectivity, some common sense of being under judgment, one judgment. We are exposing ourselves to the same signs. Like it or not, we are members of one body, and we signalize it by sharing the same sacramental life.

We all know, I think, the destructive results that follow the breaking of this aspect of the common life, the impoverishing and trivializing of belief and commitment that can attend upon the abandonment of eucharistic fellowship. At least there, at the altar, we do indeed come before our judgment, as St. Paul reminds the Corinthians. And there we show forth daily the death we believe to be the source of all our meaning and our health: the cross with all its ambivalence and silence; its openness to what may be disastrous and deadly (or just inept and boring) interpretations; its lack of clear systematic theology; its questions to left and right alike; its *thereness*, its authority, the authority of the one whose cross it is. When the face of Christ in the gospel and the body of Christ in the eucharist have ceased to be common ground, then there will be enmity. Then there will be, finally, no Christ for us. And when we do not find unity before the cross, we have lost all our hope of reconciliation.

This brings me to a fourth and final consideration. To give the cross and the sacrament this kind of authority as *binding* realities in the community is to accept that we are to be questioned by them—that Christ (however eccentrically or obscurely we talk about him) is not just there as an object of our investigation, but is a challenging and unsettling fact for all of us, interrogating us without mercy, interrogating our understanding of God and ourselves. The truth is that God is the only real and authoritative iconoclast. If your faith seems perverse and distorted, if your understanding seems naive or obscurantist or irresponsible, the only question I can put to you is, "Are you looking *into* your vision? Are you letting yourself be shaped and changed by what you see?" I'm asking, in fact, about the precise degree to which your vision is what you live by from day to day—a matter of life and death, sense and nonsense. Are you attending to your vision? Are you stripping yourself in prayer before the terrible and searching Word of God? Are you being refined in that fire? And am I? Is my vision doing that to me, breaking and remaking my thoughts and words, my heart and mind? I have no right to destroy your vision, nor you mine. I have no business to devalue your understanding or make light of your struggles, nor you mine. But we have the right—and perhaps the duty—to put the questions to each other and hear them from each other. When all the formulae, all the slogans, all the impassioned, sincere, and no doubt inevitable theological disputation is over, then we have to get back on our knees and ask about our own fidelity to God's questioning, our own readiness to go into the desert where the security of pictures and ideas fades away, where all theologies finally give way to God.

This may be very routine stuff—pleas for understanding, openness, praying together as a way of bearing conflicts—but I shall not apologize for it. The wounds caused by hasty and dismissive words about other people's theologies or spiritualities are too deep to be ignored by any of us, and the obvious has to be said from time to time. Yes, we have all shed at least a little blood or sweat over our beliefs; yes, our integrity is at issue; and yes, truth matters and doctrinal indifference is abhorrent. So these pains won't go away, and the hurts may be deep when our creed is assaulted or—worse—just dismissed. We cannot get around it just by adopting the other person's point of view: too much of ourselves is involved for that. But theology *must* bring us to penitence and contemplation, just as it must arise out of trust—trust in the abiding objectivity of the one in whom we have believed, trust that (in Augustine's words) "our home will not fall down just because we are away."

"That vision of Christ which thou dost see...." The Christ we both see, however, is the one who instructs us to love our enemies, to love even what may seem the pale shadow of his face in other people's minds, because compared with the light of his glory all our thoughts are shadows. He is the truth we shall never own; we can only hope to be owned by him.

21

The Touch of God

Revelation 2:18-29

The Revelation to John is written in two scripts. The first is chiselled in stone, with the deep and clear lines of some Roman inscription, still arresting after all the centuries.

> I am the first and the last and the living one....Behold, I have set before you an open door....I saw a Lamb standing as though it had been slain....God will wipe away every tear from their eyes....Seal up what the seven thunders have said....Alas, alas for the great city....Behold, I make all things new....They shall see his face, and his name shall be on their foreheads. And night shall be no more....Let him who desires take the water of life without price.

These are the words etched upon the Christian imagination for centuries, with the simplicity, the nakedness, of all revelatory poetry, the sense of a fusion between word and world. They *embody* what they talk about.

And then there is the other script: tightly written, pen driving into cheap paper, page after page of paranoid fantasy and malice, like the letters clergy so frequently get from the wretched and disturbed.

> They were allowed to torture them for five months, but not to kill them....Let him who has understanding reckon the number of the beast....The smoke of their torment goes up for ever and ever....All the birds were gorged with their flesh....I gave her time to repent, but she refuses....I will throw her on a sick bed...and I will strike her children dead.

Goodness knows who Jezebel in Thyatira was or what she taught; perhaps she was just an inoffensive liberal who had read something like Romans 14 and couldn't see what all the fuss was over eating meat bought at the temple butcher's stall. But whoever she was, it is the wild venom of John the Divine that has given her her unwelcome immortality. Throughout the seven letters to the churches at the beginning of Revelation, the tone swings disconcertingly between vitriol and a language of haunting authority whose images—the tree, the crown, the white stone, and the morning star—have the mysterious solidity of a conceptual Stonehenge.

Revelation has been the quarry for mystics and fanatics alike. The script of paranoia and revengeful fancy is a lot easier for most people to write, and this book has touched deep and diseased places in many psyches, unlocking streams of violence and obscenity and plain madness. It is easy to forget that scripture in its entirety is the Word we must hear; we must not attach the label "God's Word" to this or that fragment. If there is a Word from God to hear in John's Revelation—and if there isn't, it's a waste of time reading it aloud when we might have been reading something less troubled and troubling—then it's to be heard in the very tension between the two scripts.

The average, prosaic human mind cannot strike hard enough to cut so deeply in stone ("Behold, I make all things new; Take the water of life without price"). Our language is not accustomed to speaking for God—that is, speaking of some restoration and grace, some resource of beauty and transfiguring strength, greater than the sum of all things visible and invisible, some promise of wholeness that can stand like Stonehenge through all the gales of horror and failure that blow in the world. To speak like that is the result of having had one's own speech interrupted, having been thrown off course. John tells us about it at the beginning of Revelation: "I turned to see the voice that was speaking to me....When I saw him, I fell at his feet as though dead" (notice the disorientated imagery of *seeing* voices). John has seen something lethal to his ordinary perceptions, and his mind is opened to the impress of rhythms far below the surface of ordinary speech.

Yet to say this is to grasp how vulnerable the speaker of such words will be. The poet or seer speaks from a fractured sensibility, following rhythms below the surface, but those rhythms are not only the shapes of a reality creating and nurturing us; they may also be the intermediate layers between the conscious mind and its maker, the rhythms set up by our injuries or our inner diseases. When the sensibility is fractured, it isn't only God who comes through the fissures in the surface. The poet or seer may present appalling contradictions—disturbed and destructive behavior, the capacity to say insanely wounding or cruel things. In our century the poet who, for many believers, comes closest to "writing in stone," T. S. Eliot, could write what Stephen Spender called "poetic death sentences" on experiences he feared or longed to ignore—not to mention the absurd and horrible anti-Semitism of some of his earlier work. His own mentor, Ezra Pound, offers a still more dramatic example of tragi-comic contradictions. A sensibility sufficiently blown off course to be able to speak for more than a pragmatic and conventional wisdom is a mind at risk.

Perhaps, as we read the Revelation to John, we should let its ugly and diseased elements speak to us in this way. The very disorder, madness, and vengefulness of certain passages can help us to hear more clearly the depth and authority of others. Whatever we have here, it is not just the voice of common sense. Do we or don't we decide to recognize, among the fractures of this language, this imagination, some opening into the scale of God's language ("an open door, which no one is able to shut")? If we do, it will be because we have been jolted out of our good sense by this speech—by its disorders as well as its glimpses of God's order, God's rhythms. If there is to be some real communication from God, we might well expect to recognize it in a mind that has been forced beyond itself, for good and ill.

And this suggests a troubling but necessary reflection on the whole idea of revelation. The touch of God *is* dangerous, in that it can be a light too sharp to be borne without hurt or breakage; and when the perception is skewed and redirected, it may run close to the destructive and the hellish. Jonathan Smith, the great anthropologist of religion at Chicago, remarked about the horrific mass suicide of the sectarians who followed the prophet Jim Jones that at least it reminded people that religion wasn't automatically "nice." For God to come near us is for God to risk God's own integrity, in the sense that God puts himself into our hands to be appallingly misunderstood, to become the justifier of our hatred and fears, our madness. And it is to put *us* at risk, since the disorientation we thus experience can unleash some very dark things in us. Revelation itself, as the church's history shows, is bound up with tragic possibilities.

But this is not to romanticize religious irrationality, only to say that the diseases and injuries of the mind that revealed religion seems so often to produce are the price paid for some irreducible perception of what is beyond the whole world. For the Christian, that perception is that the world is sustained by mercy and generosity without limit, by a giving God ("take the water of life without price"). That is not by any means a deduction of common sense, but it is bought at a price—the price of the madness of violence unleashed in the cross of Jesus; the price of the fracturing of the imaginations of a John or a Paul; and the further disturbing price of the violence justified in the name of the cross of Jesus—the distortions, fury, and hatred that may be set free in the bruised mind of the prophet. But that cross and that bruised mind set before us the universal scale of mercy: those things that touch and stir our diseases are also the things that finally show where our diseases are to be judged and healed. The rantings of John the Divine about his theological rivals are part of the by-product of the very vision of the Living One that shows these ravings for what they are, by showing the radical and unconfined purpose of God in Jesus Christ.

Not all the Lord's people are prophets. Quite properly, our worship sets out to remind us of covenant and faithfulness, the reliability of God's mercy, and we don't expect to be blown off course by these reminders. Cathedral matins is not very like the congregations known to John the Divine, hot quarrelsome groups jammed into someone's front room in the less savory quarters of Turkish towns, intermittently praying and weeping together and screaming at each other in the tone of voice we hear in this morning's lesson. We have learned how to build the disorientating vision of the First and the Last, the Living One, who was dead and is alive for evermore, into a tradition of grace and quiet and beauty. And we have come to think that this vision of God is natural to us (no one habitually falls on their face as if dead during Anglican worship, at least outside the more dramatic bits of the charismatic movement), and that grace and quiet are an appropriately low-key acknowledgment of this. But our worship does continue to set before us the memory that discovering the Living One is dangerous, and we would know less of it without the fractured and disturbed languages of people like John the Divine and their contemporary equivalents—sometimes even those people who write their strange and painful fantasies to clergy and other public figures. We aren't called to believe and endorse all they say, only to ask ourselves what we are taught here about the strangeness—and sometimes the terror—of the Word of God to fragile minds. We who may not think of ourselves as fragile but who are not likely to think of ourselves as prophets either need to pay our debts to those scorched by their closeness to the One we observe from a polite distance. "He who has an ear, let him hear what the Spirit says to the churches."

The last word rightly belongs to the fractured awareness of the poet. Annie Dillard, the young American writer whose poetry and prose have taught many people to see the natural world and its maker with something of the terror and newness of revelation, says this about going to church:

> Why do people in church seem like cheerful, brainless tourists on a packaged tour of the Absolute? The tourists are having coffee and doughnuts on Deck C. Presumably someone is minding the ship, correcting the course, avoiding icebergs and shoals, fuelling the engines, watching the radar screen, noting weather reports radioed in from shore. No one would dream of asking the tourists to do these things. Alas, among the tourists on Deck C, drinking coffee and eating doughnuts, we find the captain, and all the ship's officers, and all the ship's crew. The officers chat; they swear; they wink a bit at slightly raw jokes, just like regular people. The crew members have funny accents. The wind seems to be picking up.
>
> On the whole, I do not find Christians, outside of the catacombs, sufficiently sensible of conditions. Does anyone have the foggiest idea what sort of power we blithely invoke? Or, as I suspect, does no one believe a word of it? The churches are children playing on the floor with their chemistry sets, mixing up a batch of TNT to kill a Sunday morning. It is madness to wear ladies' straw hats and velvet hats to church; we should all be wearing crash helmets. Ushers should issue life preservers and signal flares; they should lash us to our pews. For the sleeping god may wake someday and take offense, or the waking god may draw us to where we can never return.[1]

---

1 Annie Dillard, *Teaching a Stone to Talk: Expeditions and Encounters* (London, 1984), pp. 40-41.

22

A Ray of Darkness

My title is a paradox, and people tend to be annoyed by paradoxes—in many ways quite rightly. We suspect them of concealing muddle, and so of representing some kind of intellectual or spiritual cowardice. Those who speak in paradoxes haven't had the strength or the honesty to look hard enough at what they really want to say; perhaps they're afraid of facing contradictions in what they perceive or believe, of having to choose and sort out what does and doesn't make sense.

So when religious writers or speakers come up with paradoxes—like "a ray of darkness"—they invite just this kind of skepticism. "It's a mystery," we say feebly. And the critic may well reply, "If you really can't talk about it, don't. If you can talk about it, you can talk clearly. But if you want to escape the responsibility of having a conversation, you're welcome to go on chattering about 'mystery'; just don't expect me to do anything about it."

Of course, it is not so simple. We use paradoxes a good deal in other contexts. "I hate and I love," wrote Catullus of his tormenting passion for Clodia. More trivially we speak of people "having the vices of their virtues," "killing with kindness," "being so nice you could kick them," or whatever. Why? Because even in banal contexts, we are aware of the fact that our pigeonholes for things, people, emotions, and perceptions are often lagging well behind the fluidity of the real world, with its subtle, rapid interactions and its puzzling quality. And whether it is in theoretical physics or in poetry, we need to express some sense of this strange fact that our language doesn't "keep up" with the multiplicity and interrelatedness and elusiveness of truth. In such a setting, we utter paradoxes not to mystify or avoid problems, but precisely to *stop* ourselves making things easy by pretending that some awkward or odd feature of our perception isn't really there. We speak in paradoxes because we have to speak in a way that keeps a question *alive*.

How, then, do we know whether any particular bit of "odd" language is an honest effort to keep questions alive or a dishonest attempt to escape real questioning completely? We don't; at least, not in the abstract. It is only when you can see in the whole of somebody's life and language that they have been interrupted, disoriented, reorganized, left behind by their experience, that you may be inclined to think that, whatever else they're doing, they're not *evading* anything (they may, of course, be mad). Ordinary and colloquial paradoxes perhaps don't need taking quite so seriously. But we could say of Catullus, for instance, if we were prepared to spend a bit of time listening to that remarkable poetic voice, that at least he's not running away from the range and tension of his experience.

So, back to the "ray of darkness." The phrase was used by a fifth-century Syrian who called himself Dionysius, and this kind of imagery had a lasting influence until at least the late seventeenth century (that period after which, on the whole, western Europe succumbed to a collective amnesia about the meaning of the word "God"). In the seventeenth century the Welsh poet Henry Vaughan wrote:

> There is in God (some say),
> A deep but dazzling darkness.

Unforgettable lines, but Dionysius is saying something more. God's "ray" interrupts our blindness and ignorance; it cuts through something, as beams of light do. God is "the light of the world" in his Son Jesus, yet that interruption, that light cutting through our darkness, is not a comfortable clearing up of problems and smoothing out of our difficulties and upsets. On the contrary, it brings on a kind of vertigo; it may make me a stranger to myself, to everything I have ever taken for granted. I have to find a new way of knowing myself, identifying myself, uttering myself, talking of myself, imaging myself. In short, when God's light breaks on my darkness, the first thing I know is that I don't *know*, and never did.

Here is, if you like, the ultimate situation ripe for paradoxes. I can't keep up with what is happening, because the language I usually speak has been challenged at its heart. When God breaks in, my picture of what it is to be *me*, and my attitudes to that picture, have been deeply disturbed and confused. I am nearer than before to some sort of truthfulness, and I am plunged into confusion.

Here is *God*, then, in the event that attacks and upsets my self-image, and so confuses the whole of my speech and imagery. What such an event may be varies incalculably. There are breakthroughs into levels of fulfillment or assurance that shake us and change us (the intolerable intensity of joy), and there are breakdowns into despair or mental illness. There are moments, for the artist and the scientist alike, of a sense of, not exactly power, but attunement with the creative rhythm of things; and there are moments when the world of our experience or our memory confronts us as something utterly beyond control or understanding, leaving us shut out, alienated, and impotent. Points of intense communion with someone, points of apparently unbridgeable distance between me and others. All alike—the positive and the negative, the ecstasy and the loss—a "ray of darkness."

It is after experiences like these that people sometimes say "I've seen God." They don't mean they've seen a thing, or a face, or even a person. They mean they've been interrupted and turned inside out; they've seen a process in which *they* are put in question at their deepest level. And to talk about "moments" and "points" is actually misleading. These can be experiences of years' duration. In a way, all serious prayer and religious practice, ritual or imagery, should be a discipline designed to keep us in some degree on this edge of experience where I and my world, my regularities and securities, are always being made provisional. We are struggling for a discipline that stops me taking myself for granted as the fixed center of a little universe, and allows me to find and lose and refind myself constantly in the interweaving patterns of a world I did not make and do not control.

"I've seen God," people say, when they've seen and felt themselves and their world going into a kind of refining fire. It's the vision expressed in the great Indian image of Shiva dancing in the ring of flame. Yet that alone, perhaps, leaves us with a God who is—what? More darkness than light? More terror than beauty (even if "beauty is but the beginning of terror")? The God who is seen not only by the artist or the contemplative, but also by the schizophrenic: is this the true God? Is this the Christian God?

Yes. God is one, the crucible of divine creative darkness, the breaking in on us of what is wholly unmasterable, so much so that it forces my defensive ego out of its castle in the center of my universe: these are the marks of God wherever they happen, whether in sickness, ecstasy, madness, intuition, speechlessness. Whatever makes the world new and makes me strange to myself, forcing me to see my contingency, my participation in the world's uncontrollable flux: this is God, the one God, because there is only one reality that ultimately and creatively escapes our grasp and vision in this way. There cannot be more than one ultimate pivot on which the universe turns, turning *(converting)* my life and language with it. If we lose sight of the beauty and terror of dancing Shiva or Job's God in the whirlwind, we are taming the vision to the scope of what we can cope with, pretending that our language has caught up and that we no longer need paradoxes of confusion and subtlety to speak of it. Yes, this is the Christian God. (There aren't any others.) But we, as Christians, do have something more to say, something that boils down to two fundamental things.

First, we believe that what happens in our own experience in terms of this "ray of darkness" happened repeatedly and with deepening intensity in the story of one particular historical community until it reached a point of crisis and focus that shattered and re-formed a whole religious vocabulary—and went on subverting and reconstructing other traditions and vocabularies as its impact spread. Once (we say) there was a nation that risked living close to the fire, refused to have images of God, refused to lose God when they lost wealth and security, land and power and religious ease. And out of their history of disruption and suspicion of images, out of their stubborn commitment to the finite world and their sense of their own vulnerability to history and change, out of all that came one set of events in which all this was fleshed out (incarnated) so sharply and decisively that the way God's people thought about themselves was deeply challenged.

Once (we say) there was a man who was seen and heard as someone naked to the mystery of God in life and death. Once there was a man who lived in what seemed an exceptional closeness to the disruptive darkness of God, to the extent that he assumed the right to speak for God—for God's kingdom, the condition in which God (and not we as individuals) is at the heart of the world, so that all our efforts at defense and control are overthrown. He assumed the right to declare, on God's behalf, that our history, our world, the drama of our egos, was at an end in the presence of God. And then, in his own experience, he absorbed the dissolution of his life and his world and his speech: he encountered the "ray of darkness" as he suffered the terrified violence of those who couldn't cope with God and themselves, and he accepted even this as the oblique and contradictory sign of God's presence. Jesus crucified is our central image of the strangeness of God, consuming what comes close to it. He suffers the darkness in life and death as something that is immediate, authoritative, and inescapable, and because of that he transmits that same "ray" to us. He now *stands for* the strangeness of God. He *is* the "ray of darkness" in the world of our religious fantasy. He *is* that which interrupts and disturbs and remakes the world. That's the first thing: the story we tell.

But *second,* the kingdom he sees, lives in, and lives out is not a threat, except to those who are already deeply frightened by their own humanity and struggle to control it tightly by law and institution. It is a promise for those alive to their own vulnerability, those open to having their pictures of themselves constantly questioned and reordered by their receptive awareness of the world—a promise for the "poor in spirit," the humble, the compassionate. The kingdom is theirs; they have found and been found by God's truth. They have begun to know that when they stop taking for granted that the world revolves round them, and when they take the risks of self-questioning, clarity, equity, and pity, then they discover a harmony and an affirmation of their humanity utterly unconnected to surface happiness or security. They hear the assurance that, whatever happens, they are rooted in something deeper than "the way the world goes." They experience the "ray of darkness" as the dart of *love,* unconditional acceptance.

So too, when the herald of the kingdom goes to his death on the cross he does not turn and condemn us for our fears, nor does he leave us with the memory of his death as a reproachful and guilt-producing trauma. He takes the risk of stepping lovingly into the kingdom through death and emptiness, and thus breaks through to some unimaginable new level of being. He returns from death to gather his friends in renewed acceptance and love—to make himself the cornerstone of their new humanity. He leaves *himself*—his nature, his calling, his mission—as the great and fundamental question in the new language his disciples slowly learn to speak. But the question will only arise because of the newness that has already come into being, with its assurance of peace, mercy, and grace. We can learn to live with the vastly unsettling questions about the divine and the human posed by Jesus because of this deepest assurance: in the church of the resurrection, the darkness of the cross is a promise of a love beyond our failure and cowardice and death.

So, the ring of flame, dancing Shiva, Job's God, beauty and terror—that vision is real and fundamental. And the Father of Jesus, the good shepherd, the wiper-away of tears, is also fundamental. The Christian God is a ray of darkness, indeed, in the lives of individuals and in the story of humanity as a whole—the ground of paradox, of the oblique and puzzled language of so much Christian doctrine. And he is our home and our center, the well of life and light, our loving parent, the ultimate simplicity of pity and acceptance—"while he was still far off his father saw him." And the Christian gospel (which is *not* a religious system or a spiritual theory) affirms that we can only hold these two together by telling the story of Jesus. Without it, we have an impossible choice between terror and even madness on one side, and sentimental coziness on the other. But in the story of the cross and resurrection, darkness and light, terror and joy, loss and fullness are woven together in one word of grace and promise. The ray of darkness is not different from the dart of love.

> If I say, Peradventure the darkness shall cover me:
> then shall my night be turned to day...
> the darkness and the light to thee are both alike.

Or, in John Donne's words:

> He brought light out of darkness,
> not out of a lesser light.
> He can bring thy summer out of winter
> though thou have no spring.

Testing Questions

23

What is Truth?

A university sermon at the outbreak of the Gulf War (1991)

We have lately become used once again to the cliché, "The first casualty of war is truth." Nobody can dispute its present aptness; what is rather depressing is the way in which its obviousness is recognized without—apparently—much residue of outrage being felt. It is as though truthfulness were a luxury commodity, over and above the iron rations required to sustain human beings in pain, something sadly but indisputably dispensable in crisis, to be dusted down and reinstated when things are easier.

But perhaps this is a consequence of the phrase itself. War happens, and these are its tragic results; we are not laid too heavily under obligation to ask how war happens. What, though, if we were to turn the cliché around and say, "Peace is the first casualty of untruthfulness"? This at least would remind us that truth may not, after all, be a luxury, but the iron ration itself, an iron in the soul to fortify against the disintegrative seductions that obsess us and lead us to the slaughter of self and others.

Well, it would not be too difficult to say of our present conflict that it is in large measure the price being paid for self-delusion on a massive scale by both sides—a delusion that could be summed up in tediously simple form by defining it as the refusal to believe that acts have consequences. There is the refusal to believe that a ruthless enemy could have both the skill and the resolve to engage in steady but unpredictable escalation of the scope of conflict: the dismissal as alarmist of threats to other parties, or threats of what we are learning to call ecological terrorism. There is the underlying illusion that technological sophistication guarantees control of the course of a conflict. There is the foolish supposition that the presence of an enormous military force will allow diplomatic and economic pressures to operate effectively. On the Iraqi side is the illusion that the promise of further inhumanities will simply intimidate and the assumption that, because this is a world in which brutal aggression is habitually ignored by the self-appointed guardians of law, democracy, or justice, this particular blow to political pride and economic greed will be passed over too. Further back still are the idiotic habits of supporting the enemy's enemy as a friend, whatever that country's morals (a habit tried and tested in what was once South Vietnam, and brought to near-perfection in Central and South America), and the infantilism of the arms trade's pursuit of markets in detachment from the flesh and blood of actual international politics—and from flesh and blood *simpliciter.*

How are we to confront such a tapestry of deceit and self-indulgent fancy? This is a sermon and not a political essay, and so it must be said here that we confront it by examining it in ourselves: by excavating our own passionate deceits, our own preference for believing that the world is not, after all, independent of our will, and that we can clear an innocent space where the discharged arrow of our actions can fall. We shall not truthfully see the web of lies in which our public life buzzes away until we have recognized where the fissures of the same untruthfulness run across our own moral vision. The decay of peace begins with me and you, though alas it is far from true that our individual penitence will restore what has been globally fractured. Still, to try to identify the sin of the politician without identifying, bitterly, with it is simply to treat the world's untruth as something that does not touch me. And that denial of belonging together is precisely, *precisely,* what the untruth of our public and international life consists in. If you wish to know the pertinence of religious faith to the political realm, here is one answer, in a recognition of the need and the possibility of shared repentance.

But where and how do we learn the truth of our belonging—our belonging with one another, with the past and future of our actions, with the uncontrollable reality of the human and more-than-human environment? We can remember, perhaps, what it was for all of us first to learn to negotiate our world: to discover the resistant surfaces of things, to recognize connections, to put the world we have discovered together in play, to be talked into talking. We can remember being children and relearn those lessons. Becoming again like children, becoming stumbling and eager learners and listeners, we may find our way to the kingdom of heaven. This is true, yet it can also be sentimentally seductive, as if we could say simply, "Of course! *Now* I remember," and mend our ways. Learning is more than remembering, as Kierkegaard admonished the shade of Plato: the true teacher, the teacher of what we do not know and have never known, must create in us the very capacity to learn. That is to say that such a teacher must open in us the knowledge of lack and poverty and show us ourselves desiring, unfinished.

Need is the beginning of truthfulness: the need that recognizes I cannot talk myself into language now any more than when I was a child, that I cannot see my own face, look into my own eyes or my own soul. What I cannot do for myself is to offer the gift of difference, the only real *gift*, since it is the only thing not planned and packaged by my ego. I can't give myself what is given in a new friend, a lover, a song heard for the first time, the claim of a sufferer upon my attention and compassion, the words my daughter has learned for the first time on her second birthday. And this is a need I may only come to see when I have lost or damaged the difference of another: I am bored by my friend; I have analyzed the music; I can explain why children starve in Africa; my daughter has grown up. It is *my* face and *my* fancies and *my* words that are stuck over the once-startling, the once-alien surface of the world, and I know I shall not be enlarged like that again.

It is *difference* that has made me live, and I am losing it—need, truth. The true teacher—my friend, my child, the interruption of the sight of pain—keeps me in contact with the reality of my incompleteness, and when I begin in idleness, selfishness, or fear to absorb that saving difference into the familiar contours of my own inner geography, I must hold on to the knowledge that this familiar landscape was once invaded. I must remember how little I can do for and by myself, and work at stripping away from the world I perceive the film cast by my fantasies and surface *wants* (which I so often call "need").

But we cannot succeed in surprising ourselves by the *effort* not to be bored and self-reflexive; we can only struggle in the dark to avoid that imprisonment, struggle against becoming incapable of surprise, deaf to the unplanned question or interruption. It is, of course, intellectual candor as well as moral clarity that is at issue here. But for the Christian, both intellectual and moral vision and truthfulness are held together in the question about the spirit's life with and before Jesus of Nazareth. Into his mouth the evangelist puts the claim to *be* truth (and therefore life). Of this human being it is said that he is not to be mastered, not to be finished with: he has the resource to go on surprising and to interrupt all the self-serving streams of your language and mine. He is the truth, because before him we cannot pretend to control, and so cannot do other than see our neediness. Not that we can evangelize by working on and working up imagined needs for Christ to satisfy, because the need he meets is our need to receive a gift from a stranger and, by definition, nothing can secure that for us in advance without destroying the stranger's strangeness.

Is this, then, his "kingship," the *basileia* not of this world? His authority is not one that can be fought for and legislated. It is not for *him* that his servants fight, if fight they do, like Peter in Gethsemane—Peter who is not condemned, but only reminded, flatly and drily, of how violence breeds its mirror image, how the threat of slaughter invites the threat of slaughter. The kingship of Jesus is witness to truth: to what is inexhaustible in persons and things, Hopkins's "dearest freshness" beyond the smeared surface of our little worlds. It is witness to our belonging and dependence, the endlessness of our growing, the gift and receiving without which we do not live, the expectant waiting for the stranger. This is truth, this is his authority. He is the true teacher because he will always be strange to us, breaking into our self-referentiality to make us capable of receiving what he says. His kingship is not shown in the issuing of edicts or the promulgation of an ideology, but in those sharp and enigmatic words that oblige us to imagine ourselves anew: as child, as homecomer, as discoverer of hidden treasure, as afraid of compassion and jealous of gifts given to another, as Pharisee and tax collector. And his kingship, so John's gospel most powerfully insists, is at last shown in the refusal to answer the questions of his judges and the silence of a death, which, because of its aftermath, remains the most disturbing and interrupting question of all. What else but embodied and eternal truth can turn round its own denial and extinction and make *that* an offer and a promise?

Christ's is the kingship of a riddler, the one who makes us strangers to what we think we know. The Welsh Quaker poet Waldo Williams, in his greatest poem, called him "the one who escapes the conscription of every army...the marksman, the outlaw, the lost heir, the exiled king." Reflecting on those images, we are brought back to where we began. If the Christian gospel is more than a simplistic moral message, it does not primarily set out to insist on individual options for pacifism (though it has, in effect, said that there are worse fates). It witnesses, with and in Jesus Christ, to the truth; as *gospel,* it does not offer to make your decision for you, but neither does it simply appeal to the desirability of private good intentions or utter bland calls to more and better prayers. It claims that it tells the truth about the world that human beings inhabit and, with the parables and the silences of Jesus in mind, asks if we know what kind of price we pay for our illusions. It asks where exactly we want to locate ourselves in a universe of which a Jewish peasant dialectician is the monarch. It offers truth; it calls to truthful living; it binds us in unbreakable relation, both confrontation and kinship, with the embodied Word of God and asks, before all else, for repentance, without which there is no truth.

Violent human conflict, in this universe, is the effect of the steady shrinkage of the world to the dimensions of the ego. It is *my* interests that interpret and process what I see, and yours can increasingly appear only as a rival bid for the territory I have colonized. Peace is the first casualty of untruthfulness. But it so often takes major public and international conflict to remind us how tightly rivalry and lying are tied together. The language of war, above all of modern war, is fundamentally self-referential. It redefines its terms: who can forget the classic instance from Vietnam, "In order to save the village, it became necessary to destroy it"? It reorganizes the contingencies of fact to display conformity with some subtle plan. And, at every level, from the tabloid to the carefully "neutral" official briefing, it teaches us to forget the human particularity and strangeness of our enemy. It teaches us to expect the worst from the stranger. In short, it makes us forget fallibility, discovery, surprise, and need; it makes us forget human truth.

Modern war relies heavily on mass communication for the molding of perceptions and feelings, and in its technology it removes human agents further and further from the violent effects of their actions. If the Christian gospel has no absolute and timeless prohibition to utter against coercion (and very few Christians have consistently maintained that it has), has it at least authority to challenge the distinctive offenses to truth involved in the depersonalization of modern conflict—wars rooted substantially in and conducted by skillfully managed deceptions about the nature of the moral world? At the moment, we are being surrounded by the miasma of half-truth and open lie, by the increasing demonization not of one recognizably appalling tyrant only, but of a whole nation—and sometimes of the tradition of Islam itself—by sanctimonious reassurances of a success guaranteed by righteousness. The price is high, and this is not even to mention the price paid already by dedicated and resourceful men and women carrying out on the ground and in the air the decisions of political leaders. Their human reality is no less overshadowed by the management of propaganda, war as soap opera, than is the identity of their enemies.

If Christians construe the truth of Jesus Christ as the truth of our need to meet the stranger expectantly, war in general becomes—at the very least—problematic. But how much can we afford to pay in terms of collusion with self-deceit and the leading of others into fantasy, collusion that war in an age of technology and mass entertainment media seems inescapably to involve? This of course is a question, not an answer; but it must be heard as *Christ's* question to us as believers, if we are serious in calling him the incarnate truth. Whatever our answer, Pilate's option is not open to us.

> Pilate said to him, "What is truth?" And when he had said this, he went out.

24

Holy Ground

Recently the excellent BBC "Everyman" series gave us a film about Medjugorje, the village in Yugoslavia where the Virgin Mary has allegedly been appearing to a group of local teenagers over a period of several years. It was an impressive production, impressive at many levels: it presented, plainly and unaffectedly, the plain and unaffected faith of the young people involved, one now married, one at an agricultural college, one suffering from an inoperable cancer, one contemplating monastic life—ordinary teenagers touched by extraordinary joy and pain. No one could doubt their honesty and the depth and realism of their faith.

But the film also showed a particularly dark background to the apparitions. There is a history of bitter factional strife in the church between the Franciscan friars and the nonmonastic clergy; and, much worse, there is the memory of an appalling incident in the last war—one of many such incidents in this part of Yugoslavia when it was ruled by a pro-Hitler dictatorship that encouraged the age-old hostility between Catholic Croats and Orthodox Serbs. Near Medjugorje, large numbers of Serbian peasants, including women and children, were thrown to their deaths from a hilltop in the early years of the war by Catholic Croatians who supported the fascist government. Here as elsewhere, the Franciscan friars did nothing to save their Orthodox brothers and sisters; there were some places where friars actively joined in these atrocities and gave their blessing to loyal Catholics as they burned alive or buried alive the children of Orthodox villagers.

In other words, the Virgin Mary has been seen in a place where the church of God and the people of God have most singularly and dramatically betrayed Christ; she has been "seen" in a place where God is *not* to be seen in the history of his people—or rather, seen only in the suffering and slaughtered victims of those who call themselves his people.

What do we make of this? This morning's New Testament lesson points us to some reflections on the strange contradictoriness of holy places and their history. Jesus is impelled toward the holy city, the city of the great king, as he himself calls it, *because* it is the place where prophets suffer and die. Its history is a history of God's manifestation and God's protection, the cloud of glorious presence filling the Temple, God wheeling and hovering over the mountain top like a flock of birds. And it is a history of the rejection of God's presence in the abuse and mockery and murder of those who proclaim that that presence is a summons to judgment and to renewal. Jesus speaks out of what was by his time a well-established non-canonical tradition that prophets ended their lives by martyrdom at the hands of the powerful among the people. Accordingly, he "sets his face" to Jerusalem, toward the place of the greatest, most manifest, signs of presence (the holy place, the Ark, the cherubim, the mercy-seat) and of the greatest rejection of God. Where else are prophets to live and die but here, on this cross of contradiction where God's faithfulness and human unfaithfulness meet?

This is what the Bible finally has to say about holiness. It would be safe and consoling to believe that holiness was securely bound to an object or a place in itself, to the city of the great king, the shrine, and the Ark, timeless and changeless. But the holiness of our God does not live in temples made with hands. This city and this shrine are holy because here God has called, and human beings have stoned and burned and impaled him in the forms of their fellows. And here God has entered more and more deeply and urgently, with his judgment and forgiveness, through all this history of bloodshed. This city of Jerusalem, with its terrible history, is holy because here can be seen the victory of God's vulnerable faithfulness over the atrocities that power and religious arrogance inflict on him in his children and servants.

A human being is holy, not because he or she triumphs by will-power over chaos and guilt and leads a flawless life, but because that life shows the victory of God's faithfulness *in the midst* of disorder and imperfection. The church is holy—and this congregation here present is holy—not because it is a gathering of the good and the well-behaved, but because it speaks of the triumph of grace in the coming together of strangers and sinners who, miraculously, trust one another enough to join in common repentance and common praise—to express a deep and elusive unity in Jesus Christ, who is our righteousness and sanctification. Humanly speaking, holiness is always like this: God's endurance in the middle of our refusal of him, his capacity to meet every refusal with the gift of himself.

A Christian holy place, then, is a place where such a gift is shown and remembered in human stories. Typically, and from the first, Christian holy places have been the scenes of martyrdom—not only bloodshed, but also a deeper and repentant discovery of God through the horror. We dare not talk of Auschwitz as a holy place because no one outside of it can presume to talk of suffering accepted and transfigured; only if its victims could ever speak to its torturers could we talk of the discovery of God there, of holiness. But as Jesus goes to the holy city, he goes in memory of and in solidarity with those who have died there for God, to confront the executioners—the powerful, the pious—with the ever more urgent claims of a God yearning to forgive and welcome them home ("How often have I longed to gather you under my wings"). And in the ultimate and decisive showing of God's mercy in the resurrection, he confirms for ever the holiness of Jerusalem, not as a place where holy power is locked in a shrine, but as the setting for the showing and remembering of God's most central, final gift of himself in and beyond our sin—the fear and fury, the torture and murder by which we keep ourselves strangers to God and to our own nature.

What then of Medjugorje? It shouldn't surprise us if God is seen to act in a place whose history is one of hostility and murder: God acts in Jerusalem, with its record of infidelity, of the slaughtered children of God. It shouldn't surprise us if the recipients of visions and graces are those of average virtue and unsophisticated belief. But before we finally say that God is at work here in a specially dramatic way, there are more questions to be asked. How far have these strange events *connected* with Medjugorje's history? Is there anything here that presages some new discovery of a grace that heals these memories, that opens up reconciliation among the clergy, that makes Serbs and Croats able to face each other and live with each other in Christ? Well, perhaps. And if so, if this is seen to happen, then we shall be able to speak of a true "apparition" of the work of God. Meanwhile, five teenagers have been brought deeper into God's love and thousands more have followed them on such a journey, finding healing for body and spirit. For all this we can give thanks.

The true miracles, however—the truly supernatural, that which is authentically not of this world—are not apparitions or even healings (Jesus tells us as much, after all), but the appearing of God's glory in forgiveness, in the hardly conceivable meeting of torturer and victim so that both are re-created, and in the relentless persistence and urging of God's mercy that is shown in his saints and martyrs. Think what it would mean, in some unimaginable future, for Beirut to be a "holy" place because Shia militiamen had seen the face of God in the starving and despairing Palestinians in Bourj-el-Barajneh and had turned to them for the gift they only can give, an acceptance releasing them from the prison of their own violence. *This* is the appearing of the "holy" for Christians, as it appears at our worship when we celebrate our absolution by God, and as it appears in every act of true reconciliation ("Mutual forgiveness of each vice, Opens the gate of paradise"). This is holy ground, like the holy city, stained with the blood of God's friends, from whose holiest place, the refuse heap of Calvary, flow the streams that water the whole dry earth.

25

Intercessory Prayer

Genesis 18:23-33; Ephesians 6:10-24

Both of our readings tonight are full of the imagery of *struggle* and conflict. Abraham wrestles with God, boldness and terror almost pulling him apart, in an effort to enlarge the scope of God's mercy. He pushes God as far as he dares, to the greatest reach of mercy he can imagine: it is just possible, remotely possible, that God could be good enough to spare even Sodom for the sake of ten just men. The apostle's struggling is different: here in Ephesians is the classic imagery of spiritual warfare, wrestling with the evil powers that restrict the scope of God's mercy, the "rulers of this present darkness." And constant, untiring prayer, prayer at all times, is the central feature of this battle against slavery and illusion and sin.

Different kinds of conflict, but both are battling against the limitation of God's grace and love, both pushing out the frontiers of grace as far as they can go. We don't think often enough of our intercessory prayer as a battle, but so it is—just as, at one level, the whole of prayer and spirituality is penetrated with warfare, with the struggle for freedom and vision. The prayer of intercession at its simplest is thinking of something or someone in the presence of God. That very great saint of the twentieth-century Church of England, Dick Sheppard, once asked a friend to pray that he might spend a bit of time "thinking of nothing but Jesus and me." And put in those terms, it may be easier to see how intercession can be a battle and a struggle. *How* do we think of Jesus *and,* for example, a hundred children massacred in central Africa? Jesus *and* the senile, the dying, the dead, the mentally ill? Jesus *and* the IRA? "This present darkness" is often so dark that it seems empty formalism to put the name of God beside some appalling atrocity. How pointless, how unconnected it is. In many circumstances, the effort seems only an increasingly hollow gesture against despair. You have been praying for two years, say, about a friend going through a breakdown, about a disintegrating marriage, about Northern Ireland, and nothing is happening, or things get worse. *Then* it's a struggle all right, the struggle not to let God and the world fall apart from each other: because that is the center of this prayer, the recognition that, in spite of appearances, God and the world belong together. There is no place where the love of God can't go. And that is unbearably hard to believe.

Still, as Christians, we are bound to believe it. On the cross we see the love of God still at work—indeed, most gloriously at work in the extreme of mortal anguish. Jesus, in Gethsemane and on Calvary, "holds together" God and the world in his own suffering and dying person. And in the resurrection and the ascension, Christ's authority over all times and places is proclaimed: now there are no doors that can be locked before him. As the embodiment of God's mercy, he can be found everywhere. The cross means that Christians recognize right from the start that this faith strains the imagination to breaking point, yet this is undeniably and centrally the gospel of God. Abraham's problem is, "Can God love *that* much, even where there is hardly anything worthy or lovable?" The Christian's problem is still more acute: "Can God love and act and heal where there seems to be *nothing* worthy or lovable, when the whole world seems enslaved to cruelty, betrayal, and pain?" Yet that—as Paul is always telling us—is exactly what God's love is like; it is there *before* there is any hope, any light, any merit. It knows no barriers. "The gates of brass before him burst, The iron fetters yield."

So our intercession is a sharing in Christ's terribly costly struggle to hold together God and the world, love and suffering, light and darkness. At baptism, Christians are commissioned to "fight under Christ's banner." Intercession is part of this, planting the flag in the remotest and bleakest places, saying of this or that situation, "Lord, I know even *this* cannot defeat you or send you away." Intercession does not and must not shrink to a utilitarian thing—putting in a request, filling in a sort of spiritual form, and waiting for a simple answer, "yes" or "no." We do it because our faith absolutely demands this "holding together" operation. We do it even when we can't see what imaginable hope there might be, when we have no idea at all what might happen or how exactly things might get better, no idea, even, what we can *do* about the situation. It is a cry of naked faith: in some inconceivable way, God is here too. If we find we can't pray about something because it is too meaningless or dreadful, this is very understandable, but it is still a drawing back from the full implications of faith in Jesus crucified.

Of course, it is in no way wrong to pray for *specific* results. Who wouldn't pray for peace in Northern Ireland, for healing for the sick, and so on? We pray like this because we have a sure confidence that God's will is for peace and healing and abundance of life. It is only when intercession reaches the (all-too-familiar) stage of being a sort of shopping list that we may feel something is a little bit askew. No, when we pray, we do, naturally and rightly, pray for solutions and improvements. And to identify our will with God's is to open our will to his own yearning for the happiness of his creatures. But that is the important thing: to see our prayer within the context of this great and eternal divine passion for our well-being, not to bind it to our own limited vision and limited love. Intercession is, once again, the prayer of *faith;* and faith is not a matter of detailed plans and programs. It is sometimes said that if you qualify all your prayers with the words "if God wills," you might just as well not pray at all. But this is nonsense. Intercession, as we have seen, is the natural flowering of our life in Christ, under Christ's banner, our faith in Christ's lordship. We may or may not wish to "qualify" our prayers in this way, but whether we do or don't, the underlying reality is the same, and true and valid as ever—the proclamation of Christ's victory and the universal presence of God's gracious, reconciling love. If you don't pray, you deny that.

Very well, but what does prayer *do?* How does it work? These are inescapable questions, however crude, and quite unanswerable ones. We have one absolute instance of God's reconciling love at work in Jesus on the cross, and that is practically the only clue. It works in a man whose heart is open to God and to all the world, so open that it is broken to death. And our Christian growth must be toward that. Our hearts must grow, must be constantly enlarged in sensitivity to the world's suffering and sensitivity to the victorious mercy of God. It means that our eyes have to be fully open to the world, to see its dereliction and hopelessness, its "Godlessness"; and it means that we must know in *ourselves* how God's mercy breaks barriers, remakes and renews. It is only through such open hearts that God can work. When selfishness and greedy manipulation are set aside, and insensitivity and complacency are overcome, then there is an empty space for the wind of the Spirit to blow through. That is all we can know. If prayer "works," it is because of lives that have been crucified with Christ.

Finally, we must not forget that intercession is inseparable from all we are and do as Christians. It is inseparable from involvement in the pain of others, and inseparable from our own understanding of God's love in *us*—inseparable, therefore, from the prayer of confession and thanksgiving. And, of great importance, it is inseparable from the prayer of adoration and contemplation, the simple, loving, and trusting prayer of gazing on God and letting him work as he wills in your soul, because that is the simplest and most basic way of growing in Christian love and Christian maturity, and deepening your knowledge of God's grace. It is a great mistake—though lots of people make it—to regard intercession as "bread and butter" prayer, while adoration is left to a few professionals, holy and remote souls. In the long run, prayer is one act, not several—the act of opening ourselves as best we can to the glorious life of God, letting God live in us. It is the intensifying and daily deepening of our life in the crucified and risen Christ. Intercession is one aspect of our pilgrimage from glory to glory, and one aspect of God's victorious assault on all that hurts and diminishes his world. It is part of God's reclaiming and re-creating of all things, one small yet significant aspect of the everlasting fact of his transfiguring and selfless compassion: not just our thoughts, our words, and our wants, but, most truly and deeply, his unceasing creative and reconciling work.

26

Being Alone

There are plenty of subjects that Christians seem to treat with a consistent lack of seriousness, with a painful lack of imagination and sympathy. One such subject is loneliness. Most of the time we are so caught up in a bland rhetoric of "communion" and "sharing" that we fail utterly to confront that more puzzling and disturbing fact of irreducible human isolation. "We pray for the old and the lonely"—words heard quite frequently in intercessions, implying that loneliness is an unfortunate condition from which *some people* suffer, like diabetes or color-blindness. But what about the loneliness of each one of us?

Loneliness has little to do with what we do or where we do it, whether we're married or unmarried, optimists or pessimists, heterosexual or homosexual. Loneliness has to do with the sudden clefts we experience in every human relation, the gaps that open up with such stomach-turning unexpectedness. In a brief moment, I and my brother or sister have moved away into different worlds, and there is no language we can share. It is when I see what my words or actions have done to someone else, or when I realize what picture someone else has of me. It is when things that matter to me are met with polite incomprehension, and when I cannot hear and understand the importance of what someone is trying to tell me. It is—recalling an experience I can't forget—sitting on the floor with a nine-year-old child of normal intelligence and trying to understand what he is saying. Because he is hopelessly spastic and can't control his tongue any more than he can his head or his limbs, I can grasp only one word in ten, and he stares at me desperately and furiously, *willing* me to understand with all his might, and I *can't*.

Faith cannot solve or heal any of this, and so often it doesn't even try to make sense of it. We give way to embarrassing and embarrassed moralizing or soothing noises. Well, it's a school of patience, isn't it, and we all go through it, and it won't last long. It's just one of those frustrating facts about human nature. Perhaps all I will manage to do is to make noises like this. Yet I feel there is something more to be said, and I can only try to hint at it. It has to do with the story of our Lord's betrayal and death: a story in which *solitude* is, unobtrusively but surely, one of the most important themes. Already, before the great climactic events of Thursday and Friday, we have James and John clamoring for power, and the cleft opens wide in Jesus' reply, "You do not know what you are asking." At the supper, there is Peter refusing Jesus' service; and Jesus' plea (for that is what it is)—if you do not let me wash you, we are apart for ever. As they go to the garden, there is one of the great dramatic moments of misunderstanding in the story. (St. Luke, who relates it, for once touches a height of Johannine irony.) Jesus has bitterly proclaimed that this is the hour of violence, when a man ought to sell his coat to buy a sword, and the disciples proudly say, "We've got two swords already." Jesus' reply is as poignant and ironic as anything in the narrative: "Well, that should be fine, shouldn't it?"

The gulf becomes ever wider; Jesus seems more and more to be moving away into a world from which he can neither speak nor be understood. When the disciples have fled in terror from the stranger that their master has become, we move into the great set pieces of the trials, and, again and again, we hear the response of silence or *su eipas*, "the words are yours." Are you the Messiah? What is the truth? There are no words shared between Jesus and the princes of the people to which an answer can be given. There are no words to explain to the weeping mother at the foot of the cross. At the end, if St. Mark tells the truth, there are no words even for God, only "a great cry."

This enormous, dreadful solitude at the heart of the story of our redemption is where we must start in reflecting on any human solitude. Why is Jesus so totally alone at his end? One exchange, more than all the others perhaps, embodies the reason: Pilate's question, "What is truth?" and Jesus' answering silence. The truth stands there in flesh, a truth that cannot be contained in any words or images we may create. Jesus' isolation is the isolation of a reality that so resists definition and limitation that it can only appear as utterly strange to our world. It doesn't belong and so, as Bonhoeffer said, it is "edged out of the world onto the cross." There are no words for it, because there is no room for it in our world of common speech and agreed definition. There is no room even in the language of religion: Jesus is not the anointed son of Caiaphas's God, and by *that* God he will be abandoned on the cross. He is truly "the Word in the desert," the Word exiled from the world of words and the compromises of definition. This is the solitude of truth, the solitude, finally, of God: God as a spastic child who can communicate nothing but his presence and his inarticulate wanting.

And so, what about *our* solitude? Ours is never this absolute isolation of God, because *we* are not "truth." But can we say that we find and know solitude to the extent that there is truth in us? This seems a strange thing to say. One thing loneliness *does* teach us, after all, is the falsity of imagining that we possess any wholeness in ourselves. Loneliness uncovers for us the tedium and the poverty of our own private worlds; it lays bare what has been called the "raw surface" of our need for others and our need for communication. It seems to show us that loneliness is falsity and unreality, and that we can only find truth and integrity in relationship with others, in sharing and *koinonia*. I am not a whole person, and there is no such thing as a whole person, in the sense of a wholeness sufficient in and to itself.

This, surely, is the main lesson we learn from the experience of loneliness. It is *true*, and it *is* important. It is just that, in looking at the solitude of Jesus in his death, I find it only a partial vision and a partial truth. The collapse of communication, the lack of words and visible, tangible contact with another person, the realizing of misunderstanding, the discovery of incompatible aims—all these are reminders that there are things in each of us that cannot be made public, even if we want to make them so and struggle to let them speak. Complete openness with another, even the closest lover or friend, is a phantom, infinitely receding as our attempts at total honesty become more and more dramatic and desperate. We may believe we are speaking our truth, but we can never know, we can never measure our words, except against other words. And we can never hear them with another person's ears—hear the accent of falsity we can never discern for ourselves. We can never stand in front of the tapestry we are weaving and see its picture.

For most of our time, we belong to groups and societies and to individuals we love. In all these contexts we use the common coinage of words and ideas and accept the compromise and imprecision of human communication. Nor is this wrong; it is, indeed, utterly necessary to us, it is the way our identities act and are acted on and built up. But it is not everything, and if we think is, the results will be the grossest hollowness and unreality in our selfhood. We are prevented, thank God, from thinking this because of these inescapable disturbances, the moments of isolation, the unbridgeable clefts in the social and relational worlds. In the face of these, we cannot pretend. And this is why loneliness has to do with truth, why the impulse to seek truth drives some people into deserts and hermitages. Loneliness makes us confront the mysteriousness, the elusiveness of our own reality, makes us recognize that it is never exhausted in our relations and our words and our acts. The truth of our selves, the foundation of our selves, is something baffling, toughly resistant to all our efforts to bring it out into the open, into our sight or other people's sight. The phrase of 1 Peter 3:4 is sometimes used in this context: *homo cordis absconditus,* "the person in the hidden heart."

Suddenly to experience one's isolation, then, is to know what in us can never be spelled out in public terms, a dimension always behind and beyond. And because it is so bewildering and unsettling, we try very hard to avoid or gloss over the moments of sharpest solitude—to smooth away the misunderstandings, minimize the conflicts, fill the silences, because we cannot comprehend them, and they menace our very existence.

> Or as, when an underground train, in the tube, stops
>   too long between stations
> And the conversation rises and slowly fades into silence
> And you see behind every face the mental emptiness deepen
> Leaving only the growing terror of nothing to think about.
>   (T. S. Eliot, "East Coker," 118-121)

Any culture that is terrified—as ours is—of silence and aloneness is one in which the sense of human reality, human truth, is being eroded. I am not talking about the erosion of individual liberties in collectivist societies; that is a complaint normally uttered by those who are most terrified of the real freedom of solitude, who need society for their audience or their victim, or both. No, this is something that affects equally the so-called collectivist societies and the so-called free societies. Neither kind can afford to trust solitude. Indeed, in one sense, no society at all could completely trust it because it puts them all in question. And no society can eradicate it so long as human beings continue to talk to each other and love each other, because, as we have seen, it is in the middle of intimacy that the reality of loneliness most dramatically appears.

Solitude teaches us about our truth, but it teaches us too that our truth is not our own. It is, as I have said, "behind and beyond," not at our disposal, not to be grasped by us. And if we see Jesus as the ultimately lonely person because of his complete embodying of a truth that cannot be grasped, we are driven to say finally that he is the "home" of all our truth, our reality. To put our loneliness next to the loneliness of God-in-Christ is to see our truth in the light of what the truth is like—the truth that is (who is) irrefutably not of this world. That is disturbing, yet it is also a ground of hope. We cannot grasp or plan or organize our reality, for it is somehow in the hands of God. There is, behind and beyond, someone who not only sees and grasps, but also accepts and holds our reality. This is not to argue a doctrine of providence—God plans, even when we can't—but only a belief that we are not deserted by our unknown God, even when all our nameable and domesticated gods forsake us. When all our words vanish, the Word remains. In our silence and empty fear, the reality of our grounding in God and our acceptance by God can make itself known.

This will happen only if we let it, of course, hence the importance of not glossing over and trivializing our loneliness, but facing it and feeling it. If we *can* trust that truth has a home, an objective place in the all-perceiving mercy of God, then our hidden life is "hidden with Christ in God." What's more, if I can see *my* reality thus, I can see yours and everyone's in the same way. I shall see *your* elusiveness, your mystery, your terrible singleness and solitude. And because your solitude, like mine, belongs to God, I shall stand before you as I stand before God. *You* are holy, as God is holy, and you are unknowable and unpredictable, as God is. I must therefore give up and put away all hopes of trapping you in my words, my categories, and my ideas, my plans and my solutions. I shall offer whatever I have to offer, but I shall not commit the blasphemy (I don't use the word lightly) of ordering your life or writing your script. I shall see your boundary and recognize that love and fellowship are realities I do not constantly have to preserve by my efforts, by struggling to say and know everything. We meet in God, in whom your solitude and mine, your truth and mine, are at last at home.

In our failure at the level of word and understanding not everything is lost. Through the unhealed pain of that child and me sitting and looking despairingly at each other there can still be trust that there are other levels on which to communicate. We exchange rueful smiles as we get up to part—and perhaps that's everything. Jon Stallworthy wrote one of his greatest poems about the birth of his mentally handicapped child. Here is part of it.

> You turn to the window for the first time.
> I am called to the cot
>   to see your focus shift,
> take tendril-hold on a shaft
> of sun, explore its dusty surface, climb
>   to an eye you cannot
> meet. You have a sickness they cannot heal,
> the doctors say: locked in
>   your body you will remain.
> Well, I have been locked in mine.
> We will tunnel each other out. You seal
>   the covenant with a grin.

Out of all our failures, out of this distance and alienness, God painfully makes for us truth, integrity, and salvation—and love and fellowship, though full of barbs and ironies and unease. It is a work that has all the strangeness of those other memories of Jesus: his coming again to his friends in their locked rooms and locked minds to give them his reality, his humanity and Godhead, and more fully than ever his gift of the Spirit, creating the strange and immeasurably frustrating fellowship of the church. The loneliness dividing Christians from one another, individually and collectively, has a sting all its own, but we live by the gift of a shared Word that is not ours and a shared food and drink we have not made—the solitude of our Lord and God, by some great divine comic *denouement*, made into the means of our communion. With Christ we are torn away from the superficial communion of our own making into his loneliness; and there we find our truth in him, so that he becomes our own secure bond, our bread broken and shared, our food, our life, our prayers, our hope, and our love.

27

Loving God

Who made you?
God made me.
Why did he make you?
To know him, to love him and to serve him....

But which of us *does* "love" God? I remember, ages ago, talking to a young Chinese Marxist student, who amazed me by saying, "Of course, priesthood [I had just told him I hoped to be ordained] is unrewarding, but you won't mind that, because you love God." I was amazed and rather appalled, because I couldn't imagine why he should think I *loved* God; as soon as he'd said it, I knew it wasn't true. After all, what was it to love God? The saints loved God: their whole lives revolved around God, they wept and laughed and danced for love of him. When St. John of the Cross was staying at a convent over Christmas, one of the sisters saw him, when he thought no one was looking, picking up the figure of the child Jesus from the crib. He hugged it close to his chest and then, with eyes closed, danced around the crib for a few minutes. Well, that, it seems, is love of God: a devotion that makes people more than a little dotty, that produces an all-pervading warmth and delight, an incommunicable gladness beyond all words. "My beloved is mine and I am his"; "Jesu, the very thought is sweet; In that dear name all pleasures meet"; *Jesu, meine Freude*; St. Aelred of Rievaulx on his deathbed murmuring "Christ, Christ, Christ" unceasingly; Francis of Assisi literally crying himself blind in his long vigils of prayer.

If this is loving God, most of us don't. Even taking into account the charismatic experience of the gift of tongues or the gift of tears, for those who take it seriously, it is still only a momentary thing; and there are plenty who *don't* take it seriously and who look askance at what they think is easy emotionalism. Some of you may know Thomas Keneally's lovely novel about Australian Catholicism, *Three Cheers for the Paraclete.* In the first chapter the clerical anti-hero of this book, a wry and rather puzzled young seminary professor, preaches a sermon on the quotation applied to priests, "Because they love no one, they imagine that they love God." This is duly reported to his archbishop; kindly but quite ruthless interrogation follows. Does he know any priests of whom this is true? Desperately, he replies, "Yes, myself." At once, the tone of the examination changes: deep pastoral concern is shown by all the inquisitors, who take great pains to prove to him from all the best textbooks that of *course* he must love God, because all that "loving God" means is having good dispositions, avoiding mortal sin, and so on and so on. Eventually the poor man has to confess that indeed he does love God, and everyone is happy except him. It is all a misunderstanding, but he goes away with an obscure feeling that he and all of them as well have missed the bus somehow.

That's one practical solution: love of God is a matter of the will, not the emotions, and so it's entirely a matter of loyal churchmanship and keeping within the rules. The other simple solution is the one favored by austere Protestants, like the great Swedish scholar Anders Nygren: human beings *can't* love God, and it's a horrible blasphemy for them to try. "Mystical" ideas of this sort are a deep perversion of authentic Christianity, he thinks: *eros* corrupting *agape;* greedy, possessive human love reaching up to drag God down from heaven and make him a cozy little pet to help us feel warm and good. The only love worth the name is *God's,* and that is pure, uncaused. God does not love because he wants or needs anything: he loves the utterly unlovely and unlovable. We can't love like that, because all our love is selfish, wanting our own profit. If I pretend to love God, all this means is that I want to use God to produce nice experiences for myself. The only proper response to God's love is faith: blind trust and commitment, unadulterated by any search for experience.

Paradoxically, this comes very near the Catholic idea of "pure love" for God—a love completely indifferent to results or rewards: if God sends me to hell, I shall still love him. Incidentally, when Wesley first began to preach, he was suspected of being a Jesuit in disguise because he taught something like this—what a distinguished Anglican dignitary of the time called the shocking papist idea of "pure love." And all these solutions—good will, faith, pure love—come out at the same thing: "love of God" is an attitude rather than a feeling; we can't expect it to make a tangible difference. The words really describe an aspect of the whole of our relation to God, not an experience that is part of it.

This makes excellent sense and affirms something vastly important about the secondary place of emotions in the mature Christian life. But I can't help wondering whether we haven't missed the bus too. When all these admirable and true points have been made, is that *really* all? "In that dear name all *pleasures* meet." Were they all wrong? Were the saints simply having occasional regrettable lapses into self-indulgent emotionalism? I don't think so.

Part of the trouble is that if we say loving God is a matter of the will, we usually have at the back of our minds a very abstract idea of will, as if "will" just acted in a vacuum, and "free choice" meant total arbitrariness. But surely what we normally think of in this connection is choice, based on the simple fact that we *like* some things more than others. Being the creatures we are, we are moved by being drawn, being attracted. We may talk as much as we like about faith and pure love, but the plain truth is that we are not moved toward God except by means of his attractiveness. We turn to God because we like what we see in him—to put it in the crudest terms. If it is not a choice in which our *desire* is involved, it is no choice at all; and you won't solve this problem by talking about "faith." I can't see how even Nygren can conceive of a response to God that doesn't involve choosing, that means *wanting* what God has to give. What God wishes to say to us, do for us, give us, is not something irrelevant or tangential to being human. How could it be? He made everything to find its fulfillment in him, not in itself. So he speaks human words to us and (in Paul's expression) "makes his appeal" to the world in shamelessly human, and therefore passionate and emotive, terms. Pure will is a figment of imagination and a pretty silly one. Men and women will, because they first desire. They choose God because they see in him their hope, their life, their fulfillment. And it is pointless to call this "selfish," unless we are to call every aesthetic or even moral preference selfish. It is as truly a recognition that truth does not lie in myself, that beauty must draw me away from *my* self if my *self* is to live and grow.

And incidentally, isn't there something rather absurdly arrogant about "pure love"? If I say I love God with absolutely *no* thought of effects or feelings, am I not perhaps denying that I *need* God? Of course, I don't expect any reward (except the assurance of my pure motives): I can do without that sort of thing. No, there is no need to worry about "pure" love too much. It is easy to get into the delightfully ridiculous situation of Patience in Gilbert and Sullivan's operetta. Believing love must be a pure and utterly unselfish thing, she decides it is her duty to marry the man she doesn't love, because if she married the man she *did* love, that wouldn't be love, it would be selfish, i.e., it would make her happy. Like it or not, love is hopelessly entangled in need and dependence—the need to find in another, human or divine, human *and* divine, the happiness we cannot generate in ourselves. It is the recognition that we must let ourselves be "made," to some degree, by others, because we can't complete ourselves.

So, loving God *does* mean choosing God and wanting God, seeing one's happiness in God, not just having good thoughts and a reasonably orderly moral disposition. God is what we are for; he is that by which everything in our experience is to be tried and valued: he is himself incomparably *worthwhile*. And this desirability is something akin to other experiences of "worthwhileness." God became flesh: God-in-Christ is given us to draw us to our happiness. "Come unto me, all that labor and are heavy-laden, and I will give you rest." Christ is a stranger and a foreigner; he comes in judgment, but he is no less the desire of all nations. He is the one whom "all seek," as the apostles tell him. Whatever else we may find in the gospels, there is at least this: a compelling person—the imprint, the memory, the echo not only of the universal challenger, but also of the universal healer and consoler, someone people *long* to see, hear, be with. God spoke to the world in beauty—as Dostoyevsky said—in the beauty of that single human face.

And yes, of course, the "beauty" of Jesus' humanity remains the motive force of much Christian devotion through the ages:

This beauty doth all things excel;
By faith I know but ne'er can tell
The Glory that I now do see
In Jesus Christ, the apple tree.

But even in that lovely folk carol, the "humanity" of Jesus is in fact a long way away. This devotion does not spring so much from detailed reflection on the gospel, or speculation on the moral elevation of Jesus' character, as from a secondary kind of response: how beautiful, how compelling must Christ have been, must Christ *be*, to be the savior and healer of humankind. And that kind of conviction rests, to an important extent, on your own understanding of healing and grace, your own experience of the beauty of the life of grace.

I'm not suggesting that the gospels are "secondary" to our experience in the Christian life, far from it. What I'm trying, rather laboriously, to say is that the gospels and the figure of Jesus come alive when viewed and grasped in the whole personal and social context of Christian life. And—I suggest—the *attractiveness* of Jesus will most come alive through our experience of the attractiveness of forgiven, grace-penetrated, Christ-filled lives in those around us. And for Christians, "those around us" doesn't just mean our immediate neighbors and contemporaries, but the "cloud of witnesses" of every generation: the communion of saints, in fact. Paul can say boldly to his converts, "be imitators of me, as I am of Christ." Is Christ remote and abstract to you? After all, you have not known Christ in the flesh. Then look at his work, his reflection, his image in someone who is not remote and abstract—perhaps a historical figure, perhaps a great contemporary, perhaps just someone very inconspicuous who happens to have come your way. Christ—and Christ's beauty, and so God's beauty—can be seen in this oblique way, at an angle, in a mirror, in those he lives in. For practical purposes, we can quite often echo that idiosyncratic theological genius who said, "God's a good man"!

But not just a *good* man. It is well said that good people make you feel awful ("He's so nice you could kick him," a friend once remarked of some mutual acquaintance of ours); only holy people make you feel *better* too (though, like our Lord, they will make you feel awful enroute). They make you feel that the humanity you share with them is—in spite of everything—capable of glorious transfiguration, joy, and fulfillment. This can be true even if the people in question are poor, depressed, in pain, humiliated: there is still a quality, hard to define, a sense that life in them is somehow as it should be, rooted in the soil of the deepest and truest reality of all. They are attractive: to those who meet them, they convey some sense that their life is what we should be seekingr. They produce, oddly, a kind of longing in us, the distant reflection of what, ultimately, God is doing with the whole of his universe: revealing fulfillment and joy and peace, in fragments and hints, suggesting where wholeness is to be found, suggesting some reality so full and final, so lovely and rich and all-embracing that we can only say that all things are there for its—or his—sake, that all things are to be valued in that light.

So what we perceive in the saints is the echo of God's desirability and worthwhileness. Life in them is "well-lived" because they live as men and women grounded in the "absolute value" of God. They know (even if not all of them can say so) what they are *for*, and so point us all to that end. In the long run, they make us look not at *them*, but at the wellsprings of their life in Christ, and Christ's in God the Father. What they do is what they are; what they are are members of Christ; what Christ is is God with us, the glory and beauty of God in a human face. And the faces of the saints are his, too, as well as their own.

> I say more: the just man justices;
> Keeps grace: that keeps all his goings graces;
> Acts in God's eye what in God's eye he is—
> Christ—for Christ plays in ten thousand places,
> Lovely in limbs, and lovely in eyes not his
> To the Father through the features of men's faces.
> (Hopkins, "As Kingfishers Catch Fire")

God's beauty is to be grasped, longed for, and loved in Christ; Christ to be longed for and loved in his saints—that is, finally, in one another. If "the love of God" means nothing to you (says William of St. Thierry in the twelfth century), then love the lovers of God. Love the love of God in Francis or John of the Cross, Dick Sheppard or Mother Teresa, Aelred of Rievaulx or Charles de Foucauld. To love love-*in*-someone is, by the courtesy of heaven, to love love and so to love God. It is to turn our eyes toward, to choose and desire the truth of all truth, the beauty of all beauty. It is to look and hope in and love and serve and know the Father, the Son, and the Holy Spirit, from whom and for whom everything in heaven and earth exists, even the cold, flabby, and fantasy-ridden hearts of human beings. Even these hearts are not incapable of kindling, if given the Holy Spirit. We can only pray for precisely that gift:

Come, O fire and flame of divine love,
    and burn away all our deadly wounds.
May I be cleansed by thee,
    that I may cleanse others.
May I be enlightened by thee,
    that I may enlighten others.
May I be set on fire by thee
    that I may set others on fire.
For to this end thou wert sent from heaven;
what else is thy will but to be kindled in us?

(Prayer to the Holy Spirit from Dies Sacerdotalis)

28

Reading the Bible

This text is being fulfilled today even as you listen. *(Luke 4:21)*

As Jesus utters these words at Nazareth, there is obviously a very straightforward sense in which the text as being fulfilled: the prophet's words are now facts, what the prophet foresees is now done, and the prophetic word of the Lord has become the Incarnate Word of the Lord. Many of us have moments when we can say in reading scripture, "this text is being fulfilled today." In his autobiography Thomas Merton recalls the time when he was meditating on whether or not to join the Trappists. He opened the Bible at random, it fell open at the first chapter of St. Luke's gospel, and he read the words: "Behold, you shall be silent"! More seriously, in his journal, *The Sign of Jonas,* he records reading the book of Job with a growing and menacing sense that what that book was about was to be realized in his own life. Judging from the eloquent silences of his journal, he knew what he was talking about.

If that were all that could be said about the reading of scripture, we might have a rather lopsided view, as if scripture were invariably and simply transparent to the action of God, as if we needed no reflection, no wider perspective, in making it our own. Alongside the experience of the transparency of scripture, we have probably all equally had the experience of incomprehension or, worse, of alienation, when we feel "this text is *incapable* of being fulfilled," or, "I have no idea what this text means." When we hear a text of scripture and it is offensive to us as well as unintelligible, or when we are touched by words of exclusion, of superiority of race or of sex, then suddenly "this text is being fulfilled today" is a strange word.

So how are we to make sense of it? Must we not say something like the following? Scripture, we know, is not simply an oracle; it is not simply lapidary remarks dropped down from heaven and engraved on stone. Our lives would be a great deal easier if it were. No, scripture is the record of an encounter and a contest. Often in thinking about scripture we may be more helped by reflecting on the story of Jacob wrestling with the angel than by any images of oracles from heaven. Here in scripture is God's urgency to communicate; here in scripture is our mishearing, our misappropriating, our deafness, and our resistance. Woven together in scripture are those two things, the giving of God and our inability to receive what God wants to give. On almost every page of the gospels we read: "Jesus said, 'Do you now understand?' They said, 'No.'" And there are many moments when, in reading the gospels, it is possible to feel that the sayings of Jesus have been passed through a process of organization and meditation that, while giving them a meaning and a structure, have at the same time obscured them. The parable of the unjust steward is my favorite example, a story St. Luke does not seem to have understood particularly well. He has linked it with a number of other sayings about wealth and poverty, all very worthy, but leaving us with a sense that the parable is actually much more difficult than it is. Luke tried his best with it and so does the ill-fated preacher!

A record, an encounter, a contest, a wrestling: God chooses a people and he gives them liberty. He brings them out of slavery and gives them a law, which is his way of showing his glory to the world. What happens? The law is either neglected or it becomes the tool of a new kind of pride. The book of Nehemiah, from which the first reading today is taken, contains chilling moments of exclusivism and hatred toward those who have intermarried with foreigners. The gift of God, the liberty of God, is passed through the distorting glass of our own fears.

On 25 January we celebrate the Conversion of St. Paul, perhaps one of the most luminous moments in the whole of the New Testament, when Paul sees in the face of those he has been trying to slaughter the face of Jesus. It is a definitive moment of Christian perception. The next day we celebrate Timothy and Titus. In the letters to Timothy and Titus we can see how Paul's own insight was bundled together by a later generation with a lot of anxiety about being respectable and having a good reputation—some distance away from that blinding moment on the Damascus road.

Encounter, contest. Perhaps when we read the words, "This text is being fulfilled today, even as you listen," we can say that that aspect of scripture is being fulfilled in me *now*. In me *now* is God's gift, and in me *now* is the distorting glass of prejudice and fear. In me *now* the gift is being received, but the gift is also capable of being distorted and hemmed in, of not being given through me. All the complexity of the contesting of scripture is in us as we listen to it. When we listen to a passage that is difficult, alien, or offensive, I think our reaction should be neither to say, "This is the word of the Lord, so the difficulty is my problem," nor to say, "This is rubbish, we ought to produce a more politically correct version of scripture!" Our task, rather, is to say that the revelation of God comes to us in the middle of weakness and fallibility. We read neither with a kind of blind and thoughtless obedience to every word of scripture, as if it simply represented the mind of God, nor with that rather priggish sensibility that desires to look down on the authors of scripture as benighted savages. We read with a sense of our own benighted savagery in receiving God's gift, and our solidarity with those writers of scripture caught up in the blazing fire of God's gift who yet struggle with it, misapprehend it, and misread it.

If that sounds an inconclusive or problematic way of approaching scripture, we need, finally, to recall that scripture is not simply a long record of unfinished business. At the heart of scripture the prophetic word does become the incarnate Word. At the heart of scripture is the fire of God's presence, of God's gift perfectly given and perfectly received in Jesus Christ. We need to read the Bible around Christ, and read it, therefore, in the confidence that our own mishearing and misapprehending, our own confusions and uncertainties about the text and about the matter with which it deals, will be part of God's triumphant work in us. Through that encounter and contest we may trust that God will be victorious. At the end of the night we shall learn his name as he touches us, because we know that scripture turns upon Christ, in whom all texts are finally fulfilled, since there is in him no misapprehension, no distorting by sin of the gift of God.

Now, reading the Bible around Jesus with all that in mind is by no means easy and, as we know all too well, in the church it can lead to endless squabbles and bitterness. We do not know how to read certain passages: we do not know how to deal properly with Paul in his most rampantly sexist moods; we do not know how to deal with some texts on sexuality; we do not know how to cope with the violence in so much of the Hebrew scriptures. We say the psalms each day and quite often find ourselves wishing unspeakable plagues on our enemies. All the time we need to remember the humanity in, to, and through which God speaks: a broken humanity, a humanity poorly equipped to receive God's liberty. Yet we can recognize this not simply with resignation or cynicism. We do not read the Bible just as a record of the crimes and follies of humankind (to paraphrase Gibbon in *The Decline and Fall of the Roman Empire*), but as a record of how those crimes and follies are drawn together and plaited into a strong rope, drawn together and unified in the Word made flesh. As the text of encounter and contest is fulfilled in our own struggles, so we pray that the culmination of that text, the Word incarnate, may triumph in each one of us, in our reading, in our praying, and in our living.

29

Is There a Christian Sexual Ethic?

Given that this is a subject on which more clergy have probably made bigger fools of themselves than any other, the simple and safe answer would be to say, "Yes: several, and all of them perfectly all right," and leave it at that. But that won't do, and wouldn't please anyone. People who ask the question are generally people who (like A. A. Milne's Piglet) Really Want to Know. They want to know whether Christian discipleship makes identifiable claims on this vast and complex area of experience; whether sexuality is an area where you need thought, judgment, and discrimination; and if it is, whether the gospel is of any use in forming your thought and discrimination. A lot of our culture has decided that it isn't of any use. And, indeed, a lot of our culture seems by no means convinced about the value of thought and discrimination in any case—not to mention those who have found the issue of their sexuality so complicated or hurtful, so humiliating or energy-draining, that their attitude to this aspect of their humanity has become cynical or contemptuous and, beneath the surface, profoundly frightened. In a way, these are the people I'm most worried about. But more of that in a minute.

The trouble is that Christians or would-be Christians in a culture like this are bound to feel a bit schizophrenic when confronted with what is normally understood to be "simple traditional biblical" (or, for that matter, "simple traditional Catholic") teaching. It is not clear to many whether limits and constraints such as you find in the tradition are a good idea anyway, when the environment is one that prizes independence and experiment. And it certainly isn't clear that, even if constraints and disciplines *are* acceptable, these are the right ones. So you have Christian moralists, like others, tentatively saying that the only real constraint is genuine love and care, or not hurting others, or some such idea.

The picture suggested is a bit like this: it won't do any longer to say that sexual activity (i.e., genital intercourse, because most people seem to think that sexual activity begins and ends there, and they don't allow for the fact that all sorts of aspects of how we relate to each other, as parents, children, lovers, friends, colleagues, is activity with a sexual dimension—but that's another story) belongs only in lifelong monogamous marriage and is sinful in any other context (such as homosexual relationships or premarital love). That's no longer good enough in most people's eyes: our circumstances, they'll say, are more varied than this allows for. We need the freedom to develop by trial and error, and above all we need space to express genuine feeling, whether or not such "expression" coincides with what others or the Bible or tradition or the Pope says are the rules. The kind of discrimination that matters here is the ability to ask yourself, "Is this relationship *serious?* And is it in any way hurtful or threatening to me, my partner, or anyone else, if we go ahead and incarnate it in the union of bodies?"

> To our bodies turne we then, that so
> > Weak men on love revealed may look;
> Love's mysteries in souls do grow,
> > But yet the body is his book.

That's what plenty of people, including Christians, act on and live by. It is the conventional wisdom of the right-thinking, liberal-minded person of today. Some, especially Christians, may still feel faintly awkward, even a little bit guilty, at disagreeing with the traditional teaching, perhaps even a bit sad that they do not seem able to take it seriously. But they do not and feel they cannot, and there it is.

But faced with the choice of crisp moral precision that seems to carry such limited conviction, and gentle vagueness about not hurting people that risks domesticating, even trivializing, the whole thing somewhat, I wonder what exactly is supposed to be *Christian* about either of them. The first speaks of sacrificing your own immediate gratification for the sake of discipline, purity, or obedience; and that certainly has some echoes of things we associate with Christian discipleship. The other shows a concern for honesty and care, for avoiding injury or tragedy, and for the liberty to take an adult responsibility for your choices; and all that too sounds fine from the point of view of Christian teaching. However, both seem to go a long way toward treating this area of our experience as one where a few bits of shrewd insight and rules of thumb will give you a way of managing, sorting out, its dangerous complexities. Both show a dim and uneasy awareness that sexuality is a place of powerful emotion that needs some sorts of convention to restrain its effects, but they also suggest that we could in theory get it more or less settled once we have the principles straight. And both treat it just a little as though the main thing were for *me* to get it right, to get it sorted out.

And the Christian gospel is very skeptical about *me* getting it right. It's skeptical, on the one hand, about the safety and usefulness of rules, and it's just as skeptical about sentimental self-deceptions in regard to my needs and feelings and intentions. Christian morality is always lurching between a touching faith in the power of rules to secure your place with God and a rather vacuous reliance on "inner" convictions and sincerity. But the gospel addresses itself to a level where neither strategy will do—the deepest strata of injuredness and self-dividedness. It says that the places of pain, powerlessness, injury to self and others, despair, and bewilderment are laid open to a God who does not condemn or desert, but who works tirelessly in the middle of our very betrayals and evasions to bring life. The gospel is faintly cynical about our motives for keeping rules (how nice to *know* we're all right), and it suggests as well that we're not up to much as judges of our own feelings and needs, our own seriousness or maturity, of the consequences for ourselves and each other of what we do. If this is right, then neither legalism nor good intentions will deliver a properly *Christian* ethic of sexuality.

What if we start from somewhere else? The gospel is about a man who made his entire life a sign that speaks of God and who left to his followers the promise that they too could *be* signs of God and *make* signs of God because of him. Even in this unpromising world, where we are so prone to deceive ourselves, things and persons can come to show God's meanings—to communicate the creative generosity and compassion that, we learn from revelation, is the most basic reality there is. In more theological language, Jesus is himself the first and greatest *sacrament,* and he creates the possibility of things and persons, acts and places, being in some way sacramental in the light of what he has done.

Now, if my life can communicate the "meanings" of God, this must mean that my sexuality too can be sacramental: it can speak of mercy, faithfulness, transfiguration, and hope. Whatever the temptation, we are not to give up on this aspect of ourselves, as if it couldn't speak of God. For all the danger and complexity, it isn't outside the sacramental potential given us in Christ. And it might be worth saying here that the celibate in the Christian church isn't giving up on sexuality, but exploring one particularly demanding way of making sense of it.

All right, but this is very abstract, isn't it? What are we supposed to *do* (and not do)? Well, the writer of the letter to the Ephesians tells us that married love is an image of the love between Christ and the church—a "mystery" in which we learn something of God's dealings with us in Jesus. And it is so, apparently, because Christ "gives himself up" for his people, becomes dispossessed for the sake of another's life—and this is supposed to be something that can be shown by the male partner in the marriage relationship, and is mirrored by the "surrender" of the female partner. The writer is struggling to hold together the insight of the gospel story with a set of more or less unquestioned assumptions about male power and female submission, but the logic of the image is of mutual "dispossession," rather than command and obedience. Nowhere is this more clearly set out than in the remarkable passage in the seventh chapter of 1 Corinthians where Paul speaks of mutual rights and mutual belonging: neither partner owns or governs his or her own body, but makes it over to the other—a very startling idea indeed in Paul's culture. So we can begin to see that, in this context at least, sexual love becomes sacramental when it involves a lasting (not just momentary) resignation of *control,* a yielding to the other, a putting your own body at the disposal of another for that other's life or joy. God's surrender to us in the weakness and nakedness of Christ, especially Christ crucified, is what generates in us the courage to put ourselves into God's hands. What God has done for our life and joy, we learn to do for God's joy, the joy there is in heaven over the return of the lost. A sexual relationship that lives from this gift and joy is properly "sacramental."

The New Testament texts referred to (and others too) assume, as has most of the Christian tradition, that this mutual surrender normally takes place in marriage. Why? At least partly it is because of the instinct that warns us about the destructive energy that is the shadow side of sexual passion. The borderline between control and surrender, possession and dispossession, is so obscure and elusive in our lives that "making myself over" to another is always risky. It may *not* be a movement of mutual gift, but an asymmetrical matter, giving myself over to someone's greed or egotism. In any long-term sexual relation, there will be acts and moments where the balance is different, and the considerations of power and belonging and vulnerability don't issue in a fruitful reciprocity. All our sexual acts are "haunted": when do we ever know what role we might be playing in someone else's imagery or fantasy?

This is where the Christian tradition has wanted to talk about *fidelity* as the thing that makes sexuality most fully meaningful in relation to God. Our own yielding to God would be terrifyingly uncertain if we did not take it for granted that God was "faithful"—bound to us by covenant, by solemn self-commitment, a covenant recalled and represented when we celebrate the eucharist and remember the way in which God returns Jesus to us even after our most dramatic betrayal of him. Promise does not take away pain. It may even intensify it in all sorts of ways, but it frees us to give ourselves. While we won't know what that might involve in every detail, we know we are not going to be abandoned, written off, if we make a wrong move. This is somewhere near the heart of what Christian sexual commitment is about.

God's faithfulness makes our risky faithfulness possible, and mutual commitment has the same freeing effect in our relationships. The grace that is to be discovered in nakedness, in yielding, is released to be itself when we give up the self-protecting strategies of non-commitment, experiment, and gratification, and decide instead for the danger of promising to be there for another without a saving clause that would license us to abandon the enterprise as soon as the other declines to be possessed unilaterally by us, as soon as the other's otherness gives us difficulty. In such a perspective, we have *time* for each other. A commitment without limits being set in advance says that we have (potentially) a lifetime to "create" each other together. By giving ourselves over to each other, we make something *of* each other. But without the former, the latter would be in danger of becoming a sort of Pygmalion enterprise, one manipulating another into what one wants.

You know the obvious problems in all this without my spelling them out. There are marriages that simply institutionalize this and other sorts of manipulation and oppression, marriages whose continuance simply *doesn't* reflect the grace of God. The creative liberty of the woman in marriage is something neither church nor society has come anywhere near catching up with. Some marriages are a means of mutual destruction, while there are relationships other than Christian heterosexual marriage that show far more of the grace of mutual dispossession and creation than many duly and religiously blessed unions seem to.

You might also say that such images and hopes are so strange in a culture like ours that few people learn anything about them except by making their own trials and mistakes, and they are unlikely to take anyone's word for all this. I don't disagree with this. But equally I don't believe we can have a Christian sexual ethic without repeating the challenge the New Testament's language carries: Can this area of our lives come to reflect and communicate what Christ's incarnation and cross tell us—that it is faithful gift and costly promise that set us free to return such a gift and such a promise with the fullness of which we are capable? If not, something of the richness of the image of God in us is not yet brought to life.

Our main question about how we lead our sexual lives should be neither "Am I keeping the rules?" nor "Am I being sincere and non-hurtful?" but "How much am I prepared for this to signify?" You could well say that we are slow in letting other areas of our lives come to express the generous fidelity of God, and that we don't discover all this in the void. True, but here are two thoughts on this. First, experimentation for its own sake in this area is an ambiguous business at best, given that other people's deepest vulnerabilities may be the raw material of experiment. And second, it simply makes *some* difference if, whatever our subjective struggles, whatever our uncertainties, our discoveries of what we can and cannot do, our self-deceptions and disappointments about what we thought was commitment, we are still able to look hopefully at our sexuality and remember that it *can* speak—more powerfully than practically any other aspect of our embodied lives—of the most fundamental things in the Christian vision of God. Our sexual lives are about making sense of the oddities and uncontrollabilities, tragedies and farces, of bodily existence; a Christian sexual ethic ought to be saying before all else that there is a distinctively Christian sense to be made, the sense God makes in the life, death, and resurrection of Jesus, where flesh itself carries the meaning of God's Word.

Callings

30

Vocation (1)

The trouble with the idea of vocation is that most of us, if we are honest, have a rather dramatic idea of it. I don't mean dramatic just in the sense of *self-dramatizing*, but dramatic in the simpler sense of *theatrical*—vocation as casting, you might say. God has a purpose for the world, a very long and very good play, even longer and better than Shaw's *Back to Methuselah,* with plenty of juicy parts in it. The nuisance is that he draws up the cast-list before doing any auditions. We find ourselves *called* to fulfill a definite role, but we haven't actually seen the script, and as time goes on we may suspect we would do better in another part. We think we could play Hamlet very effectively if only our talents weren't so successfully concealed by the fact that we have a two-minute appearance as Second Gravedigger. Or else we find the burden of learning all the lines for Claudius rather too much and think we would prefer an impressive walk-on part like Fortinbras. What I mean is that this not uncommon way of talking about vocation as God finding us a *part to play* is actually rather problematic: there will always be the suspicion that we're not really being used, stretched, and so on, and a flicker of resentment at being consigned to undue prominence or unjust obscurity. In short, we are uneasy about the hint of arbitrariness in all this.

And it is quite true that this kind of language has deep roots in our faith. There is Isaiah's call: the King says, "Whom shall I send?" and the prophet replies, "Send me." There is a task to be performed; it is offered, who may dare refuse? There are souls like Jeremiah and Paul, set apart from before birth for the work of God, writing and crying under the terrible, merciless pressure of their burden, unable to ignore their calling—"If I say, 'I will not mention him, or speak any more his name,' there is in my heart as it were a burning fire shut up in my bones, and I am weary with holding it in, and I cannot" (Jeremiah 20:9)—and yet tortured and almost destroyed by it. There are those who try to escape: Herbert's great poems of revolt ("I struck the board and cry'd, No more") or Hopkins's sonnets testify to the passion to get away from the unbearable pain of uselessness, loneliness, and frustration. Or think of the Curé d'Ars, trying again and again to run away to a monastery to get away from the relentless crowds of penitents, and always being prevented.

Vocation here is indeed a dreadful falling into the hands of the living God, being bound upon a wheel of fire. God has decided; I may struggle or revolt, but here is this clear will, to be done whatever the cost. All I'm asked for is compliance: in a real sense, I have no *rights* here. I obey, I bear the crucifying consequences, because I have, however dimly and weakly, chosen to love God and to do his will, chosen to see obedience as the one ultimately, unconditionally worthwhile thing a human being can do. It may seem arbitrary, but the clay doesn't argue with the potter. And behind it all is the unimaginable promise just glimpsed—"Me thought I heard one calling, child"; treasure in heaven; the hundredfold recompense of God's fatherly acceptance.

All of that is, I believe, quite genuinely central to the Christian doctrine of vocation, but there is a lot that it *doesn't* say. On this pattern, the will of God is seen as still being something very like the *preferences* of God: God would like so-and-so to be a priest or a nun or something, and that is what so-and-so must be. And, once again, if there is a complaint about arbitrariness, the answer is ready to hand that God's ways are not ours. "Why does X have to be a nun? What a marvelous wife and mother she would have made!" But God is inscrutable, and he has decreed frustration for X on one level, for the sake of greater fruitfulness on another. He chooses what he wills: there is no set of conditions for his grace. We are to rejoice in the fact that, weak and sinful and silly as we are, God has chosen us for the privilege of loving and serving him. Grace upon grace: how wonderful that God *is* arbitrary—at least for those of us who are chosen. There is a bit of a problem about the rest.

Grace upon grace, but what about nature? Does grace necessarily interrupt and overturn and deny and frustrate? Isn't it supposed to fulfill? Once put the question in terms like this, and the dimensions of the problem become clear and very alarming: grace and nature, creation and redemption, election and reproba-tion—inescapable and horribly complex matters. In the long run, we can't think usefully about vocation without some thinking about these wider things.

It's very important, for instance, to remember that in the Old Testament *calling* and *creating* are closely associated. Look at Isaiah 40:26—God creating the stars and calling them by name—and the echoes of that in the psalter. And think too of the image of God creating and recreating human beings by *naming* them. God, say the prophets and poets of Israel, has called you by name. As at first, when Jacob wrestled with the angel, God calls, consecrates to his service, by giving a name. And though there's nothing specific in the New Testament that says we should, we still reflect this sense by associating baptism, God's grace calling people into Christ, with the giving of a name. As the Greek fathers liked to say, God creates by uttering a multitude of *logoi*, designating words, names: creation springs into being in or-der to *answer* God's speech, God's call, so that his Word does not return to him empty (Isaiah 55:11). So in the most basic sense of all, God's call is the call to *be:* the *vocation* of creatures is to exist. And, second, the vocation of creatures is to exist *as themselves*, to be bearers of their names, answering to the Word that gives each its distinctive identity. The act of creation can be seen as quite simply this—the vocation of things to be themselves, distinctive, spare, and strange. God does not first create and then differenti-ate a great multitude of roles within creation: in one act he cre-ates a multiple, noisy, jostling, and diverse reality.

So with the human world; God does not create human ciphers, a pool of cheap labor to whom jobs can be assigned at will. Each human being called into existence by him exists as a distinct part of a great interlocking web of identities. Each is a unique point in this great net. To be *is* to be where you are, who you are, and what you are—a person with a certain genetic composition, a cer-tain social status, a certain set of capabilities. From the moment of birth (even from before that) onwards, you will be at each mo-ment that particular bundle of conditioning and possibilities. And to talk about God as your creator means to recognize at each moment that it is his desire for you to be, and to be the person you are. It means he is calling you by your name, at each and every moment, wanting you to be you.

And this may be the clue to the problems we have in thinking of vocation. It isn't that God looks down from heaven at a certain moment and just drops a vocation on you, as if he were utterly uninterested and uninvolved in what's actually there. If we take seriously the idea that God is faithful and doesn't change, we need to think of him speaking over and over again the *same* Word to us—our true name, our real identity—and making us be, over and over again, in that speech of his, in his Word. In other words, vocation doesn't happen, once and for all, at a fixed date. Paul himself, who seems to be the classic instance to the contrary, recognises this precisely in talking about being set apart *from his mother's womb*. It happens from birth to death, and what we usually call vocation is only a name for the moment of crisis within the unbroken process.

It is a moment of crisis, because answering the call to be oneself at any given moment is not at all easy. In spite of how it may sound, it isn't a bland acceptance of the status quo in your life, or a license to surrender to every possible impulse. God asks for his Word to be answered, he asks for response. To exist really is to exist as responding-to-God. Each of us is called to be a different kind of response to God, to mirror God in unique ways, to show God what he is like, so to speak, from innumerable new and different standpoints.

So one clue to our identity is this, the idea of *mirroring* God. We have to find what is our particular way of *playing back* to God his self-sharing, self-losing care and compassion, the love because of which he speaks and calls in the first place. Crises occur at those points where we see how unreality, our selfish, self-protecting illusions, our struggles for cheap security, block the way to our answering the call to be. To live like this, to nurture and develop this image of myself, may be safe, but it isn't true: insofar as it's unreal it's un-Godly. God cannot reach me if I'm not there.

The crisis comes when we put the question, "What am I denying, what am I refusing to see in myself? What am I trying to avoid?" This is where we have to begin really to attend to ourselves and to the world around, to find out what is true and what is false in us. It is not just introspection, because we don't merely live in private selves; we have to reckon with the needs and expectations of others, with the practical realities of life, society, family, and so on. And it is not just collusion with those needs, because we have our own secrets of memory, and temperament, and desire. We have to listen harder than ever—to each other and to our own hearts. And what emerges is perhaps that sense of near-inevitability, that obscurely authoritative impulse that crystallizes for some as "a vocation," the sense that being myself will demand of me a certain kind of commitment. The process can be rapid or slow, it can work at a conscious or a subconscious level with or without a single recognizable point of decision, but this is, I think, the basis of what goes on.

Those whose job it is to assess the reality or adequacy of vocations can really do no more than attempt to say, "Have you reckoned with *that* aspect of yourself, with *that* feature of your relationships? Is this actually *you* we've got here? Or is it another defense, another game?" That is one reason why it's so important to have some kind of shared life bound up with vocational training. None of us, I imagine, can discover the truth from the perspective of an isolated individual existence. Our hearts are infinitely cunning in self-deceit; we need others to let the cold light of accuracy shine on our evasions and posturing. All of us have to ask one another at times, "Tell me who you think I am," and all of us are obliged to answer that with as much candor—and as much charity—as we can. Someone's life depends on it.

It's all a way of restating the idea that vocation has to do with *saving your soul*—not by acquiring a secure position of holiness, but by learning to shed the unreality that simply suffocates the very life of the soul. It has to do with recognizing that my relation with God (and so with everybody) depends absolutely on making the decision to be what I am, to answer God's Word, and doing this without fuss and existentialist drama because what I am is already known and loved and accepted in God. As Karl Barth loved to say, "God has chosen us *all* in Christ: at the deepest level we are all called Jesus in the eyes of the Father" ("Methought I heard one calling, child"). Sometimes this will look and feel arbitrary. There will be few continuities, no readily graspable pattern in it all, the crisis will be severe and shattering. That is a measure not of God's whimsical and capricious despotism, but of how far I have really been from myself. (Augustine's *Confessions* has some wonderful things to say about this.)

And I may rage and cry at the frustrations of my calling and yet know beyond doubt—like Herbert, Hopkins, Jean Vianney, Jeremiah, and all the others—that while this may be dreadful, anything else would be worse—an invention, a game. Here at least, whatever the cost, I am *in the truth*. The nun may say (as I have heard nuns say), "I *know* I'd be a wonderful wife and mother. I know I have it in me to live that out successfully and happily because it fits my temperament. And knowing that doesn't make things easier. But I know too that, for me, that would be playing, messing around with a tame reality I could control, and reality is not like that." Vocation is, you could say, what's left when all the games have stopped. It's that elusive residue that we are here to discover, and to help one another discover.

Here is a little story to conclude. Rabbi Yehuda Loew ben Bezalel was the greatest rabbi of his age in Europe, the man who, in his house in Prague, created the Golem, the animated form of a man, to which he gave life by putting under its tongue a slip of paper bearing the unutterable name of God. One night, Rabbi Yehuda had a dream: he dreamed that he had died and was brought before the throne. And the angel who stands before the throne said to him, "Who are you?" "I am Rabbi Yehuda of Prague, the maker of the Golem," he replied. "Tell me, my lord, if my name is written in the book of the names of those who will have a share in the kingdom." "Wait here," said the angel. "I shall read the names of all those who have died today that are written in the book." And he read the names, thousands of them, strange names to the ears of Rabbi Yehuda; as the angel read, the rabbi saw the spirits of those whose names had been called fly into the glory that sat above the throne.

At last he finished reading, and Rabbi Yehuda's name had not been called, and he wept bitterly and cried out against the angel. The angel said, "I have called your name." Rabbi Yehuda said, "I did not hear it." And the angel said, "In the book are written the names of all men and women who have ever lived on the earth, for every soul is an inheritor of the kingdom. But many come here who have never heard their true names on the lips of man or angel. They have lived believing that they know their names; and so when they are called to their share in the kingdom, they do not hear their names as their own. They do not recognize that it is for them that the gates of the kingdom are opened. So they must wait here until they hear their names and know them. Perhaps in their lifetime one man or woman has once called them by their right name: here they shall stay until they have remembered. Perhaps no one has ever called them by their right name: here they shall stay till they are silent enough to hear the King of the Universe himself calling them."

At this, Rabbi Yehuda woke and, rising from his bed with tears, he covered his head and lay prostrate on the ground, and prayed, "Master of the Universe! Grant me once before I die to hear my own true name on the lips of my brothers."

31

Vocation (2)

Last time I talked about "vocation" as, in part, a discovery of some sort of truth about oneself, some level of honesty deeper than the one we usually operate on. I want now to delve a little further into some of the problems this raises. It could be said, "Recognizing a vocation may well be recognizing something deep and true in yourself now, but if it means committing yourself now to a fixed style of life, a determined role in church and society, isn't this a very negative thing, a pre-judging of the identity you may have in ten or twenty years' time?" In short, isn't thinking of *lifelong* vocation very hard to reconcile with some of our ideas about the unpredictability of God and the freedom he gives to men and women? This is me *now*—being ordained, or marrying, or taking a vow of poverty, or what have you, "but it doth not yet appear what we shall be." How can I speak for that? How can I answer for my future self?

I can't. There's no other answer possible. In abstract terms, I don't know; anything may happen. And I may indeed—because the world is a risky place—have become a different person in twenty years, and who knows what truth and honesty may then demand? And in a sense, at the same time, that doesn't matter a bit. To commit myself is not to make a prediction; it is not to lay down the kind of person I shall be. It is precisely because that is how some people see it that commitment is so frightening in the eyes of many. How can I be sure this is how I shall be? A bad question. How do I know I can be faithful to *this* picture of my-self? I don't. How can I pawn my freedom in this way? That's not what is being asked.

If that sounds as though vows and commitments are light and casual and dispensable things, that is not what it means. We need to look harder at this idea of freedom. In Zeffirelli's awful (if pretty) film about St. Francis—*Brother Sun, Sister Moon*—Francis is asked by the Pope to explain what his aims are, and he replies, "I want to be free, like the birds...." This is a travesty, not only of Francis, but of Christian freedom. It assumes that freedom means a kind of lack of definition, a lack of edge and shape. "Free like the birds," to go where I will and say what I will and be what I will: uncommittedness, not having to make choices, to say "yes" or "no." That is the root of the trouble: it is a view of freedom that goes backward rather than forward. Its ideal is the freedom to be unreflective, to follow your instincts, to be liberated from the intolerable burden of thinking about what you're doing. Its ideal is literally a childish one, at best. And in trying to free us from the pressures of judgment and reflection, it joins hands with its apparent opposite, totalitarian authority; it says, with Dostoyevsky's Grand Inquisitor, that humankind cannot bear very much responsibility. The fulfilled human being is the happy child.

Well, we are told to become as little children, but we are told no less forcefully to leave behind the *bondage* of childhood and take up our inheritance in the household of God. Why is childhood "bondage"? Why is that kind of freedom really unfreedom? For one thing, there is the problem of communication—one aspect of childhood, if we think about it, is the very important limitedness of what children can *say*. We learn, indeed, from the perception and unexpected and hilarious communication of children, but we learn because *we* are able to set it in the context of a wider language and experience. I'm not talking just about intelligence: there's surely a sense in which children don't yet *know* what they want to say, they're trying out roles and styles and languages. That's important, but—by definition—it isn't an end in itself.

Adult commitment seems to me to have a lot to do with learning what you want to say and being free to say it because you have found the language in which to say it—the particular "set" of life and intention or direction that gives the space, the peace, the structure, whatever we want to call it, in which I can be and make what I am to be and what I have to do. It is like Wordsworth's sonnet on writing sonnets: once you have the shape, you have a real freedom from distraction and woolliness and wondering what to do next. You can concentrate, yet not in a strained and effortful fashion. You have a "home" to work from. To refuse commitment or discipline or structure because you want to safeguard freedom and keep your options open is rather a misunderstanding of freedom. If you never learn a language well, you will be able to say nothing. That frustration is a kind of servitude—slavery to a tyrannical self that so fanatically protects its individuality that it never ventures outside the front door.

(All this happens at the collective level too, if I can digress for a moment. The struggle to preserve or revive national languages—Welsh, Hebrew, Basque—is not as comic or self-conscious as it may sometimes look. There is an important element of discovering what as a human *group* with a particular history you want to say. This also throws some light on our liturgical problems at the moment. We've lost a language which in its way was strong and flexible. We certainly haven't found a new one that is at all comparable, and so we don't know what we have to say in worship and retreat into inoffensive banality. Petitions about the Prayer Book seem really to be asking less for a particular book than for a language in which certain vital things can be said with confidence, honesty, and imagination. But that is another story.)

So, coming back to the heart, what does it mean to talk about the service of God being perfect freedom? It means that living with or in or from God provides the structure and shape that most frees us from distractedness and fragmentation of life and thought. As the Christian Platonists were always saying, this is a life in which we are "simplified"; the threads are drawn together, not in an intellectual synthesis of concepts, but in some kind of unity between heart and mind. We become sufficiently "at home" in ourselves-in-God to act and respond to others with clarity, without the bondage of our power-hungry, fantasy-ridden instincts clouding our vision. That is the kind of simplicity that can live with the terrible contradictions, the multiplicity and conflict, of Christian theology and Christian images, of the church itself and its relations with humanity at large. In the center of freedom is the language of compassion, prayer, self-offering, self-forgetting, crucifixion, and resurrection, the language whose "grammar" is the life and death of Jesus.

There is our paradigm of simple freedom: the service of God in a sense so intimate that we cannot see Jesus' identity apart from the reality of his Father. And this is the intimacy at the root of his boldness and sureness, his freedom—something the fourth gospel returns to over and over again. "My Father is working and I work. My Father speaks and I am what he speaks; he acts and I am what he does." I work, I speak and it is the Father's own free creative Word that is thus given to the world. That is the simplicity and freedom of Jesus, the only-begotten in the Father's bosom. *He* is the language we must learn to be free to speak and act as human beings, even though his "freedom" reaches its fullest point when he is nailed immobile on the cross. There he is most free because he is most truly the compassionate and loving Son of the Father.

That is the freedom we inherit in our baptism, the freedom that has to be actualized in the particular decisions we make. It has little to do with birds or babies; it is not rooted in a nostalgia for indeterminacy. It is creative because it engages with real limits and constraints, with discipline and attention. And so it can never be opposed to commitment, to the self-limiting decisions we make. None of us "just grows": we grow in certain ways and not others because we find a language and a style or structure. We choose to interpret and develop our shifting and fluid consciousness thus and not otherwise, in order to make something of it that is free from the private dialect of self and so is free to be given to others and to God.

So it is natural and intelligible to seek to realize this freedom in working out disciplines of life. The most fundamental discipline is discipleship itself, but beyond that come the specific forms of what we usually call "states of life." Ordination, like marriage or monasticism, is a "state," something still pretty general, still needing further precision: there is no *one* way of being a priest, any more than there is one way of being a monk or nun or wife or husband or father or mother. These are wide categories of interpreting and molding experience. I remember someone saying about a mutual friend, a priest, who had great musical gifts, "Perhaps he needs to discover his priesthood as a singer." An odd remark, you may think, but an important insight lies there.

Yet whatever further exactitude needs to be learned or devised, it is a serious task. If our friend were going to be a singer, he would be involved in a very demanding discipline. And for most priests these days—as for most religious and most married people—there is no agreed discipline to be learned. Once it was clear what shape the good priest's life should have (at least in some traditions: if you ever find a copy of that Anglo-Catholic classic, *The Priest's Book of Private Devotions,* you'll see what I mean). But it's not so clear now. I'm not advocating the adoption of old styles because they're clear, or anything like that: the contemporary priest (or religious or married person) who consciously adopts the style of another generation may well be suspected of taking a short cut—just as the flight to the 1662 Prayer Book is a short cut. No, just at the moment, for a wide variety of reasons, we have to work quite hard at finding a language, and we may find ourselves not particularly successful or consistent.

The point of what I've been saying is that it's never, for us, a choice between discipline and happy, regressive chaos, but a matter of finding the appropriate structure and discipline. There may be some fairly constant elements, but the rest needs thought and work, and sometimes help and exchange and discussion, even "direction." Once we have disentangled the ideas of discipline and legalism in our minds, all this may begin to become clearer. We should at least recognize that it makes sense to bring to our daily lives the same serious attentiveness we give to any demanding activity, so as to let the whole of our lives be free to communicate what we have to share.

How do I know such and such a commitment or discipline is right? People do, it seems, get it wrong: vows are broken, paths are changed. And what can we say about this except that it happens? Something perhaps has been suppressed or ignored, and then suddenly emerges. Or, in some strange and extreme cases, the very commitment itself seems to develop in a direction away from all its familiar forms, even outside conventionally recognizable varieties. In such conflicts and crises, there is nothing to be done except to see how truly and how much your discipline is *you,* how deep it has gone, whether your first decision was made in drastic and destructive ignorance of yourself or not. But all these things are by definition unpredictable. All we have to do now is decide what the next step is, which way to turn, and then act, trusting in God's faithfulness to us. "What is that to thee? Follow thou me."

Making choices means ruling things out as well. Part of the pain of it all is the sense that we might have been more fulfilled, more real, if we had or hadn't...something or other. A colleague pointed out a couple of weeks ago that the advantages of living in a nice, orderly, bright community are purchased at a high price. The advantages are real, and the losses are just as real. Judging whether the cost is worthwhile is no simple task. And so it is more widely: choices are made that rule out certain actions, even rule out certain people (marriage, after all, does just that). Part of choice and commitment is the death of some hopes and projects—a death to be accepted, because it is the death of that infantile aspiration to omnipotence that longs to live without boundaries, without human, finite identity. A death to be welcomed, yet recognized by us for what it is: a tragic thing (in the strictest sense) that can only feel—most of the time—like a diminution of our reality and of our freedom.

True and false freedom are all too easily mixed up, and the elusive and cunning ego clings very obstinately to an ersatz and ultimately crippling idea of freedom as uncommitment. Accepting what even the most ordinary choices of daily life teach us (I can't go to the movies tonight *and* finish a 10,000 word dissertation by 9 o'clock tomorrow morning) is hard. We have to trust that finally, through action and decision that is properly committed and properly detached, we shall find our freedom. Vocation may be to be *what* we are, but that doesn't leave us *where* we are. We shall need to work to find the structure and form of life that is most our own because it leaves us most alert, most responsive, most open to the never-failing grace of God. We have to find the meter for our poem, the key in which to sing our song to God, the cell where we can pray to him, the person in whom we can love him, so as to give "a local habitation and a name," face and flesh, to our own particular following of Christ.

32

True Deceivers

We are treated as impostors, and yet are true. (2 Corinthians 6:8)

Or, as the King James Version more sharply puts it, "as deceivers and yet true." That has not changed over the centuries. Do not let us delude ourselves by imagining comfortably that the gospel and "the world" are any less in opposition than they ever were. The world still reproaches and derides the preachers of the gospel—today more than ever—with this accusation. We are not merely harmless spinners of fantasy; we are *deceivers*, seducers, frauds, misleading men and women in the most significant and vulnerable areas of their lives.

Nothing is easier than to respond by preaching a gospel that cannot be disagreed with, that is not open to the charge of deceit because it affirms nothing. It does not lead us to "tumults, labors, watching, hunger," and it is content to accept the world's definition of the world. But whatever it may be, it is not Paul's gospel. In this great epistle—perhaps more than anywhere else—Paul insists with passion that the gospel he preaches is a gospel whose blind paradoxes will constantly leave the preacher exposed and helpless, unable to predict or control its workings, "in honor and dishonor, in ill repute and good repute." The Holy Ghost transforms us from glory to glory in hiddenness and humiliation: the apostolic credentials are sealed as the apostle is bundled over the wall in a laundry basket.

These are only the reflections of the vastly controversial assertion at the heart of everything: the assertion of *reconciliation*. God in Christ has reconciled the world to himself, and our ministry is the proclamation and the realization of this. It is controversial because this is a world in which reconciliation of any kind is liable to seem a fantasy. The reality of the world, we shall be told, is composed of self-interests and their conflict, of threat and defense. To preach that reconciliation has been achieved and can be experienced is to blind men and women to the fact that their condition is tragic, and so to prevent them from coming to terms with it. It is to deny them the possibility of the courage and honesty in the face of meaningless suffering that are the highest human dignities. The gospel degrades human beings, feeding them with sweets like children; it will not let them grow up.

That is one kind of attack. Another, expressed with special force and clarity in Dostoyevsky's parable of the Grand Inquisitor, is that the gospel deludes men and women with the hope of freedom. The truth is that freedom—free compassion, free forgiveness—is destructive. People need security and firm government; their manic greed must be controlled by force. They are trivial and selfish, but at least they can be made happy by wise and benevolent autocracy. The gospel destroys human beings, insisting that they grow up into a responsibility that will forever take away their happiness.

Those are two kinds of realism, two descriptions of the world, and the gospel is equally alien to both. To understand the intense seriousness of these objections should be the task of all Christian ministers, because if they do not realize fully how far the gospel does run against the world's judgment—even its most compassionate or reasonable judgment—then they will preach "cheap grace." They will fail to see what it means for the gospel to call men and women to the cross, to intensify their darkness before driving it away. "To be restored, our sickness must grow worse," as Eliot put it. Or, as Wesley wrote:

Deepen the wound thy hands have made
  In this weak, helpless soul,
Till mercy with its kindly aid,
  Descends to make me whole.

Maturity, says the gospel, is not a stoic confrontation with death. Happiness, says the gospel, is not a life without responsibility. Maturity is the vision of death as the last and greatest cleansing of the self by God, the final rooting-out of self-will and self-absorption. Happiness is the undertaking of the vulnerable and risky enterprise of loving acceptance, living by the hope and possibility of a reconciliation that will be our total fulfillment, and exposing ourselves to the great hurt of failure in our dealings with others and theirs with us.

We should never, never be blind to the enormity of these definitions, the enormity of what we, in the name of Christ, call people to. When we have seen the shipwreck that Christian belief and life can make in the lives of some—the pride, the guilt, the confusion, the self-hating—we can only preach in fear and trembling. Our questioners are right: we are *not* harmless. How do we ever have the right, the authority, to preach all this, to say, "Take the cross, repent, be baptized into the dereliction and death of our Lord"?

Let's go back to the Revised Standard Version: not only "deceivers" but "impostors." Here is our answer, such as it is. We have no right, no authority, but the authority of the Lord in whose name we speak. Our imposture is our daring to stand where Christ stands, and it is yet another invitation to the world to accuse us. You speak in the name of Christ's supposedly transforming power? Paul cried out to the Galatians, "Henceforth let no man trouble me, for I bear in my body the marks of the Lord Jesus," but it is a bold Christian indeed who can protest *that*. No, there is no good answer. The question will always drive us back in penitence to prayer and struggle. But we have no authoritative holiness of our own, we have no option but to admit the charge. We *are* impostors, traveling in borrowed clothes under an assumed name, the name of Jesus.

Why? Because we are baptized in that name and we stand before God with that name on our foreheads. He has lent us the name, lent us our baptismal garments, and told us to go and preach forgiveness of sins to all nations *in his name.* Of course, we may look ridiculous or pathetic in our borrowed finery, these ill-fitting trappings of a spiritual authority that belongs to Christ alone. But do it we must, out of obedience and love, out of that strange "constraint" Paul speaks of in the previous chapter of this epistle, the constraint of the love of Christ, ours for him and his for us.

> If I say, "I will not mention him, or speak any more in his name,"
> there is in my heart as it were a burning fire shut up in my bones,
> and I am weary with holding it in, and I cannot.

Absurd it may be, and it will make us look foolish. But that is the folly God wants in the ministers of his gospel, like the folly of his own love. It will risk sounding empty, a dangerous deceit; it will risk harm and failure, but if we must, we must. If we do not feel, however obscurely, this compulsion, this desire to break and share the bread we have received, the loving acceptance of God, *then* we are in danger. *Then* we can begin worrying about imposture.

Is this to make "good" preaching dependent on "good" feelings? God forbid. Surely what this teaches us is that the compulsion to preach the gospel takes no account of our inclination or lack of it. It is simply *there*, if we have once given our heart and will to God. "Woe is me if I preach not the gospel," with all the risk of silliness, insensitivity, and delusion. Yes, indeed, we are meant to do all we can to avoid bludgeoning stupidity and lack of understanding, and we need so much to see the world in its horror, which seems to mock what we say of love or forgiveness. But still, even in the greatest incomprehension or bitterness, we have to say the "nevertheless" that is the gospel of the cross. We are commanded to be impostors, to "dress up in Christ" (as one might render another phrase of Paul's). This is no new or exceptional thing for the preacher. What, after all, is the first and simplest of Christian prayers? "Our Father." In those words, we put on Christ, we act as children who share the family relationship of Jesus to God. The familiar introduction to the Lord's Prayer in the historic liturgies makes no bones about it: "As our Savior Christ hath commanded and taught us, we are *bold* to say...." *Audemus dicere*, we presume to say, we have the nerve to say, because our saying it is part of our loving obedience. Implausible as it is, we *are* reconciled to God; unlikely as it sounds, we *can* call him Father. It's simply a matter of believing the assurances of love—never easy, never tangible, but "constraining us" all the same.

Deceivers? Yes, at least potentially. Impostors? Yes, though under obedience. In either case, we rest nothing on our "private" truth and our "private" identity; we can look only to the truth incarnate, the truth in whom we are baptized and named, and in whom we find our true identity as God's children—"having nothing, and yet possessing everything." For Christ *has* brought us into reconciliation, into family fellowship with his Father; it is an inheritance we shall always be growing into and never wholly comprehend.

33

My Neighbor's Business

Peter seeing him saith to Jesus, "Lord, and what shall this man do?" Jesus saith unto him, "If I will that he tarry till I come, what is that to thee? Follow thou me." *(John 21:20-21)*

Although we are all egoists, very few of us are so utterly consistent that we are capable of doing without a supporting cast. A sense of the dramatic, after all, is not a purely individual matter; it demands not just that we be in the center of the stage, but that other people be excluded from it, standing around in suitably subordinate and decorative positions. "Behold, we were binding sheaves in the field, and, lo, my sheaf arose and also stood upright; and behold, your sheaves stood round about, and made obeisance to my sheaf." Thus young Joseph, surely one of the most obnoxious characters in holy writ. We are seldom content simply to know where we stand; we are eager to know where others stand in relation to us. We want to see the script and the stage directions to make sure we are not being—as they say—"masked," that we are still the focus of the dramatic action. Peter has been given his part, and it is a dramatic and essential one, that of the faithful shepherd following his master's example to the point of martyrdom. But the nagging suspicion remains: what if this is not quite as important as it looks? So, incidentally, and while we're on the subject, and purely as a matter of interest—what shall this man do?

Without the immediate presence of Jesus to pull us up short here, we have our own solution to the problem. We can, after all, rewrite the play ourselves. "What shall I *make* this man do? Who shall I make this man *be?*" If the definitions are not going to be provided for us, well, then they must be provided *by* us. We can without too much difficulty construct an eminently satisfying scenario for our world in which other people's roles are neatly and pleasingly determined by ours. We need not be so crude as the hero of one of Tony Hancock's brilliant little dramas, who is given the opportunity of writing one episode of the radio soap opera in which he regularly takes part and gleefully arranges for all the other characters to fall down a disused mineshaft. We are usually a bit more subtle than that. But the fact remains that we no less gleefully write ourselves into the center of the stage and insist that the reality of those around us depends upon our good pleasure, our offering of ourselves as a standard and a point of reference, a fixed point in the flux of other people's lives. The priest, the doctor, the teacher, even the artist, all those traditionally cast in explicitly dramatic and "pivotal" parts, will be hard put to it to avoid some such "creative revision" of their experience and their environment.

But sooner or later we are bound to come up against one very unpalatable fact: other people are unwilling to play the parts for which we have cast them—as unwilling as *we* are to let ourselves be defined by *them*. Even without a conscious clash of wills, even when someone else is simply unaware of our attempts to define or dominate, we shall meet resistance—the resistance of the sheer otherness of the other person. We shall find ourselves confronted by the utter unexpectedness, the unpredictability, of others. It is easy enough to write our script in the neat formula of a half-forgotten moralism or a half-digested psychologism that begins from the vast lumber-room of categorizations our religious and cultural heritage makes available to us. And when we have tied up the matter in this way, what is left? *Everything* is left: all the intractable, odd, baffling, resistant *singleness* of a person whom, with all our pigeonholing, we have not even begun to know. There will be moments, not only in our immediate loves and intimacies, but also in the classroom or the confessional, in our "public" lives, when suddenly and with dreadful clarity we shall see the infinite distance between self and other opening up and a great gulf fixed. We cannot pass over to the other; we cannot at any level enter their solitariness or submerge it in any tidy scheme, and it dawns on us that our minds and imaginations cannot, after all, dictate to reality, or even begin to comprehend it. An alien and absurd world mocks and threatens us.

One of the great paradoxes of being human is the fact that we discover solitude not just by going out into the desert but by living with others, living in community. No one would go to the desert if he or she had not first learned about solitude in the terrifying silences between people in society. This discovery of our solitariness, our distance from and strangeness to each other, is the beginning of human seriousness, the moment at which the infantile omnipotence of the self is checked and questioned and we begin to see ourselves in perspective. Now this sense of distance and strangeness is shocking and menacing at first, and for many it never ceases to be so. But that is not the whole story: the question is whether we are able to find liberation in our solitude, whether we are able to see the distance between us as a space in which to grow toward God, the space of our freedom. This means understanding that our solitariness is the measure of our *uniqueness*. Our singularity, our strangeness to each other, our resistance to categorization point to the fact that the life of each person is unrepeatable, radically distinct from all others; it cannot be mapped out and legislated in advance. And if God is in any sense at work in the lives of men and women, he must be seen as working in and through this uniqueness; in his unimaginable humility, he cooperates with the freedom of each one of us.

Vocation is not something that obliterates the self "in God," however much it may, at times, *feel* like a violence done to our nature. The Holy Ghost calls us to be more, not less, ourselves—teaching Peter to be more Peter, John to be more John—and leads us to explore our space of freedom. Exhilarating as this sounds, however, realism bids us remember the implications: there will be no safe predictions, no unambiguous models, no script for us to learn. Cooperation with God is a matter of constant recourse to his presence, so that he—like any loved one—may help us know ourselves. Our following of Christ demands, at the deepest level, a receptivity to the Spirit that is without images, ambitions, and preconceptions: a "night of faith" as St. John of the Cross has it. Only thus can we grow in and with his will, free from the wild imperialism of selfish imagination. And only thus can we avoid what so many writers have spoken of as the worst of betrayals—the judgment of others. "Such is the inexplicable variety of internal dispositions, that the same course and order in all things will scarce serve any two souls," writes Father Baker in *Holy Wisdom*. If this is so, it is foolish indeed to believe ourselves capable of writing another person's part and assessing that person's progress in learning it. "What is that to thee? Follow thou me." "I only tell you your own story," says C. S. Lewis's Aslan to the inquisitive child.

Is the work of God, then, restricted to this lonely and uncharted area—solitary flowers blooming in separate walled gardens? Surely not, for we are constantly being reminded that the Lord knits together his elect in one communion and fellowship, that his work is not to isolate but to unite us. The problem arises only because we still instinctively think of our uniqueness in terms of an exclusive, individual self-assertion. The hard lesson to learn is that of seeing ourselves as unique agents within a world whose patterns neither we nor any other human being can trace, cooperating not only with our Lord, but also with each other, learning our freedom with one another, without preconception and manipulation.

When, on very, very rare occasions, the veil is lifted and we seem to grasp some small part of an overall story, it can be distinctly surprising. When Joseph saw his dreams come true as his brothers prostrated themselves before him, he must have felt the enormous irony of the situation: his power and glory, the "Arabian Nights" splendor, all this is his *in order* that he may serve his once despised brothers. And he is able, in one of the most glorious passages of the Old Testament, to say to them, "Be not grieved, nor angry with yourselves, that ye sold me hither: for God did send me before you to preserve life... to preserve you a posterity in the earth, and to save your lives by a great deliverance" (Genesis 45:5,7). Here is a memorable paradigm of the freedom of God working slowly through and with the free interrelations of persons, though it is not so memorable as the greatest and harshest paradox of all, the great deliverance wrought by God in the crucifixion of Jesus by his brethren.

The model we need is not so much that of a classical drama with one figure at its heart, but that of voices in harmony, collaborating and interweaving in a single, dense, and subtle texture. More precisely perhaps, we might think of the old-fashioned partbooks, each singer being able to read his or her part only, so that the richness of the harmony will be new and astonishing to all. Even if we seem to spend far too long in uncertainty about the key, or waiting for the resolution of a cadence, there will, by the grace of God, be moments when, in spite of all, we have some inkling of a "direction" in what we are singing. Raymond Raynes used to say that "life is a love-song we sing to Jesus": a little sentimental, perhaps, but fundamentally true. Only it is not a solitary serenade, but a madrigal. Those of you who have sung madrigals know the importance of learning that there is a right and a wrong way of listening to the other voices, and that a dedicated and critical attention to what everyone *else* is singing is conspicuously unhelpful. You have a part to sing that no one else can supply: concentrate on that, in the light of Christ, and, for the rest, "What is that to thee? Follow thou me."

Celebrating People

34

St. Oswald of Worcester

For the celebration of his millenary

Every day in Lent each year, says his biographer, Oswald would wash the feet of twelve poor men, reciting as he did so the "Psalms of Ascent"—the fifteen psalms associated for so long in monastic spirituality with going up to the heavenly Jerusalem and with longing for the vision of God in his holy place. Well, yes, we may say: he would. Any medieval saint worth his salt washed the feet of the poor; it's a conventional gesture and a conventional motif in saints' lives, as much a part of the good medieval prelate's timetable as meetings of the diocesan board of finance are of the modern priest's. We wonder, in an abstracted sort of way, about the miracles of ecclesiastical progress and enlightenment across the centuries. But, before we pass on to the more interesting features of Oswald's life, bracketing clichés like this, we'd better pause for a moment. Is it a cliché? And, in any case, what exactly is being said to us by a detail like this?

Oswald performed this task on the last day of his life, on a cold February morning in 992; and, the biographer tells us, on this occasion "he began to wipe the feet of the poor, not only with the linen towel, but with his hair as well." It is a picture that is at once faintly grotesque and enormously moving, the tonsured skull rubbing against the knobbly ankles of some old Worcester pauper, moving because of its evocation of the sinful woman in Luke's gospel unplaiting her abundant tresses to dry the feet of Jesus as she anoints them with her ointment and tears. Oswald at the feet of the poor is not simply Jesus washing the feet of the disciples; he is the penitent before the judge, the penitent whose absolution is found only in the love and service of the injured. It is as if Oswald's awkward gesture acknowledges that, in the presence of the poor, the powerful—even the good and well-meaning among the powerful—stand under judgment. Sddenly the cliché is no longer so remote or boring, and it becomes uncomfortably modern. Christ asks of us not simply a Godlike benevolence toward the unfortunate, but a recognition of our involvement in the world that makes poverty and want. Our eyes are to be opened; our power is to be called to account. The wretched and needy become an authority before which we must bow, a place where we meet and are converted by the authority of Christ.

The story of that last February morning, a dying man making his peace with God by prostrating himself before the raw facts of need and hunger, puts flesh on an earlier remark in Oswald's biography. Conventionally again, we're told how the poorest of the poor loved him because of his generosity to their souls and bodies; he had fixed in his heart the text of Matthew 25:40, "Inasmuch as you have done it to the least of my brethren, you have done it to me." But, again, there is more: "while he obediently submitted to the authority of the earthly king, he took all the more care to bow down before the feet of the poor of Jesus Christ." Obedience, in other words, is very far from being a passive yielding to earthly force; it is interwoven with, and tested by, another sort of obedience—attentive response to need. The roots of "obedience" are found in the Latin word for "listening": obeying is having our ears open, in readiness to hear how the commands of God are uttered to us in the facts of suffering. It is not that God crisply passes on instructions, so that we know just what the right thing is to do: *how* we respond requires thought and care, patience and—sometimes—depressingly hard and compromising labor. Obedience begins in responding to a primary summons to *look* and *listen*, not to lie to ourselves about the kind of world this is.

To obey in this way will certainly entail for us a fair degree of skepticism about what other authorities may say, about all the ways in which we are encouraged *not* to see the concrete human cost of our decisions or our priorities. Do we ever think that watching the television news or reading the newspaper thoughtfully and receptively, resisting both media trivialization and our own longing not to know about unmanageable suffering and brutality, might be an exercise in *obedience,* in refusing to let the empty reassurances of the powerful distract us from the questions that pain and poverty set before us? We are enmeshed in patterns of political and economic authority that regularly tell us about the unavoidable price of national security, banking, stability, economic recovery, international order. The church may be, and usually is, helpless to come out with a detailed counter-analysis, but lest we "obey" these messages comfortably and uncritically, we must all the time direct ourselves back to two stubborn and unshiftable facts—what the price is in specific flesh and blood, and what our complicity is in our own flesh and blood. "While he obediently submitted...he took all the more care to bow down before the feet of the poor of Jesus Christ."

Obedience is a monastic virtue, and Oswald was a Benedictine, one of the most compellingly attractive in the great English Benedictine renaissance of his age. He learned his obedience in communities that did not understand obedience as passive submission to an authority answerable to no one. The Benedictine Rule requires the monk to see Christ not only in the abbot, but also in the guest at the door, above all the guest who has no worldly wealth to buy respect and comfort. It requires the abbot to learn how to meet the spiritual needs of each one in the community: that is, it requires the superior to model in the community a patient listening and attentiveness to the messy particularities of every person, and to avoid the tyranny and laziness of generalizations. And so too it requires of each one a reverence toward all others, a mutual reverence that was indeed called "obedience" by one of the greatest Benedictines of the Middle Ages, Bernard of Clairvaux.

Obedience as attention to *particular* human need, *this* flesh and blood, not law in general or even humanity in general, this is what lies behind the picture of the old man saying, "I was glad when they said unto me, Let us go into the house of the Lord," as he presses his thin white hair against a damp and dirty foot. It is what sustains his labor and vision and the life of his communities—here and at Westbury and Ramsey—through the decades of dynastic intrigue and murder (poor young Edward assassinated on the orders of his proverbially stupid brother) and the weary persistence of buying off and fighting off yet another Danish invasion (half off-stage in Oswald's life we can hear the Battle of Maldon and one of the great masterpieces of Anglo-Saxon lament). Oswald had learned an obedience that kept steady his gaze upon the hard realities of betrayal and carnage: a place to stand where it was not possible to lie about human violence, and where, in consequence, you have no choice but to bow down to the wretched as the prostitute bowed in tears at the feet of Christ—to bow down before the Somalian or the Bosnian, the abused child or the jobless parent, the refugee, the migrant....

And how is such repentant attention learned? In St. Benedict's rule, as in so many classics of the monastic life, two things go in step: reverence to each other and receptivity to God. If we learn to attend, to listen to God in liturgy, in silence, and in the prosaic tasks of life together, we learn to forget our own clamorous dramas, our own noisy efforts to impose on the world *our* story, *our* version of how it all is. Our eyes are cleared and our ears unblocked for attention to each other. Then, as we practice patience with each other, as we become used to the generosity of receiving, forgetting the urge to insist on our version, we come to God with a new openness and a new thirst, a new silence. What we're talking about, of course, is contemplation—so alarming a word at first, but inescapable if we want to think about Christian maturity. To grow up as a Christian is to learn the twofold silent openness to God and God's world that is the heart of Christ's own life as we see it in the gospel: obedience to the Father (so that the posturings of earthly monarchy, whether Herod Antipas or Ethelred the Unready, can be ignored, as they deserve to be) and obedience to the hunger or sickness of the person before you ("What do *you* want?", that often-repeated question from Jesus in the gospels). Without the first, our engagement with the world's needs will be clouded all along by our self-serving fantasies; without the second, we will be using obedience to God as a pretext for disobedience—inattention to God's creation, above all to those whom Jesus calls brothers and sisters.

The great Benedictine saints of Oswald's age, when so much of the renewing energy of the church came from monastic pastors and teachers, remind us forcefully of what the Christian community needs both for its prophetic task and for its pastoral calling. Obedience: the listening heart, the eyes unafraid to see, open at once to suffering, to sinfulness and to the faithful love of God; attention bred of silence. The old man on that cold morning, a few yards from here, a thousand years from here, believed that he saw God as he washed the feet of the poor in penitence, that *his* feet were standing in the gates of the heavenly Jerusalem. On that February day, those gates opened to receive him, as we pray they will for us, if we seek to stand where he stood.

35

John Wesley

And yet this is the mystery, I do not love God. I never did....Therefore I never believed in the Christian sense of the word. Therefore I am only an honest heathen,...and yet to be so employed of God! and so hedged in that I can neither get forward nor backward!...I am borne along, I know not how, that I can't stand still. I want all the world to come to—I know not what. Neither am I impelled to this by fear of any kind. I have no more fear than love.

So wrote John Wesley to his brother Charles in June 1766: bizarre words from a man so frequently charged with irresponsible emotionalism, with wallowing in subjective apprehensions of guilt and forgiveness, and stirring up unhealthy excitement in the susceptible hearts of the uneducated. (It was still possible in the late nineteenth century for an Anglican parish priest in Cornwall to attribute the prevalence of illegitimate births in his village to Methodist influence, because Methodists encouraged ignorant peasant girls to give way to their emotions.) But these are moving and sobering words, perhaps the most eloquent account in our language of justification by faith. In the same letter, he went on "O insist everywhere on *full* redemption receivable by *faith alone!* Consequently to be looked for *now.*" This is no summons to cheap emotionalism, but the plea to preach complete trust in God in the midst of coldness, unhappiness, confusion, boredom. Never mind that: you may still decide to put yourself in God's hands, to be employed for him or to be laid aside for him, as the wonderful prayer in the Methodist covenant service has it.

John Wesley had good reason to know this. His life is a record of what many—not only his politely contemptuous Anglican contemporaries—have seen as muddle and silliness, false starts, disastrous misjudgments, wrong turnings. The desperately scrupulous young don, growing his own hair lest a wig should be an extravagance, encouraging his intense and admiring coterie in prayer and good works; the aspiring missionary in Georgia, entangled in a humiliatingly awful love affair, utterly unable to disentangle pastoral responsibility and personal need, offending most of his flock, returning miserably to England; the new convert touched at last by the good news that God *gives* what we shall never earn, and then writing to a former guide and teacher letters of such censorious and pompous arrogance that he must have blushed for them all his life; the missionary again, compromising (they said) the dignity of his cloth by preaching in the early morning to laborers on their way to work, in the open streets and fields, earning mockery and physical assault; the aging and lonely pastor, contracting a disastrous marriage with a quite Hogarthian widow lady who bullied him and shouted at him and sneered at him and struck him before his friends; the harassed organizer, frustrated by the church at every turn, desperately deciding to ordain with his own hands a "bishop" to further the great work in America, and so ruining his last hopes of cooperation from the English hierarchy.

"And yet, to be so employed of God!" This neat, nervous little man, with his impulsive judgments, his endlessly betrayed reliance on his fellow men and women, his passionate and confused sexuality is, arguably, the greatest saint, the greatest witness to Jesus Christ, produced by the eighteenth-century Church of England—the last place you'd expect to find fools for Christ's sake. He has rightly been compared with the great monastic reformers, Bernard, Francis, Ignatius. And that, paradoxically, gives us a clue to him. It is possible to score an easy point by saying that, in a Catholic culture, John Wesley would have been a monk or friar or Jesuit, and so would have been spared his muddles and humiliations. His faulty judgment would have been submitted to a confessor, his chaotic enthusiasm channelled by obedience, his uncertainties about a call to the single life settled once for all by a vow. But how much less he would then speak to us!—to us, who (Catholic or Protestant) live in a context in which the traditional disciplines of piety are not readily accessible, where even the religious life, some say, is hard to live without a sense of self-consciousness or even inauthenticity. In another setting, Wesley would have known what to do, how to be good: his models would have been provided for him. As it was, he had no assurance from outside. Boldly (or foolishly) he digested what he knew of the tradition of spirituality and tried to rework it not only for himself but also for semi-literate weavers and miners of his own country and century. He knew he was a fool, that his life was a mess; he set that to one side, because the imperative was to preach what he could only have learned *in* his folly—that God is to be trusted. "The best of all is, God is with us," he said as he died. With that assurance, he could afford to experiment, to take risk after risk, to walk into disaster. "I want all the world to come to—I know not what."

Martin Luther, two centuries before, had grasped the great temptation at the heart of the observances of Catholic spiritual discipline—the illusion that we can by good observance create order in our souls, shape our identity. Wesley was less inclined than Luther simply to reject all these observances with repulsion, but what his witness says to us is that, once you have *seen* this temptation, there is no safe place. The order of the cloister, the well-drilled exercises of piety, these cannot now be undertaken without a certain ironic awareness of how they may be a means of evading grace. Wesley does not *expect* to be able to produce order in his soul, to make a coherent identity before God. His life, his identity is in God's hands, hid with Christ. What holds him together, from moment to moment, is only the trust that his "wholeness" is kept and formed by God. The errors, the humiliating mistakes, and wrong turnings are all there, woven by God into a work of grace, a sign in the world of his victorious mercy.

So he speaks; he is, unexpectedly, a very modern figure. We are tempted to nostalgia for a time when Christian (Catholic or Protestant) rules and practices made a clear map of the moral and spiritual life, because few of us experience it *now* with that sort of clarity. We—as individuals or a church—are nervous about the risk we run in experiment: new kinds of community or ministry, new kinds of engagement in our public life. We are understandably afraid of *losing* something—if we allow (for instance) the ordination of divorced men or women to the ministry, we fear we shall lose our grasp of God's will for the sanctity of faithful marriage. Yet we may well be privately confused, faced with the sister whose marriage has ended or the son who postpones marriage with his partner for fear of empty formalism. We should like the rules and the roles to be clearer, but they seem not to be. We are all post-Luther in that sense, anyway!

Wesley's gospel is that our *first* task is to trust God and not to invent ourselves as if we were to be clear-cut characters in a drama: our identity before God will come from God, insofar as we simply *go on* with him, patiently opening ourselves to his patience with us, and patiently staying with each other in our risky and muddled lives. This is not a Christianity without struggle, without discipline, and without judgment. It is hard to keep that openness, that habit of trust—we need disciplines for that, silent listening for God, standing before the Christ of the gospels, joining in the church's act of praise. We need to learn real repentance and honesty, to accept our mistakes as real and never to be so paralyzed by or ashamed of them that we are afraid of ourselves and our own perceptions and choices. "The best of all is, God is with us." Beyond this stumbling and confusion, the awkward innovations whose rightness or wrongness we simply don't know, the risky judgment based on fallible or lazy perception—beyond this, God still holds a future for us in his hands. Thank God for a saint who had to live his life so embarrassingly beyond the conventions that had marked out sanctity in Christendom! Thank God even for the eighteenth-century Church of England, so clueless about how to handle a man irresponsibly devoted to God that it forced him into wandering and exploration, folly and blundering, *and* unshakable witness to free and full grace.

Wesley's hectic life makes him look like a Martha in terms of this morning's New Testament reading (Luke 10:38–11:13). Mary, the silly, time-wasting sister, doing the unexpected (women did not sit and listen to rabbis in well-conducted households) is in fact more of a prototype: she wanted, not to impress or to do a good and conventional job, but to absorb the loving presence of Christ, to be with him who has chosen to be with us, to find an identity only in that presence, that love.

But there is another echo of Bethany in Wesley's story, a fitting anecdote to end with. Mary anointed Jesus "for his burial"—a story itself echoing the anointing of Jesus' head by the sinful woman of Luke 7. We read that once, when Wesley was preaching in some derelict corner of a city, a drunkard staggered toward him, intent on embarrassing and mocking him. He then broke down in tears, and began to stroke the old man's long white hair. "How soft it is," he stammered, "How soft it is!" Some perception of a complete vulnerability that we can only call Christlike had broken through God knows what wretchedness and self-loathing. That is what we praise God for today, as we remember Wesley and his brother: the vulnerability of the man whose life was so chaotic, who almost could say that he didn't know what it was to love God, "and yet to be so employed!...I can't stand still. I want all the world to come to—I know not what."

36

The Abbé Huvelin

A university sermon for All Saints' Day

High on the list of those who might rightly be said to deserve the name of "saint" must surely stand the Abbé Marie-Joseph Huvelin. For over twenty years, he served as curate in one of the great Parisian parishes and performed the ordinary duties of a vicar in the nineteenth century—catechism classes, sick visiting, and so forth. In addition, he bore the load of the spiritual direction of countless people, French and foreign, and included among his penitents both Baron von Hügel and Charles de Foucauld. Two drastically different spirits: the intense, affirmative, humanist intellectual, and the radical ascetic and solitary, moving inexorably toward his Jerusalem and his Calvary in the Sahara Desert. These two men met in Huvelin because there was enough of them in him for both to feel at home in him. That alone is indication enough of the man's stature.

Many will know von Hügel's famous description of Huvelin, prostrated with gout, migraine, God knows what besides, lying on a couch in a darkened room, receiving his flock for hour after hour and giving the same patience and attention to each. Huvelin ministered in circumstances of chronic and debilitating ill-health; and our admiration grows still more. Less well-known are the facts documented in the most recent French monograph on his life and work. It is not surprising to discover from his private letters and journals that he suffered acutely from depression. More disturbing is the knowledge that the thought of suicide was a recurrent obsession (the word is not too strong). Most startling of all is a section of one of his notebooks, eleven pages long; every page is covered with his signature, scribbled again and again, in various forms, interspersed with chilling little phrases.

"Il n'est": he does not exist. The conjugation of the imperfect tense, *"J'étais, tu étais, il était"*: I used to be....

Huvelin, in other words, was not what many would call a whole man. He was dramatically lacking, it seems, in proper self-love, that authentic self-valuing which, according to John Cassian, saves us from despair. Huvelin lived with a sense of his own worthlessness almost unrelieved by the hope and assurance he transmitted to so many others. Not a whole man; and so, we must conclude, in some sense a deeply injured and fearful man, psychologically scarred.

The question is this: can we, with our rhetoric about holiness and wholeness, begin to cope with the "sanctity" of a man whose mental and emotional balance was so limited? A man less than perfectly sane? Here, we have to deal not simply with the question of the *holy fool,* but with the question—harder for our day—of the holy neurotic. We often talk as though the creative love of God can work through us only if we remove the fear and self-hatred, the pathological guilt, that stifle the freedom of love: the more we advance in integration, the more we advance in sanctity, which is essentially health of mind and spirit.

Yet here we have a man whose love is very far from stifled, who, whatever his inner condition, actively transformed the lives of those who came into his presence. Is it then enough to see holiness as health, like those American liturgical revisers who would have liked to have rendered the ancient eucharistic invitation "Holy things for those who are holy" as "Healthy things for healthy people"? In such a context, of course, we are at once reminded that Christian holiness is a property belonging essentially to Christ and derivatively to his people—not simply an empirical quality of individuals. *"One* is holy, *one* is Lord, Jesus Christ."* But this is not the full answer. The holy "neurotic" challenges us further, challenges our conception of wholeness itself.

The truth is that, if each of us has a past that cannot be undone or unmade, our wholeness is also the acknowledgment of that whole past. And if the past is indeed a memory (however deeply buried) of traumatic injury, there is no way in which grace will relieve us of that truth. A man like Huvelin bears witness to the fact that our sense of self and our love of self is irrevocably molded by an experience that remains unaffected by any later confirmation or consolation. Basic directions are fixed, and to speak of "healing" is not necessarily to envisage the possibility of wiping out all such distressing and negative recollections. *Of course,* we struggle ourselves to create relationships and societies where traumatic injury is less likely; *of course* we cannot love what we see when we look at the obscure little coldnesses and cruelties that so diminish men and women. What we cannot deny or ignore is that this is a world of scarred and emotionally diseased people, full of corporate dread and self-hatred.

These are the realities of our world. The hurt and rejected will not cease to be people who *have been* hurt and rejected and who are incurably diminished by that experience. But the crucial issue is what is to be done with this experience, this memory. For many, the condition of being hurt and diminished, of having one's self-esteem blocked or removed, can be turned into a defense: I am a victim, therefore I am innocent. Guilt and sin lie around me, but my suffering isolates me and declares me righteous. The fact that I have suffered gives me privilege, power, moral initiative. I am not answerable for others or for what I do to others. All this is what we mean when we speak of the neurosis that is endlessly damaging of others, destructive of all who come within its range. This is a sickness that cannot be reconciled with holiness, that must indeed be dealt with before love can flow.

But this is not the only response possible. If I recognize my pain or my dread as the issue of injury, my eyes may be opened to see with compassion the sickness of spirit produced by half-forgotten hurts. Far from isolating me, my suffering creates an intense solidarity with the whole human world; I can recognize my condition as more than mine alone. I can become truly "catholic," responsive to the needs of all. My pain has given me a key to love. And what is more, that love can coexist even with the continuation of feelings of fear and self-doubt. There will be for many no resolution into painlessness, into a "health" in which scars and injuries will vanish. The wholeness of holiness is not that. In terms of emotional response, even in terms of superficial ease of communication with others, some will be incurably damaged and frustrated. But for such a sick person, holiness is not an empty or irrelevant ideal. There is another kind of wholeness—a wholeness of identification with the needs of the world, the self-generated and self-perpetuating tortures of the human race—a wholeness of compassion, a catholicity of sympathy, knowing one's own incompleteness in a way that reaches out to the incompleteness of others.

So with Huvelin, it seems. A sick and "diminished" person who could yet pour himself into the lives of others for their enrichment, in a wholeness of life and action and gift that somehow includes and makes sense of the deep unwholeness of his inner self: "poor, yet making many rich." Huvelin would not have articulated the roots of his compassion in just these terms of recognizing dread and misery as the issue of trauma, but he certainly recognized in his spiritual direction, the risk of employing suffering and the memory of pain as a weapon against others. His own recognition seems to be implicit in his statement that, "The more you suffer, the more you understand that souls are above all beings that suffer, and that they stand in need more of relief and consolation than of rebuke and correction." And so the apparently mutilating, "shrinking," suffering of inner doubt and emotional self-hatred may lead to enlargement—more of an enlargement (as he says) than we might want!

Many live now with this inner darkness, with the sense of worthlessness that cannot be emotionally resolved by any amount of acceptance of the theoretical proposition that we are supremely valued and given worth by God through his Son. In a world where the worth of human persons is constantly denied by economic and international policy, it is not surprising that our societies show signs not only of sickness but also of the deadly and irresponsible moral isolation of the injured and rejected. Can suffering turn to holiness for such damaged and frustrated persons? If there are to be saints in Britain—and in the whole world—today, if the feast of All Saints has a more than antiquarian interest, we are driven to ask these questions. And it is the injured and traumatized men and women of God who come closest to suggesting an answer for us, assuring us that there are those whose pain and rejection has made them a meeting place and a home for others.

But how? Granted that this is possible, *shown* to be possible, how is it realizable? What is it that makes a person whole in their compassion, their alertness? The Christian can only reply that it is Jesus: there are Christians simply because of an act of violence transformed into an unconditional gift. Because of his loss and dereliction, Jesus gives himself in complete poverty of spirit and abandonment to his Father, to be given to the whole creation.

"From his fullness we have all received." And this is learned not in words, not in theoretical assertion, but only in the truth that our poverty and frustration has been met and held and turned into compassionate understanding in a human association struggling to live by mutual gift. We believe not because our scars are magically wiped away, but because we see and feel love and enrichment poured into our emptiness from the acknowledged, manifest poverty of others. For all their fear, their twisted sense of self, their pathologies, they are open to us, and they give to us with authority and without self-consciousness. From Christ's dread and humiliation flows the grace that can work in our dread and humiliation. It does not demand from us passivity or resignation, but the acceptance that will turn us in a new enlightened understanding to the crooked heart of our neighbor; so that my memory of privation and hurt itself becomes part of what I can offer, in intelligent compassion, to the hurts of others. That is sanctity: the wholeness of giving the gift of *all* your self, while not waiting till that self is fine and moral and healthy and balanced enough to expose. And if there is healing or growth toward integration, perhaps it can only come in the giving.

If the "wretched of the earth" are to hear our gospel, perhaps they will only be able to hear it from those who are themselves victims, diminished people who have yet understood their poverty through the gifts they have themselves received in the compassionate company of Jesus' family and body, who have understood their poverty as one with the poverty of others, who do not come with possessions and ideas to distribute, but come to offer a fellowship of giving and receiving. They will be people who see the deprivation of others not as a sign of their subhuman and hopeless status, still less as a regrettable but inevitable result of "the way the world goes," but as something crying out for solidarity and understanding, for a word of hope that itself includes and shares the protest, the injury, the sense of incompleteness. The only preachers, the only lovers with anything to say will be the ones who can make the frustration of the despised their own because they have recognized—with tears, with irony, with anger perhaps, but also with acceptance—their poverty. They know that, whatever the outward securities (social, professional, religious), they too are mutilated. These are the preachers who can speak a gospel that is never a word of condescending encouragement from the possessors to the dispossessed, but the generation of a new community, the fellowship of poor men and women, at work to make each other rich, to make each other *human*.

That is the communion of saints on earth and beyond, nourishing one another because they are nourished by the poor Christ. They are holy with *his* holiness, with a sanctity and authority not found in some preconceived fantasy of healthy normality, but in the wholeness, the catholicity, of an endless network of gifts. Our conversion is, most simply, to open our hands to this gift, so that we may give it in turn, passed through the medium, clothed in the form, of our own poor and maimed selves. If we are tempted to be shocked by the oddity, the neurosis, or inner wretchedness of a great man of God, we should pause and begin to discover how we are made rich by that poverty, and how we may make of *our* poverty a gift to God's world in the fellowship of his Son Jesus.

37

Lazarus: In Memory
of T. S. Eliot

Would it have been worth while,
To have bitten off the matter with a smile,
To have squeezed the universe into a ball
To roll it toward some overwhelming question,
To say: "I am Lazarus, come from the dead,
Come back to tell you all, I shall tell you all"—
If one settling a pillow by her head,
    Should say: "That is not what I meant at all.
    That is not it, at all."

It is easy enough for the hostile critic to complain: Eliot is a Manichee, a despiser of the world and its joys, a death's head at the feast, passing "poetic death sentences on millions of ordinary lives," in Stephen Spender's words. Is he incapable of love? All those wretched clerks and secretaries, the amateur seducers and the amateur whores, the tired neurotic ladies in their endless afternoons, the old men in a dry month, Prufrock, Sweeney, Phlebas the Phoenician, all of them pictured in that unique mixture of scorn and pity—does Eliot never see a fuller world, a fuller life beyond this? Cannot he at least wish them joy? But no, he stands and looks at these figures with perfect clarity and total helplessness.

Well! and what if she should die some afternoon...?

Eliot does not, in these early poems, turn from the world; he anatomizes it, unveils the skull beneath the skin. Is humanity no more than apeneck Sweeney and the Thames-daughters, the exploiters and their victims? For a man with this vision to become a Christian must have seemed so bitterly appropriate to his restless and protesting friends, the activists—literary and political—who believed that if the human condition was painful, it must be changed, not alternately wept over and despised. Eliot's baptism, in those people's eyes, merely set the final seal on his devaluing of humanity: the pose of the helpless observer was now fixed for ever by the myths of sin and redemption. All that nature can do is sit and wait for grace.

"Ash-Wednesday" and the Ariel poems, Eliot's first Christian writings, must have confirmed this ten times over.

> Those who sit in the stye of contentment, meaning
> Death
> Those who suffer the ecstasy of the animals, meaning
> Death.
> and
> I should be glad of another death.

Lazarus had died, baptized into the death of Christ, and was yet condemned to go back to the world, a world unchanged from the one he had known before, pitiable and trivial, and now more alien than ever. It is not wholly surprising, then, that the first reactions should be these naked reductions, the longing for a return to the grave. And so the pilgrimage away from reality continues, reaching its climax in the abstruse mystical paradoxes of the *Four Quartets*—the final escape into a motionless eternity.

> To be conscious is not to be in time.

It is easy enough to say all this; and critics will continue saying it for a long time yet. It is less easy to enter into the sensibility of a man for whom the consciousness of being human was so constantly and nakedly the consciousness of pain and failure, loss of simplicity and single-heartedness:

> Where are the eagles and the trumpets?
> Buried beneath some snow-deep Alps.
> Over buttered scones and crumpets
> Weeping, weeping multitudes
> Droop in a hundred A.B.C.'s.

It is easy to complain of Eliot's negativity, or "pessimism," because most of us do not have the honesty to risk seeing the world in that way—the vision of a heart of darkness, of people devouring and being devoured, where we are all old, weighed down with terrible knowledge and guilt.

After such knowledge, what forgiveness?

The man who wrote these lines was a man who spent years living with the slow and irreversible mental breakdown of his wife. Who, in such a situation, would not be tormented with self-doubt and self-reproach, asking always, "Could I have made it otherwise? Have *I* done this?" It is hardly possible to estimate what it cost Eliot finally to separate from his wife in 1932. It is the experience of those years especially that we read in these appalling early poems, the geography of an emotional and spiritual desert that most of us are spared. What is the gospel and the church to such a man? Before all else it is, indeed, a *refuge*, "the Garden, Where all love ends": the place where God mercifully kills and dismembers, leaving the scattered bones "under a tree in the cool of the day with the blessing of sand, Forgetting themselves and each other." Lazarus is asleep; if he sleepeth, he shall do well.

Eliot was also a man who was exceptionally alive to the possibilities of illusion and self-deception in human lives. He had come to baptism seeking not only rest, but also truth. He was well aware that it is a terrible thing to fall into the hands of the living God. Christ the tiger: us he devours. "Teach us to care and not to care," he wrote, knowing that the detachment of the enlightened soul was, at most, half of the Christian life. God still calls to us *in* time, *in* the world, calls to "care," to the continuing pain of involvement, calls to a future.

> ...let me
> Resign my life for this life, my speech for that unspoken,
> The awakened, lips parted, the hope, the new ships.

No, Lazarus is to be allowed no luxury of rest, no easy and total rejection of the world, no "death sentences...on...ordinary lives." "Redeem the time": God's word has been spoken in and to the unclarities, trivialities, bestialities of the world of history; there, and nowhere else, is the poet to hear and proclaim it. "Would it have been worthwhile?" Who can say? But Lazarus is commanded out of the grave, "come back to tell you all," and that command, the command of the fleshly and worldly God who wept for the dead man he loved, cannot be refused by a man who knows he has risked exposure to a terrible and unanswerable truth.

It is the crucifying demand of this incarnate truth that Eliot set out to explore in what was consciously his last major poetic enterprise, the *Four Quartets*. This extraordinary sequence, constantly turning back upon itself, replying to itself, qualifying, correcting, has regularly been read as if it added nothing to Eliot's earlier poems, as if it simply repeated his weariness and longing for a reposeful death. In fact, these poems state, not always clearly, but always with both clarity and passion, the full implication of the struggle to "redeem the time." "Burnt Norton," not at first intended as the beginning of a sequence, explores the idea of the escape from time into the timeless within the momentary stillness of ecstasy. It concludes, however, in near despair. If the truth is only in the timeless moment, the flash of meaning, what of the "waste sad time / Stretching before and after"? It is not redeemed or transformed, only forgotten, and that is not enough because (as "East Coker" and "The Dry Salvages" make clear) it cannot cope with, cannot heal, the pain of mortality, the anguish and despair of human beings living in a senseless world that seems no more than a vortex of destruction.

Where, then, is healing? Here Eliot is at his most stark: there is no escape, except into fantasy. There is only a penetrating further into the blackness and destructiveness of the world. Face the truth; face the fact that the world is a world of meaninglessness, of destruction, violence, death, and loss, that no light of ecstasy can change this. Only when we stop projecting patterns on to the world can we live without illusion, and living without illusion is the first step to salvation. "Only through time time is conquered." And here the starkness gives way to gospel. If there is a God whose will is for the healing of men and women, he can heal only by acting in the worldliness of the world, in and through the vortex of loss and death. He must share the condition of our sickness, our damnation, so as to bring his life and his fullness into it.

> The wounded surgeon plies the steel
> That questions the distempered part;
> Beneath the bleeding hands we feel
> The sharp compassion of the healer's art
> Resolving the enigma of the fever chart.

This is the pivot of the *Quartets:* God has borne all that we bear and so has made the fabric of history his own garment. The world has no discernible meaning or pattern, but into it there has entered the compassion of God. Give up the futile struggle to dominate and organize the chaos of the world in systems and mythologies, and realize that the empty destitution of confronting darkness is the only way in which *love* can begin. Only if we are honest about the world can we see the choices that confront us. Either there is only destruction and death, or there is destruction and death that we take into ourselves to let it burn away our self-obsession and so make room for active love, compassion, mutual giving, life in communion. And the only sign of this possibility is the ambivalent memory of a dead and betrayed man.

> The dripping blood our *only* drink,
> The bloody flesh our *only* food.

We have to choose, but *these*, no other, nothing easier, are the choices. If *all* time is to be redeemed, it must be by giving up of self in all times and places, accepting the horror and the darkness, and not trying to evade them by fantasy or by philosophy. The way has been shown by the action of the world's Maker and Lord emptying himself and taking servant's form, putting aside his lordship to suffer our wounds, so that his compassion becomes the food by which we live.

If we can consent to this, to making out of chaos a network of compassion and of giving to others, then there is redemption and reconciliation in the world of history. Past and present alike may be folded into this; we shall be able to see ourselves as living from the love of previous generations, in communion with living and dead. We shall be able to give ourselves for the life of the living and the unborn. "Little Gidding" pictures unforgettably this fusion of death and life, the fire and the rose, the transformation of inevitable death by offering it for the world. The pain will not go away; the horror will remain. Yet it is shot through with the hope and the possibility of compassion and reconciliation, a simplicity "costing not less than everything."

Eliot was a great preacher of the gospel because he had the integrity not to close his eyes to any of the real horror of the world; preaching is cheap if it fails to meet human beings at their darkest points. The reconciliation he writes of is utterly costly, mortally hard: our sole nourishment in the task is the blood of God's costly love, the assurance that even death, loss, disorder are not stronger than the compassion of God. "Prayer, observance, discipline, thought and action," all our responses to God, are not just our efforts; they are *drawn* by love, made possible by love, fulfilled by love—our compassion created and sustained by God's.

> We only live, only suspire
> Consumed by either fire or fire.

No optimism, no activism will do that does not grow out of the vision of these two fires, the unbearable violence and the unbearable compassion. The Christian will be content with nothing else: Christians are baptized in the sign of the cross and celebrate in their eucharist the violent death of God until his coming again. For Christians, the fire of which Eliot writes is the fire of the Holy Ghost, by whom and in whom Lazarus—and all of us—shall live for evermore.

38

Michael Ramsey

I have not found your works perfect in the sight of my God.
(Revelation 3:2)

More recent translators have preferred to render the failure of the church at Sardis as "having brought nothing to completion." They have not finished their task, so their reputation is empty and they are in real spiritual peril. The church at Sardis is being exhorted to effort and action, lest its members meet Christ unprepared. The church at Philadelphia, on the other hand, is assured of what *God* has done and is encouraged not to effort, but to patience. Though many commentators have suggested that the "open door" before them is the opening of missionary opportunity, the use of this imagery elsewhere in Revelation has more to do with the plain vision of God's glory and his victory at the end of time. The Philadelphians have only to keep their eyes steadily fixed on the altar in heaven to which the way is opened; their victory, their conquest, is simply their faithfulness to that image of the open heaven, the doors flung wide on the Holy of Holies where atonement is made.

The letter to Sardis alone might imply that discipleship was a matter essentially of accomplishing, achieving—very odd, when we think of Luke's Jesus commanding us to say, "We are unprofitable servants" when we have finished our duties. But perhaps the letter to Philadelphia can fill out for us what it is to "finish" the work of faith. At Sardis, the words of the gospel are familiar, and the plan or project of the gospel is enthusiastically received, so enthusiastically that the church has a name for liveliness. But what if its failure is the failure to do what the Philadelphians have done—to allow the vision of the open heaven to dominate the whole of our mental horizon?

It is possible to "know all the words and sing all the notes and never quite learn the song," to quote from a rather beautiful pop song of the late 1960s; it is possible to sing robustly and joyfully and not know the song. There have been many different forms of confident and successful Christianity—the Catholicism of the late Middle Ages, the Protestantism of nineteenth-century England, the Fundamentalism of our modern age, and so on, even the beautiful and dignified tradition of liturgy and music of our cathedrals, though it does not speak as clearly as once it did of social stability and control. All have given the impression of vitality and durability; all have, in some measure, come to judgment, and their judgment has something to do with their inability to allow the gospel, God's open door, to form their whole understanding. All of them have been confident in dispensing the grace of God, structuring and channelling the dealings of God with persons.

For the fifteenth-century Catholic, this meant a technology of merit and reward. God had freely but finally covenanted to reward certain deeds, and there could therefore be the possibility of achieving a surplus, a transferable stock, of good standing in the eyes of God. As for nineteenth-century English Protestantism at its strongest and worst, look at George Eliot's chilling depictions of the "household gods" of Maggie Tulliver's family in *The Mill on the Floss,* or the clerical guardians of the workhouse in Dickens's *Oliver Twist.* For them, failure—moral or financial—is unforgivable and pity is a foreign language. For the fundamentalist, the will of God is clearly ascertainable for all situations, either through the plain words of scripture (as received in a particular but unacknowledged convention of reading) or with the aid of supernatural direct prompting. Christian revelation is there to offer clear and important information—how to be right.

In terms of numbers and influence, such styles of belief look impressive. But the paradox is that all are in a good position to claim achievement, to claim to have perfected their work, when, in fact, all have failed to bring faith to completion. By moralism, by the accumulation of pious duties or of clear ideas, they have sought in different ways to close the open door held by the living Christ. They have succumbed to that great longing to know who's in and who's out, who's all right and who's not, how we are all doing relative to one another, forgetful of Jesus' rebuke to Peter's curiosity, "What is that to thee? Follow thou me." And if we give way to this, we show our inability to believe in the God who shows himself in the gospel—the reckless sower, casting his seed everywhere; the undignified father rushing to meet the prodigal son; the one without dignity and without defense, who is seen in the face of Christ crucified. As Auden writes, in celebration of Bonhoeffer:

> Meanwhile a silence from the cross,
> As dead as we shall ever be,
> Speaks of some total gain or loss,
> And you and I are free.
>
> To guess from that insulted face
> Just what appearances he saves
> By suffering in a public place
> A death reserved for slaves.

We, however, run to defend God's dignity, to remonstrate with his senile carelessness, because *our* dignity is at stake. Like Maggie Tulliver's aunt and uncle, we cannot conceive of a God less self-protected than ourselves. I am good and goodness is a secure place to stand; God is (probably) even better and so even more sure of himself. Hence the awful language, beloved even of some of the finest theologians and preachers of an earlier age, about God's "offended holiness" that needs to be mollified.

St. Teresa was nearer the truth when she mercilessly derided Christians for their sense of dignity. She insisted that our only honor comes from God, and only when we know that with our whole being can we presume to be concerned for the honor of God as his loyal friends who share his reproach, not as his crusading defenders. That is why we might be *glad* to be told—as we are by some—that our church is demeaning its dignity through its uncertain and often confused forays into politics and sexuality. For if we held back from these undoubted risks for the sake of *dignity*, we should be strange disciples of the insulted and injured Lord of Calvary.

So the church at Sardis needs to wake up and *work:* not as it has imagined, by fulfilling a set of controllable requirements and fixing the terms on which it knows it can succeed, but by struggling to throw off the incubus of a pressure to *make* something of discipleship, struggling therefore to keep the vision of the open door alive. The open door is the door into the heavenly temple of the Apocalypse, the door into what is abidingly true beyond the world and its vicissitudes: there stands the slaughtered Lamb who embodies God's will to bear the entire cost of our healing, the healing of *all* people. Our primary task is to show that open door to the world, not to shut it and negotiate the terms on which we shall open it or disclose what lies behind it. The church at Sardis must work at the realization that, in God's eternity, all has been done that is to be done for our sake. To the Philadelphians it is said, "You have but little power": this loyalty to God's open door will look a good deal less impressive than a smooth program for religious achievement, whether medieval Catholic, nineteenth-century Protestant, twentieth-century fundamentalist or charismatic (or, for that matter, dogmatically rootless "liberal" as well). Sardis will only finish its works before God, when it has let go of the urge to stop short of God's own exposure, God's own vulnerable openness to all the creation. And only the lively vision of the *glory* of that eternal openness, the glory of God in the insulted face of Jesus, can release us from our eagerness to tidy up the work of God and protect his status and his dignity.

The Glory of God and the Transfiguration of Christ was the title of an early work by Michael Ramsey, who died on Friday and now walks by sight, not by faith. There and elsewhere, this greatest of our twentieth-century archbishops set forth for generation after generation of seekers after God the vision of God's glory in the face of Jesus in a theology that was both a theology of the cross and a theology of glory—the one, indeed, *because* of the other. It is no accident that he led the Church of England through the storms of the 1960s, learning from the radical challenges that constantly arose, not writing off any honest enquiry—not because he was a chaotically minded pluralist who cared nothing for the truth, but because he kept his eyes on the glory of God in the face of Jesus, knowing that all truth and beauty will at last be found at home there, that all the doubts and questions and anguish will be contained there. He gave to many—including your preacher—the sense that it was possible to be a *passionate* Anglican, to see Jacob's ladder even between Lambeth and Church House, to be no less committed to the riches and glory of God's dealings with us in Christ while bearing patiently with all those asking angrily how these connected with the secular confusions of our time. There would be no glib and point-scoring riposte, nor would there be a despairing abandonment to that anger and confusion, only a steady witness to the open door in heaven, shown in a life that spoke of open doors: the opening to ecumenism and the deep commitment to reconciliation with the Free Churches as well as the "historic" communions of eastern and western Europe; the opening to a share in painful theological debate in the aftermath of *Honest to God*, when Michael Ramsey so humbly acknowledged the inadequacy of his earliest response; the opening to the experience of the oppressed, especially in Africa, where his sharp denunciations of the tyrannies of white Rhodesia and white South Africa earned him the contempt and hostility of the unthinking Right.

Michael Ramsey was an archbishop for those who sought, however clumsily, to be Philadelphians, aware that what was intolerable in the church was to close the door God had opened. It can be said of him that he "finished" the work of the gospel committed to him, by his unremitting loyalty to the vision of heaven opened in the wounded side of Christ, and his willingness to let this pervade all his thinking and acting. He was able to be a catholic Christian radical at the heart of the establishment without ever giving grounds for accusations of compromise or lack of integrity. As we praise God for Michael Ramsey's life, we must also commit ourselves to his church, the church at Philadelphia loved by Jesus. The spirit of Sardis, the smooth short cut to a manageable, managing, successful, and intolerant Christianity, is amply in evidence in the Church of England at present. But God has given us, yet again, a sign that the sterile pseudo-perfection of Sardis will not triumph. He has given us the memory of "a pillar in the temple of my God," one on whom is written the name of God and God's dwelling place. Let light perpetual shine upon him.

Celebrating Occasions

39

Unveiled Faces

For the wedding of John and Alison Milbank

We all, with unveiled face, beholding the glory of the Lord,
are being changed into his likeness, from one degree of glory to
another. *(2 Corinthians 3:18)*

One of the great dramatic points in an old-fashioned wedding
was the moment when the bride removed her veil from her face,
and whatever the original symbolism of this, it is a remarkably
telling sign of what marriage involves. Unveiling, undeception—
clear and just vision. John and Alison are promising to *look* at
each other for the rest of their lives, and to *be looked at* by each
other, lovingly, faithfully, and, above all, truly and honestly. The
married man or woman has opened the doors to let another person in. "My beloved put his hand to the latch, and my heart was
thrilled within me. I arose to open to my beloved."

It would be silly to imagine that this meant, in the often-heard
phrase, that "married people should have no secrets from each
other," that husband and wife have no individual space of privacy
and solitude. That is a misunderstanding. But it does mean a
commitment to listen to each other's questions, to face the
other's search for your truth and theirs, and the (perhaps harder)
commitment to asking questions, searching out the other, not
letting them deceive themselves. Heavy privileges, heavy respon-
sibilities, bearable only because they are ways of building and
nurturing one another in love—each one helping to *create* the
other in his or her glorious singleness, uniqueness, and delighting
always in that.

Because there can *be* no love without truth. Without clear vision, love is a business of projection and fantasy. And there can

be no truth without love. Without trust and tenderness and courtesy, truth will vanish behind the walls of fear and pain. Marriage presents to us, more clearly than any other human relationship, the unity of truth and love, clarity and charity. That is one of the many reasons for the fact that it has been found so rich a metaphor to describe the relation of God and humanity. There can be no reconciliation between God and humanity until they see one another face to face. God and humanity must meet in truth, must be unveiled to each other. And so God unveils his face to us in Jesus—"the glory of God in the face of Jesus Christ," as St. Paul has it—and the light of his presence shows us the truth of ourselves, strips away our deceptions and illusions. There is risk and pain involved here: God shows his true face to us and risks rejection—the rejection of the cross—because we cannot stand the offer of unconditional love. There is pain here for God. There is pain for us in recognizing ourselves as loveless, afraid, divided and trapped; yet we are called to admit all this before God, to recognize ourselves as the light of Christ shows us to be. Painful as this is, it is bearable because that light is shown in the face of a perfect love, a perfect acceptance, a faithfulness that violence and death cannot destroy. Truth makes love possible; love makes truth bearable.

Dear John and Alison, that is what you have undertaken to show us. Your life together will be a sacrament of the unity of love and truth in committed faithfulness. What you will make of each other will be the image of that glory Paul found in the face of Christ, the glory of a love that can be utterly trusted, because it sees clearly and justly and without illusion, and it *still* remains. You are going to be a sacrament of this for us. But even more powerfully and richly, you are going to be a sacrament to each other of that astonishing, wonderful acceptance, compassion and involvement from which we all live, and without which we would all starve in the prison of guilt and doubt. You have found this love in the face of Christ, and now you turn to find it in each other and offer it to each other. This is your way of growth in the life of Christ's Holy Spirit; this is how you will become Christlike. Unveiling your faces, your bodies, your minds and your spirits to each other, in moments of strain and hollowness, in moments of delight and generosity—for richer, for poorer, "being changed into his likeness, from one degree of glory to another; for this comes from the Lord who is the Spirit."

40

Finding Wisdom

Commemoration of Founders and Benefactors,
Clare College, Cambridge

"Where shall wisdom be found?" One of the paradoxes of what is
called the Wisdom literature of the Old Testament is that it returns constantly to the idea of wisdom's *inaccessibility*. It can't be
bought; it can't be discovered lying around; it can't even be un-
earthed by effort and skill. The book of Job presents the most
ironic conclusion of all—the wisdom of God is seen only in the
full range of the world's variety, including its arbitrariness, its
senselessness. The wise Creator savagely boasts to Job of the
lack of moral order in things, when Job has demanded evidence
of justice. The very literature that celebrates the perception of
harmony in things ends up subverting its own language. The
more you train yourself to look for the order of things, the more
the arbitrariness of the world strikes painfully. When you have
been disciplined to look for order, the savagery of the world, the
empty pointlessness of phenomena, however regular and describ-
able, come into more merciless focus.

Is "wisdom" then precisely this double perception—not
merely the identifying of an order in things but the clear awareness of an absence, a question, an unsettlement about the moral
import of what we see? Perhaps the point of studying the world
to find its harmonies is to discover where harmony is an inappropriate and useless category, as if, when you set side by side the
structure of the DNA molecule and the death of a child from
famine, you will at least understand that *explanation* is not the
way to respond to the latter. When a death has been explained—by the analysis of the biology of starvation or disease,
by economics, by history—it remains, or should remain, unas-
similable, a bruise, a challenge. The more we see what is in-

volved in the *material* rationality of the world, the more we see it is that kind of rationality that is lacking in the moral world, the world where we ask about making sense of the fate of persons, subjects like ourselves.

The life of the intellect must sharpen, not deaden, our moral discomfort in the world. It is no accident that the modern formulation of the problem of evil developed in step with the Enlightenment's sense of the possibility of understanding and controlling the environment. It has become possible to see how far short the world is of moral order when we are—exhilaratingly—tracing more and more complex levels of physical order. Bluntly put, the training of the intellect should make us more vulnerable; moral disorder should hurt us more, not less. Wisdom is more than explanatory skill on the one hand and intuitive penetration on the other; wisdom is knowing the scope of tragedy.

The intellectual community, therefore, cannot be monochrome. It must be devoted to explanation, to the search for structure, rational skill, and control, *and* it must have the opportunity of reminding itself of what skill and structure throw into stark relief, the uncontrollable, proportionless world of human disorder. The intellectual community needs to give place to the imagination—one among many considerations that should make us resist contemporary pressure to reduce the university to a training school for specific and "productive" skills. What is not often enough realized is that it is the passionate and disinterested search for order that is the condition for a truthful vision of the moral world—and thus for effective moral activity. Without the questions of rationality and explanatory adequacy being raised, we should be too easily satisfied; not knowing the rigors of good explanation, we should give way to easy rationalizations of the moral world. If the post-Enlightenment intellect has been largely hostile to religion, it is because religious rhetoric has been seen as second-rate explanation, bypassing the discipline of scientific analysis and anesthetizing the pain of truthful moral perception, justifying the unjustifiable and intolerable.

Job tells us that the fear of the Lord is wisdom. Whatever else that means, it cannot be that the fear of the Lord provides better explanations or makes fuller sense of what is, like Job's suffering, morally outrageous or irrational. The "wisdom" to which the book of Job directs us veers away, as we have seen, from interpreting Job's suffering; at its end, Job is commended for refusing the rationalizations his friends offer him. His "answer," if it is that, lies in that haunting and troubling passage where he accepts that the sight of God is itself the resolution. Is this simply a passive acceptance of "mystery" (that great intellectual and moral alibi of the religious)? No, what Job has done is to look into the world and perceive a boundless resource of generative gift behind its chaos. The order of things that wisdom presses toward is not a static pattern that can be safely contemplated from a distance, but a continual bringing forth of life: it is not possible to look for explanation in the moral world, but it may be possible to hope for a future.

If, as we look at a morally disordered world, we ask not "What is its explanation? How do we make a pattern of this?" but "What is its future? What is to be made of this?", we begin to address a challenge to ourselves. Wisdom leads toward that question poised between the theoretical and the practical. "What may we hope for?" a question which inevitably turns into the question of how I as a person make contact with the generative resource, the grace of reality. It becomes a question about my own transformation—my conversion, if you will. "To depart from evil is understanding." Wisdom points me to my place as part of the independent pattern of the world, part of its flux, its chance, and its "necessity." It shows me how the perennial human struggle is to be more than this, and how this struggle for absolute distance and mastery cuts me off from the generative gratuity on which my existence rests. Wisdom can teach me to be a creature among creatures, neither passive nor dominating, finding my life in the life of a whole material order and in so doing knowing more fully the response that is appropriate to agony, meaninglessness, and disorder—the response of compassion or solidarity, of action in protest and in hope, instead of the search for consoling explanation or for the "final solution" that will rid the world of human disorder.

Wisdom is the celebration of order and the cry of protest at what is without order; it teaches us the pattern of creation and how to act and hope from within that pattern. Wisdom is not the opposite of passion or of imagination. For the Christian, the converting discovery of what we are and may be is bound to the memory of how, through the risk and agony of a human story, a creaturely story, the Creator brings to birth a new human community, freed from the constraints of race and status, enabling every human being to claim a common hope and a common liberty with all others; and it is because of this that the hanged criminal is called the power and the wisdom of God.

But faith obsessively slips back into explanation, which is why the religious use of the modern intellect is crucial for faith in showing what is and what isn't an explanation, in refusing the pseudo-explanations of optimistic piety. Whether we are Christians or not, though, the religious use of intellect demands our reflection; we are desperately in need of learning wisdom, wisdom as a fusion of analysis, contemplation, and passion, wisdom as the skill of being a creature. Our search for intellectual structure is humanly fruitful only if it brings that vulnerability to truth which is the wisdom of Job, and that awareness of our own capacity to find and act out the generative grace in our existence which opens us to compassion and engagement.

We are here in this building on this occasion because of a particular vision of the intellectual life, a conviction that wisdom is learned in a variegated community capable of being friends—learned, in other words, in a context where the proximity of other persons, in their untidy contingency and difference, is always around on the margins of intellectual enquiry. The benefactors we commemorate thought it worthwhile to foster the life of intellect by fostering the conversation, the relations, of moral persons, rather than simply endowing the pursuit of intellectual exploration on its own. Behind that lies ultimately that integral morality of wisdom to which Job points—both explanation and protest, both contemplation and hope. You may translate as you will "The fear of the Lord is wisdom"; but if we are tonight celebrating the memory of our benefactors we should also celebrate the fact that we still have some access to what those words mean. In a world increasingly characterized by the functionalizing of intellect and the trivializing and barbarizing of religious faith, this is no small thing to celebrate.

41

Remembering for the Future

Earlier this year a major conference was held in London and Oxford under the title "Remembering for the Future." It was a conference that attempted to confront the long-term legacy of the Holocaust, and it featured among its speakers the great Elie Wiesel, a writer who has seen his chief task as gathering and preserving the fragments of memory that hold for the world the reality of this century's chief outrage. Wiesel's novels turn, more than once, on the figure of a narrator crushed by memory to the extent that he wants only to remain silent; how, after all, do you find words for what eludes sense and order? Yet the narrator's silence risks becoming a collusion in the silence of a world happier to ignore what has been transacted; the dead must, after all, be named, or else the reality, the weight, of their living and their terrible dying is set aside for the sake of our illusory comfort.

The dead must be named, for two reasons at least. First of all, human beings in each generation need to know that the world they inhabit is a world shared with others they cannot fully know, and made by others. It is not a pristine place, a clean slate: what it is it has become, and that becoming constrains our freedom to do what we please with it (whether we recognize it or not). That is a fairly banal observation. But the second reason is harder to assimilate. Our world has been made what it is by many kinds of decision, including acts and policies of unimaginable violence and terror. Peter Levi in his haunting book *The Flutes of Autumn* remarks that there is hardly an inch of the English countryside without its heritage of bloodshed; no amount of nostalgia can quite bury that fact. No quantity of "heritage centers"—for which the past truly is a foreign country—can obscure the truth that history is a record of *cost*. The naming of the dead may say to us what the apostle says to his new converts: "you were bought at a price." Not just the "price" we enjoy celebrating—the generosity of benefactors, the self-sacrifice of heroes—but the fact that we are, willy-nilly, the heirs of a process of violence and pain, power built on the back of suffering.

The past is what we cannot change (what even God cannot change), but the memory of cost can be deployed in more than one way to change the present—hence, presumably, the phrase "Remembering for the *Future.*" The past can be a *vindication:* I identify with the past's victims and present the account to the world for payment; the present is in my debt, and so the past has become a tool for claiming power. The difficulty with this wholly intelligible and attractive strategy is that it seeks to give me, in the complex present, a position of supra-historical innocence: I need not ask about my decisions and motivations, because my moral position has been assured. Yet the power in the present to seize this position often means that I am the heir of the oppressor as well as the victim. Where I now am is determined by the history made by the oppressor, and though my identification with the victim may be real and liberating, it is not the whole truth. Used as a means of access to unassailable innocence, it becomes a destructive illusion. Because it is *right* that the Jewish people, women, blacks, and others should now be reclaiming their history, naming their dead, it is dangerous for anyone more manifestly identified with the history of the powerful to ask this question about the search for innocence; it can so readily conceal the desire that the history of the powerless should be forgotten. Yet it is necessary to ask it—if only in the knowledge, drawn from the history of the powerful themselves, that the claim to stable innocence, the claim to be a moral creditor, is one of the most resourceful tools of oppression.

Here is the second use of the past, then: not to search for vindication but for *understanding.* The world moves forward, it seems, by unregarded acts of violence; yet by bringing such acts into the focus of memory, we acknowledge the unspoken cost and become capable of asking in our present where the victims of today's "historical action" are to be found. Who is now paying the price? If we are able to name the dead, we shall become more free to name those now dying of powerlessness. Our naming of present victims is a chancy thing: many things conspire to keep us from the truth, above all our interest in maintaining the power we now have. But to know the past in its costliness is to know that the voice of the violent, the powerful, and the oppressive is not left eternally unchallenged.

The French anthropologist René Girard has observed that, while our history is still anything but free from violence, there is a shorter and shorter time span in which the oppressor's perspective prevails. The Greek or Roman slave-owner, the medieval anti-Semite, the Reformation witch-hunter had a long time to wait before their victims were named. At least in our century, so prodigal of victims, the gap has narrowed to decades or less (even Stalin's dead were morally exhumed within twenty years, though only now is their number slowly being reckoned by Stalin's heirs). The more we know that there is a limit to the triumph of the oppressor's perspective, the more we shall look with proper and apprehensive suspicion at our present system of power. And this knowledge may give some solidity to the notion that the historical human community might be able to be free of the compulsion to victimize, to build power on the back of exclusion and oppression. "History may be servitude, history may be freedom," wrote T. S. Eliot. History as the quest for vindication is servitude; history as the quest for understanding, for the imagination to find out the lost perspective of the victim, may be at least the beginning of freedom.

These are somber reflections for a celebratory occasion. But if our grateful recalling of a college's past is to be more than a piece of modestly re-routed self-congratulation, we need to know what is involved in confronting the past and why it is important—why we must all "remember for the future." We need to understand why those most concerned with naming the dead as a morally serious activity are those who know something of the victim's perspective.

And there is more. As a society, we currently have a strangely muddled view of the past. It is strange and picturesque (I've mentioned the blossoming "heritage" industry), and therefore static and without moral tension. It is a fertile source of pastiche, architectural and behavioral: to talk of restoring "Victorian values" is, of course, the moral equivalent of Stockbrokers' Tudor. It is also a source of disquieting administrative untidiness. Our political institutions (I include educational and religious institutions under this head) have developed in piecemeal response to specific needs. The institutions of social welfare in particular have a history that has something to do with imagining the perspective of the victim. At the moment we see on the one hand a passion for the centralizing of control in all these areas and the application of monumentally inappropriate economic criteria to their operation; and on the other an unintelligent and sentimental defense of our legacy.

If we are interested in defending the legacy of open education with serious provision for research, of health care for all, of the proper independence of localized and particular decision-making bodies (in industry or local government), we shall need a strong sense of the way in which the absence of such things can shore up the perspective of the powerful and create victims for history. We shall need to remember the stagnation and servility of an educational system largely restricted to the wealthy and uninterested in critical learning (the unreformed universities of 200 years ago); the human cost of health care dependent upon financial access alone; the tyrannies of industrial entrepreneurs in an unregulated environment; the struggles for a proper equipping of local authorities to meet local pressures in housing and sanitation.

To remember this is not to seek for innocence and moral safety, not to identify all present battles with past ones or to pretend that ritualized recollection solves present crises. It is simply to be able to learn from the past how easily the voice of the powerless, the *true* bearers of cost, is ignored, and accordingly to listen harder for that voice in the present. Any institution committed, like our college, to celebrating a heritage has the potential to be a critical and a creative voice in the present, if it knows what its memory is *for.*

Memory, said St. Augustine, is "spirit." Our spiritual life consists in the moral imagination, the capacity for compassion and penitence that a proper sense of the past can give. It is also, he claimed, what we must pass through in our search for God, for "we have not found this outside of the memory" (*Confessions,* Book X). God is found through the memory, in one sense, because memory makes us aware of how little of ourselves is at any one moment accessible to the light of consciousness: we see what we thought was our selfhood as a small point in an incalculable network of forces. That this incalculable network can yet sustain the reality of spiritual movement that issues, for Augustine, in the confession, the acknowledgement, of an everlasting love, holding together the fragmented, deceitful, and directionless self—this is how memory leads us Godward.

"Remembrance" is the central image in the central act of Christian worship—the naming of the dead Jesus as the lord and judge on whom all lines of history converge. In one of Charles Wesley's great hymns, the Holy Spirit is addressed as "Remembrancer Divine," the one who makes Jesus' past present to us now. Jesus, as victim of the powerful of his day, victim of political and religious systems of meaning, stands as the paradigmatic bearer of the cost of history, whose name is the name of all the lost and the voiceless. He is killed because he speaks of the unbearable hope for a humanity free from violence; because he speaks of and speaks for a purpose and a future for humanity beyond the goals of sectional and local interest; because he speaks of and for God.

We remember not simply this paradigmatic act of violence but the fact celebrated in the title-feast of our college. In the resurrection we learn that victims are not lost: God takes their side, their "perspective" becomes one with God's. In raising the reviled and executed Jesus, God pronounces that there *is* an end to the perspective of the oppressor, and that history can move beyond victimage and slaughter. There is a future, a voice for the voiceless. For the Christian, to remember Jesus is the heart of "remembering for the future"; the past of Jesus is what constructs the future of men and women, above all, the future of the powerless.

At Auschwitz, the words engraved on the monument are: "O earth, cover not their blood." The empty rhetoric of both Christians and humanists may be an attempt to cover this blood, to fill this appalling silence. But, while we cannot speak of explanation or meaning, both Jew and Christian are committed to a God who has made the crying-out of that blood from the earth his own. In that belief, it becomes possible to live with the real horror of the human past in truthfulness but without final despair. History does *not* ultimately lie in the hands of the slaughterer. The dead *can* be named; the past must be known. In that naming and knowing, God is to be met; and in God lies the possibility for us of a different world, a different apprehension of power, a voice for the dumb.

42

Administering Justice

For the Wales and Chester Judges' Circuit

The idea that justice means giving to all what is due them is a philosophical chestnut so ancient that it hardly seems worth examining. Yet is it, after all, so obvious or boring a thought? Think for a moment what it takes for granted: that it is a proper and vital part of human existence to *reflect back* to others the truth of what they are. This in turn suggests that we may not, as individuals, know that truth and need each other's reactions and perceptions to discover ourselves. Whatever the fashion in self-help books or glib devotional language, we don't "find our true selves" by individual will or introspections. When our vision of each other is truthful, not clogged by selfishness and laziness, we are all set free to see our own faces in each other's eyes, and to learn our real nature. "Doing justice" begins here, in our effort to respond to the *reality* of one another, not to the projections and fictions that suit us. We know that we shall not find our *own* reality unless we live in a world where this kind of costly and careful attention is the currency.

"Give God the things that are God's," says Jesus; and thus that greatest Christian theorist of justice, St. Augustine, could (in the light of that) speak of "doing justice" to God. Our task is truthfully to reflect back to God what God is, to mirror God's glory—not because God without us is ignorant, but because we have already begun to see what we are when we look toward God. The vision of God is the cornerstone of justice: when we know ourselves to be before God, we know ourselves to be the object of a costly and careful attention, searching out the whole of our truth, accepting it, and engaging with it. We experience the way that grace opens our eyes to what we would rather not face in ourselves, gently brings us back to confront our failures honestly, and gathers up what is fragmented and forgotten. In the light of that divine attention, we know what we must offer to each other and what we need from each other—truth sustained by grace.

Augustine believed that justice in society was unthinkable without "doing justice" to God, returning God's attentive, loving gaze in silence and in praise. A society that doesn't understand contemplation won't understand justice, because it will have forgotten how to look *selflessly* at what is other. It will take refuge in generalities, prejudices, self-serving clichés. We are shocked by the scandal of false or forced confession or manufactured police evidence because we sense the real world being devoured by the stereotypes and myths of the ignorant and violent. And thank God we *are* still shocked and not yet prisoners of cynicism. It means that we still know, somewhere in our hearts, that when we give up the struggle to show to someone else as fully and adequately as possible what their reality is, we become barbarous. That struggle can only keep going if we are confident that there is a depth and a reality to persons because they are the objects of an eternal attention that has no selfishness, fiction, or illusion.

It may seem a long way from the contemplative regard between God and the praying mind to—well, let's say Rumpole at the Uxbridge Magistrates' Court. But the practice of the law in a humane society, however dull and routine, goes on reminding us that human beings deserve the truth, deserve the attention of grace: that we cannot live humanly, in self-awareness, without truthful and grace-full relation with each other—without proper compassion, in fact, since that is what truthful and loving attention promises. There are societies, like South Africa five or ten or twenty years ago, that are held to humane values only by a thread, the thread represented by the possibility, never fully extinguished, that the courts will acknowledge the truth, even if only once in a while. And if today there is a widespread sense that this country's humane values suffered an appalling blow in the announcement of last week's pit closures, it is largely because of the often inarticulate conviction that the decisions have haste, carelessness, and disregard of individuals and communities written all over them. Once again, for many people, it was the courts that honored patience and truth, that honored the stubborn sense of what is *owed* to men and women, created in God's image.

The administration of justice—as this century frighteningly shows—becomes harder and harder the more we cease to take it for granted that God is to be honored. Ultimately, all that can be said by the Christian about justice rests on a doctrine of God, not simply as the God whose truthful love is directed toward us, but as the God whose very life is "justice," in the sense that Father, Son, and Holy Spirit reflect back to each other perfectly and fully the reality that each one is—"give glory" to each other. God's own life is one in which the truth of who the Father is becomes manifest as the Son responds totally to the Father's reality, and in which the life of the Son, perfectly reflecting the self-giving of the Father, is shown in the pouring out of the Spirit. Abstruse issues? Perhaps. But if we don't believe in a God whose life is in mutuality, the reciprocal reflection of a depth of life, it's harder to see why the image of God in us should require that showing to one another of the truth of who we are, so that we literally can't *be* truthful without the loving regard we offer each other. Of course, even beyond trinitarian Christianity, human law is grasped in other religious contexts as resting on the interconnection of patterns in the universe and in the mind of God. It is simply that the Christian vision sees that interconnection as itself resting in turn upon a movement and a relation that *is* God.

So the Uxbridge Magistrates' Court and its local equivalents point us toward the contemplation of the Holy Trinity, and that contemplation, with all it says about truth and reciprocity, grounds the vision of a just society for the Christian. Administering justice is a ministry of the truth of God's life to our imaginations, whether we know it or not, whether the administrator of justice knows it or not. And, whether recognized or not, the administering of justice paradoxically keeps alive the awareness of human distinctiveness and even irregularity, the anarchic diversity of God's images. Good judgment weaves together the drawing of connections and analogies with the recognition of obstinate particularity as it appears here and now. In this demanding art, good judgment gives to God, in its own way, what belongs to God, by giving God's images the attention they claim, some small reflection of the attention of God.

A final thought. Today the church commemorates St. Luke, who, according to scripture, was a physician and, according to tradition (unreliable and irresistible), was an artist. Perhaps, in the light of what has been said, the minister of the law might find an unexpected kinship with both doctor and artist. All are called to attention, immersion in particulars, and to uncovering for others a truth they could not know for themselves. And the lawyers may understand, perhaps, that "doing justice" can be a healing art, restoring bonds that have been broken, endeavoring to mend and maintain a *trust* that our greed and self-absorption repeatedly shatter, creating and recreating a picture of a truthful and gracefull humanity. This is why neither a purely retributive nor a purely individually rehabilitative view of punishment and sentencing will do: there is a therapy directed to a whole society in the practice of good law.

The law rests, in every sense, on honor—trust between persons as well as the active honoring of each other as persons who can be healed and illuminated by the art and medicine of truth. And, finally, the law rests on the honoring, worship, and praise of God the Holy Trinity. At a time of rampant dishonorableness—the slick, evasive marketing and massaging of the egos of the powerful that so threatens our public life and discourse, and that has its nemesis and negative image in a prurient, trivial, malicious culture in so much of our media—we ask a great deal of those who do justice. But that we ask it reveals us as beings who, in spite of all, remain obstinately hungry for the bread of truth, and that is a thought to nourish failing hope.

43

Keeping Time

For the Three Choirs Festival

Imagine, if you will, an advertisement for a new recording of the
St. Matthew Passion, or *The Magic Flute* or Shostakovich's Fourth
Symphony that ran something like this: "We all love the great
classics, but think how much of your busy life you can waste listening to *slow* recordings! At last, thanks to the latest technology,
we can offer you a recording that takes ten percent less time
than any other on the market, with no reduction in musical quality...." Would you rush out and buy it? There's something odd,
isn't there, in the suggestion that sheer brisk speed is a virtue in
itself where music is concerned, even with the most bouncy
original instrument versions of baroque works? While it may be
true that current technology *does* allow us to skip around from
one bit of a CD to another and to save time with a random selec-
tion program, we couldn't pretend that we'd heard a work in its
integrity by such a method. Still less could we imagine *performing*
a work "randomly." There is, you see, a bedrock fact about music:
it takes time, and it arrogantly imposes *its* time on us. It says,
"There are things you will learn only by passing through this
process, by being caught up in this series of relations and trans-
formations."

Take an elementary example. In the first Prelude of Bach's
Forty-Eight, the first and fourth bars are identical, yet the fourth
is wholly different, because time has passed. The resonances of
bars two and three surround what was once an innocent and simple phrase and give it darkness, density. The same would be true
of the return, at the very end of Mozart's *Requiem*, of the opening
themes of the fugue subject of the Kyrie. To hear the beginning
and the end alone and to say "They're just the same" would be

to misunderstand completely. Time has passed, and we cannot at the end hear what we first heard.

Why labor this point? Philosophers have so often been absorbed by the kinship of music and mathematics that they can forget the gulf between them. Mathematical relations are timeless, can be grasped visually on the page, work backward and forward; but music keeps and is kept by time, and requires my time—my flesh and blood, my life—for its performance and reception. Its "meaning," if we can speak in such terms, depends on its movement. Selected highlights tell us nothing. And if music is the most fundamentally contemplative of the arts, it is not because it takes us into the timeless but because it obliges us to rethink time: it is no longer time for action, achievement, dominion, and power, not even time for acquiring ideas (you could misinterpret attending to drama or poetry in these terms). It is simply time for feeding upon reality, quite precisely like that patient openness to God that is religious contemplation.

In an essay of 1989, Ursula le Guin, one of the most reflectively profound modern writers of fantasy, observed that the very act of telling a story tells us "that things change; that events have consequences; that choices are to be made; that the king does not live forever." The same is true of music, because all music is a kind of narrative. It does what it does by extending itself over a period, transforming positions and relations, indicating possibilities that may or may not be realized, then doing this rather than that, choosing, closing, but then setting up new possibilities of change. A Christian celebrates this gift, this art, because she or he believes that this is how we learn who we are, how we learn the wisdom of creatures.

Our wisdom is not God's; or rather it reflects God's in a wholly different mode. We can know and share in the joy and harmony that is God's eternally only as growing and changing souls, by being patient with uncertainty, the need to choose, and patient with the slow labor of change. When we forget this and make a bid for the timeless wisdom of God, we become desperately impatient with the work of choice, the cost of living in a world where things and persons resist our will. We turn to the nightmare mathematics that destroys the moral world—"Final Solutions," nuclear terror, ethnic cleansing—in our scramble for purity and safety. We have no time to waste in attention to those realities we don't choose and control.

A musical event is—whether we know it or not—a moral event, a recovery of the morality of time. We can, of course, ignore this, or even distort it into a soothing interruption of habitual evils. But it retains its unarguable claim: it takes time, it will not be rushed. And it is—whether we know it or not—a religious event. It tells us what we are and what we are not, creatures, not gods. We are creators only when we remember that we are not the Creator, and so we are able to manage the labor and attention and expectancy that belongs to art.

If the Christian feels a particularly powerful commitment to music, it is because Christian identity turns so much upon the encounter with God's reality in a narrative, a movement. Each year, the church renews its understanding of itself and its world in the process, the story, of the Christian year. Above all, in Holy Week and Easter, it takes us inexorably through a series of changing relations, shifting perspectives, that cannot be rushed: it leads us through the passion and resurrection of Jesus, which is the center and the wellspring of what we are. We can't do this with selected highlights, saving time; this is a contemplation, a feeding, that requires our flesh and blood, our patience, our passion. It requires that things are done to us, that we allow ourselves to be changed and enlarged.

To listen seriously to music and to perform it are among our most potent ways of learning what it is to live with and before God, learning a service that is perfect freedom. We choose to yield something of ourselves, a portion of our time, a period of our life; no one forces this, no one and nothing can compel our contemplation except the object in its own right. In this "obedience" of listening and following, we are stretched and deepened, physically challenged as performers, imaginatively challenged as listeners. The time we have renounced, given up, is given back to us as a time in which we have become more human, more real, even (or especially) when we can't say *what* we have learned, only that we have changed. To borrow that old musical anecdote, if we're asked after a performance, "What did that mean?", the only answer would be to perform it again—and even then, that would itself be a new and fuller meaning, not just a repetition.

The authority of music, what silences and holds us, is one of the fullest parables we have of the authority of God: not in commanding and imposing from outside, but in asking for our time, so that it can become a time of mending and building. In that double gift—time given away, time given back—we are taken more deeply into the wisdom of God and freed from the destructive illusion that we are supposed to be God. There is no wisdom for us if we cannot receive it as gift; because the beginning of wisdom is the knowledge that we must come to the reality around us and the reality that sustains us in expectancy with open hands, not with the lust for domination.

We open ourselves to the gift, yet it doesn't make us passive; it draws out our most strenuous energy. What we learn in music, as in the contemplative faith of which music is both a part and a symbol, is what it is to work with the grain of things, to work in the stream of God's wisdom. That is why contemplative faith makes us *more*, not less, human—human with the humanity of Jesus, in whom wisdom built a house in our midst; human in patience and expectant attentions, free to give because we have taken time to receive. Our busy ambition and our yearning for control are brought to judgment. The time we wanted to save for our obsessive busyness becomes the time in which grace brings us to maturity—toward the fullness of Christ's stature and the liberty of God's wisdom.

Mission and Spirituality

These addresses were first given at the Berkeley Divinity School at Yale University in 1991.

44

Doing the Works of God

Our tendency is to think of "mission" and "spirituality" as pointing in different directions—the communicating of faith and the cultivation of faith. Think about what they evoke. The first brings to mind special Sundays for collections, or perhaps weeks of revival; foreign settings and exotic heroisms; the embarrassment of crude doctrines of salvation. And the second? Prayer and books on prayer and spirituality; religious orders and retreats; perhaps the distinctive new genre of psychospiritual self-help books (personality types and prayer, or the profile of a spiritual leader or teacher). At best you might see the second as "servicing" the first, a kind of fuel for active communication. I don't think this dichotomy is particularly adequate or helpful, and one of the things I want to do in these addresses on mission and spirituality is to challenge it on the grounds of what I think is a fuller and better-anchored account of what the two words mean. In their most common usage, they are essentially modern terms, describing modern projects, but they need some reconnecting with their origins.

"Mission" is not a word found in the New Testament, nor is "spirituality." They may be none the worse for that, but it is illuminating at least to ask where we might want to "plot" them on the New Testament map. "Mission" does not occur, but there is a lot about "sending," and it is primarily God who does it in respect to Jesus, and Jesus in respect to us. Once, and very remarkably, in Hebrews 3:1, Jesus is called "the one who is sent," the *apostolos*, but on numerous occasions in all the gospels we find reference to Jesus speaking of being "sent"—into the world, to the lost sheep of the house of Israel, to do the Father's will. The sending of Jesus, into which Jesus' followers, also "apostles," are now drawn, is the act of God toward the people of God, calling them to a new level of unity over and above the common keeping of the law. It is the action of God toward the marginal and unrespectable in Israel: by trust in and fellowship with Jesus, they become Israelites as good as the legal experts, perhaps better. And in the aftermath of the paschal crisis, Jesus' rejection by the Jewish and Roman political systems together and his restoration and vindication by God, the community gathered around him increasingly interprets his "sending" as the action of God toward *all* who are outside the people of the law. His sending and the sending of the apostolic community coalesce in God's act of creating a new and universal people bound together by the divine promise and commitment, the new and everlasting covenant.

If we want to locate mission in the New Testament frame of reference, then, this is how we must do it: it is, before all else, God's authorizing or empowering agents of the divine purpose for the world, a purpose now made known as the formation of unrestricted community. Negatively, this means the destruction of barriers between hostile or indifferent groups of individuals, and the challenging of all ways in which human beings enshrine separation from each other and superiority to each other. Positively, it is the construction of communities in which diversity serves to nourish, not threaten, and in which behavior is tested above all by what it contributes to the common life—whose goal is to realize in everyone the love and boldness, the intimacy and authority that Jesus has in relation to the God he called *Abba*. Ethics is about forming this likeness of Christ in each other; it is neither simple law nor undifferentiated or utilitarian benevolence, but the shaping of a humanity that can show God's faithfulness and God's transfiguring compassion as Jesus did and does.

This is what is involved in being an apostolic church, a community sent by God through Jesus. But what this picture entails—and what we are not always alert to—is that mission is not first of all communicating information or persuading people to adopt your point of view. The mission of Jesus *is* his concrete reality: God's purpose is satisfied when the lost and the lawless come into a specific relationship with Jesus (accepting the possibility of fellowship with him, especially at table) and are thus brought into the people of God. There is no mission that is not this sort of involvement: this is what has led some to the very significant insight that, in Jesus, mission and *person* are identical.

Who Jesus concretely is is specified by the act of God sending him as the focus of a renewed Israel.

Hans Urs von Balthasar has developed this insight more fully than any other recent theologian. He has underlined the difference within the biblical narrative between the lives of the prophets and saints, in whom the divine calling is superimposed on an existing biography with which it is in some sort of tension, and the story of Jesus, in which the sheer presence and identity of Jesus at each moment communicates the divine purpose because it is the real and potential focus of the new relation that will constitute the new people of God. Thus Balthasar can write,

> The Father is the one who sends and who, in the act of sending, grounds the entire earthly existence of Jesus....Jesus' self-awareness thus coincides with his awareness of being sent.[1]

If we want to understand the "divinity" of Jesus in this perspective, we must see it in terms of a human identity shaped wholly by the divine purpose of reconciliation through communion.

Through this we are led to a further recognition. Divine action, action whose origin is not in the world, but in what sustains and makes sense of the world, is by definition free—the product of nothing but God. Following this through, we come to see that the act molding Jesus' identity is no "temporary" thing in the divine life but is rooted in what it is to be God. This movement into communion that is embodied in Jesus is the everlasting motion of divine life: a life that can never be abstracted from the will to give. All of which, of course, is essentially no more than a paraphrase of "begotten of the Father before all ages" in the creed. In Balthasar's terms once again, there is here an identity between being and becoming—what God always is (a life of gift and communion) and what is true of Jesus as a figure living in time, living toward a goal (the *making* of communion within the time of human history). The historical mission of Jesus is identical with the life of God as Word (self-impartation), yet identical in difference, since the latter does not depend on the former.

---

1 Hans Urs von Balthasar, *Theodramatik II: Die Personen des Spiels;* Teil 2: *Die Personen in Christus* (Einsiedeln, 1978), p. 140.

While a mission can only be fulfilled in the course of a particular period of time elapsing, and while in the mission of Jesus the greatest possible weight attaches to the idea of a key phase, a crucial "hour," in the consummation of this mission, there is also in this existence-as-mission a paradoxical identity between being (always there in advance) and becoming.[2]

This opening out of the mission of Jesus onto the horizon of God's life in turn makes sense of the shape and direction of that mission. If the divine act of living in communion is what sustains the identity of Jesus, then the goal of that historical identity, that toward which it moves, could not be other than unrestricted communion. A church, yes, but a church constantly chafing at its historical limits and failures, drawn toward the universality of communion it celebrates and proclaims in its eucharist. What the life of God constantly works against is the state of mutual isolation in which human beings habitually live: the human individual as such inherits a program of restriction. Not only in virtue of the restrictions of time and space, but also in virtue of the consciousness inherited from a history of division and mutual violence, we learn to be human in step with learning to be "here" over against "there." As René Girard has brilliantly spelled out, we become human as we imitate, do what we see being done, and in that very process come to see ourselves as competitors.[3]

The Christian belief is that Jesus' life is not determined by this inheritance. He proclaims and enacts an existence that is not undermined by the dread of otherness, the paralyzed hostility of rivalry. In his historical ministry, he offers a concrete parable of this, not restricting his companionship but forming communion with the morally and socially "excommunicate." To believe in his resurrection is to say that what that policy points to is now a literal reality in the world: he is risen and goes before us. There is no situation into which he cannot enter to create new relatedness. The believing community exists for this, even though the possibility of saving communion does not always depend literally on the presence and activity of the church.

---

2 Ibid., p. 144.
3 For example, in *Things Hidden Since the Foundation of the World* (London, 1987).

So the presence of Jesus is the presence of whatever under-mines the familiar reality of division, competition, fear of living in so restricted a space that we are bound to be struggling always for *Lebensraum.* It is, in the language of our traditional theology, the presence of the *trinitarian* life. If we want to speak ade-quately of mission, we have to speak of the trinity, of God's life as communion. To engage in mission is to be touched by the life of the trinity, to be engaged in what the wisdom of God pur-poses, the polyphony of diverse created voices, human and non-human, reflecting back to God his own generous outpouring. Thus, mission is also fundamentally a matter of *dispossession.* God's sending of Jesus, like the eternal coming-forth of the Word, is a giving-away, a holding nothing back: all the Father has is given to Jesus (John 16:10), all the divine authority is shared with Jesus (Matthew 28:18). That authority is shown in Jesus' complete "givenness" to the Father, his response to the gift by holding nothing back, being at the disposal of the divine will to communion, making his flesh and blood the concrete occasion for community to happen. To belong in the apostolic community is to be involved in a complex act of giving away: to be at the dis-posal of God's will, to give away the life we have, so that God's life can be given through us. The church receives the divine full-ness, yet the church can only exist in a kind of poverty.

This prompts us to look at some of the consequences of such a theology for the church now. One can talk abstractly about the church's wealth and poverty, about its involvement in the divine communion, and so on, but we need to reflect on what difference this may make to our apprehension of what we do, especially in the Decade of Evangelism. I want to look at three implications of the model I've sketched, implications that point in different ways toward the cognate issues of "spirituality" we must address.

First of all, everything I've so far said should make it plain that there is no gap between the gospel and life together. A proclama-tion of the gospel that does not call into judgment specific forms of hostility and exclusion is empty. This ought to be obvious enough, but, at a time when there is renewed enthusiasm for widening the gulf between the gospel and the political order, it is important that the social witness and protest of the church rest upon a firm theological foundation, not simply a fashionable hu-manitarianism. Nikolai Fyodorov in nineteenth-century Russia said that "the doctrine of the Trinity is our social program"; we could equally well say that the bare fact of the church is our social program. The divine life moves toward communion, and it rules and judges the entirety of our lives, soul and body. All that colludes with competitive hostility, wherever found, is challenged simply by the existence of a community whose sole rationale is the breaking down of partitions. The actual life of any given Christian community will be, no doubt, shot through with division and fear, yet whenever it reminds itself of what it is, in the celebration of word and sacrament, it makes a statement about its horizon. Whether we like it or not, it thus makes *each* of us a provocation, an irritant, to a divided society.

This doesn't mean that we are somehow committed to peace at all costs, to reconciliation rather than justice, or whatever. Sometimes "to be restored our sickness must grow worse." Being a witness for peace and for a corporate life in which we are responsible for each other's growing up into the freedom of Christ requires an exposure—in ourselves as in the world in general—of hidden deceit and destructiveness, and a critique of easy harmonies. Anyone who has ever had anything to do with racial issues will know something of the pain of persuading people that local friendliness isn't enough in a society of pervasive injustice and may even be corrupting. And during the international conflicts of the Gulf War, some of us found ourselves unhappily skeptical about the new enthusiasm on the part of western governments for a United Nations at last compliant with their goals. Our *images* of peace and reconciliation may need to be wounded quite deeply in this process.

The point remains, however: that there is a church at all speaks of something that relativizes the loyalties we take for granted. While the church itself is perennially conscripted into the service of division and corrupted by its own exclusiveness, thus revealing the difficulties of constructing a "perpetual peace," its distinctive words and acts still remind us of the Godlessness of our assumed hostilities. The hard thing is to be neither passive nor utopian, but truthful and persistent. Some words come to mind from Jean Bethke Elshtain's superb book on *Women and War:* We need, she says,

> a *way of being* in the world that promotes civic identity and connection, even—at times, especially—if the form it takes is to reject the politics of the day....I have in mind the complex

filiations of *private conscience* brought to bear on public and private lives and actions, offering tragic recognitions of necessary, even insoluble, conflicts, and, consequently, of limits to understanding and deed doing alike....At odds with the all-or-nothing pronouncements of utopians and apocalyptic prophets, the articulators of limits create space for meaningful action by persons in the situations in which they find themselves.[4]

The church can, in this sense, be an articulator of limits at the same time as being a relentless critic of the self-imposed and self-maintained limits of compassion or communion that keep us from each other. We should perhaps think back to Balthasar's words about how mission can be fulfilled only in time. Christ's time comes to a moment of crisis and convergence, the cross, where history ends and starts. There is fullness and definition in this life, yet what it nourishes and defines is a life (ours) that remains vulnerable to change and betrayal and is sustainable only because of trust in the divine commitment made clear in the Easter event. We are thus bound by the gospel to political witness, witness in the context of how human beings order their corporate lives, and bound equally to political repentance, to the breaking of images—sometimes even good images. Mission in this connection guarantees that the Christian will be an uncomfortable presence, but also a hopeful one. Nicholas Lash, at the end of his recent book, *Easter in Ordinary*, observes that the Christian task is to say and to show that human beings can "make a difference" to the world in the way in which they labor to sustain the gift given them of living in a community endowed with hope and truthfulness. This matters despite the fact that they cannot make *all* the difference.[5]

Second, the church, if it is to be apostolic, has a very specific responsibility to those disenfranchised from community. This has not only to do with the "option for the poor," fundamental as that is: it requires a particular kind of attention to those who are disenfranchised by whatever context they live in, and, even more demanding, an attention to those who will not ever, in fact, func-

---

4 Jean Berthke Elshtain, *Women and War* (New York, 1987), p. 248.

5 Nicholas Lash, *Easter in Ordinary: Reflections on Human Experience and the Knowledge of God* (London, 1988), pp. 280-285.

tion in our society as the kind of adult decision-makers we assume as normative. Let me try to spell this out.

The option for the poor rightly seeks to identify those with no power over the conditions of their lives and histories, and to be in solidarity with their struggle to find such power. That this is part of mission, a preaching of the gospel, should be beyond question. But once again, we shall need some theological content to this if the church's mission is to be more than a sounding-board for the assumptions of a liberal society. "Unrestricted communion" is not simply a synonym for more and better democracy. We are called to communion with the elderly, including the senile; with a dying child; with those children and adults in the so-called developing world, especially in Africa, for whom no amount of liberationist rhetoric is going to make any difference in the face of disease, famine, national debt, and the economic chaos that goes with them; with people with AIDS; with the disabled, including those we classify as mentally "subnormal" or "retarded." And so on.

In Jesus' day, the sick in mind and body were as a rule excluded from public participation in the rituals of the law because they were so often classified as pollutants—making a public sacrifice on recovery was not only an act of thanksgiving, but also a sign of reentry into the community. Jesus' healings involved touching the polluting outsiders to bring them into communion. We don't operate with categories of ritual pollution, but we might well ask whether we don't effectively work a very similar system in the kinds of cases I've mentioned. We certainly do not want such people intruding into our public and private frames of reference if we can avoid it.

This is why the reality of mission and the true social consequence of the gospel are identifiable in the children's hospice and the L'Arche community as much as in the more narrowly political witness. The politics of the kingdom involves those for whom not even the most liberal politics of the secular order could have room: those who simply don't have a "normal" human future to speak of. Though I am not convinced that opposition to abortion in all circumstances is the only possible Christian option, I want at least to raise the question here of what "communion" we have with the unborn, as material individuals equipped for relation. I don't know what we should say, but I cannot leave this out of account. And in case it should be assumed that this is a problem pertinent only to abortion, the issue also arises with a pregnancy that miscarries. The Christian is, I think, bound to say that her or his identity in the communion of the new humanity is bound up with these lives too.

Whatever we do say here—even if it is only an admission of inarticulacy—we must not lose sight of how relation to those *terminally* disenfranchised in all the ways I've mentioned, and more, is an inescapable dimension of Christian and apostolic identity. Beyond the usual definition of the political is the *polis* of Christ's body, where we look to nourish and be nourished by any and every creature ("Preach the gospel to *every creature*"). In this city, dignity is given not simply by an acknowledgment of rights but by giving others the freedom to give others the possibility of growth into Christ, freedom that is at the same time part of *their* growth into Christ.

Third, I've made much of the fact that the communion of Christians is a flawed and often profoundly unimpressive historical reality. Discovering the gospel, and thus the church's mission, involves us in repentance. The first image to be shattered is that of the "successful" church: as we recognize in ourselves the impulse that belongs to God—the yearning of Christ's spirit in us, if you like—we recognize the barriers we have not yet crossed. To see lives left systematically untouched by the general policy of the church is certainly to be brought to penitence. One of the deepest paradoxes of Christian faith is that our continuity with the Christian past lies not in repeating what earlier generations said, but in bringing ourselves before the same point of judgment and asking, with them, for conversion—which may mean that we do and say things they did not.

The church before and after its general change of heart on slavery is not two different churches. The post-emancipation church had received from the pre-emancipation church a faith that had enough depth and resource to put its own history in question because it had received the knowledge of a God faithful, merciful, and inexorably demanding truthfulness. We could do worse, surely, than apply this to some of our present areas of hurt and anxiety: women's ordination, for example, and the pressure to rethink our attitudes on homosexuality. Change is only betrayal if we forget that the center of tradition, the heart of what we hand on as saving faith, is the possibility of new beginnings and the truth that our errors of interpretation are not the last word in a community which exists because of a belief in the indestructibility of God's commitment. Perhaps this is where the particular gift of Reformed Christianity to the church in general is most significant: believing in the church catholic must mean believing in the church penitent.

This suggests some thoughts about dispossession again. We are inclined to try to communicate the gospel with full "instructions for use"—a set of approved ways of responding. Yet this really makes sense only if the gospel is information before it is communion. Jesus' activity gives the reality of a new "way of being in the world." It *effects* the restoring of community (the cleansed leper's offering, the hospitality of Zacchaeus); it does not of itself prescribe immediately a whole range of conclusions and attitudes. The New Testament makes it abundantly clear that the implications—theological and ethical—took time to clarify, and the history of the church confirms the trial-and-error element in this over all the centuries of Christian existence.

If this is true, mission does indeed involve a particular sort of dispossession. We are authorized to transmit or embody God's longing for life in communion here as a reflection of the perfect mutuality of the divine life in eternity ("Thy kingdom come on earth as it is in heaven"). We can offer a share in this life but we cannot *control* the response to this offer. It may be rejected, violently or apathetically, ignored completely, or received in unpredictable ways. It is rather sobering to look at the church's history and see how often the message has been—in effect—"You can't really have received the gospel because you're not doing what we're doing." ("Master, we saw a man casting out demons in your name, but he was not one of us, so we forbade him.") We might ask how *their* way of receiving the gospel enlarges what we can see and know of the gospel, but we don't, as a rule.

It is rare to come across a missionary or theologian like Vincent Donovan, whose entire theology of mission rests on a conviction of the integrity and power of God's gift as a real *gift*,[6] offered without controls so that we can have the freedom to watch ex-

---

6 Vincent Donovan, *Christianity Rediscovered: An Epistle from the Masai* (New York & London, 1982); *The Church in the Midst of Creation* (New York, 1989 and London, 1991).

pectantly, not anxiously, to see what shapes and structures of communion emerge. Of course it *is* possible, and sometimes essential, to ask whether what purports to be a response to the gospel is authentic: as we've seen, the history of the church makes plain that the gospel can be misappropriated. What justifies such a judgment are surely idioms and practices that undermine the rationale of communion itself, whether at the level of theory (denials of the truly relational nature of God, restrictions on the scope of Christ's saving work) or at the level of practice (racist and xenophobic distortions of Christianity, such as the "German Christians" of the 1930s, or the old NGK in South Africa). Heresy is possible, but before we throw the word around, we need to remember that orthodoxy is common life before it is common doctrine.

The attempt to join in God's work, forming the communion of the kingdom, hovers between celebratory confidence and painful iconoclasm. If confidence predominates, mission becomes a kind of corporate egotism, the effort to bring the world under the dominion of a system administered by an institution possessed of exclusive rights. If iconoclasm becomes an end in itself, we have no impulse or rationale for the hope that sustains the effort to move toward communion and no shape for the humanity we want to see formed in this communion. Properly understood, our language about trinity and incarnation is one that refuses to become a system for our intellectual or institutional possession: it is only plausible or authoritative, only makes sense, within the practice of dispossession, an authentically self-forgetting practice that allows and nourishes the otherness of others.

I have argued elsewhere that Augustine's great work on the Trinity does *not* in fact propose that the image of the Trinity is to be found in the bare self-awareness and self-love of an individual mind. The image is in the mind solely of the saint—those who, in knowing and loving themselves, know and love God in the same act because they know their dependence on God's gift. And, in knowing themselves in this light, they know and love themselves as participating in that generosity and thus as radically oriented toward and involved in the life of others. It is a formulation that brings us very close to Balthasar's idea that Jesus' self-awareness is the awareness of mission: the Augustinian saint is precisely the person growing into this condition.

Since mission is not intelligible apart from some grasp of what holiness is—the radically other-directed life of God lived in finite and vulnerable subjects—we do indeed have to reflect on "spirituality" in our theologizing about mission. More specifically, the language I have used about dispossession and the breaking of images belongs traditionally with spirituality, and I want to concentrate quite closely on this. Once again, I hope to question some conventional dichotomies, especially that between an apophatically-oriented contemplation, the profoundly critical and negative orientation of a Dionysius or a John of the Cross, and a spirituality of action or engagement or positive valuation of the created order. If God's action is single and coherent, there must be a coherence to the shape of Christian holiness, a coherence we can look for in the pattern of Christ's action and passion. If mission can't be understood apart from holiness, the search for holiness and the disciplines of the spirit can themselves only make sense in the context of mission—God's mission, God's sharing of the communion that is the divine life.

Mission—to sum up—is not the work of persuasion, of getting someone to adopt your views or join your group. It is only persuasion in the sense that an extended hand, a smile, an opening door, a greeting, could be called persuasion. All of these are acts that at least potentially change where we stand in relation to each other. Christian faith believes that the entire event of Jesus' life, death and resurrection is such an act, God's act, and that our identity "in Christ" is likewise the process of being taken into or activated by God's act. (This is what we mean by talking about the life of God's Spirit, which is the Spirit of Jesus in us.) Our mission must, like Christ's, ultimately be the "who" that we are, action and gift, for the sake of a new humanity; and for this we need courage both to act and to repent. Learning this is our sanctification.

45

Against Anxiety,
Beyond Triumphalism

"Spirituality" is a much harder word to locate on the New Testament map than "mission," but if we ask about the resonance of the word "spirit," we may get somewhere. The word oscillates between divine and human reference, yet there is no suggestion that the two referents simply coincide. In Romans 8, Paul can say that "the Spirit bears witness along with our spirit" to the fact that we stand where Jesus Christ stands: as if our spirit were whatever in us apprehends the truth of the new world brought about by Jesus. This is echoed in Paul's frequent antithesis of flesh and spirit, where life "in the flesh" and "works of the flesh" almost invariably designate the state of self-protective mutual hostility, the culture of achievement and possession, the definition of each other's identities in terms of their place in such a culture (knowing someone "according to the flesh," as in 2 Corinthians 5:16, which follows the injunction not to "live for ourselves"). In Galatians 5:13, using freedom for the sake of "the flesh" is opposed to the mutual service of life in the spirit. The desire of the spirit is at odds with the desire of the flesh (5:17), because while the flesh wants rivalry and rapacity (financial, sexual, magical, material), the spirit wants *communion* (5:19-23).

This, then, may be the best definition of "spirit"—that which is oriented to the new humanity, to the unrestricted communion that is the divine life communicated to mortal bodies. (Does the reference in 2 Corinthians 4:10-11 not just to flesh but to "mortal" flesh suggest that bodily life aware of its own frailty or finitude is a proper vehicle of spirit, whereas "flesh" as an absolute term means finite life *forgetful* of its vulnerability?) We could take this a stage further and say that spirit is what is oriented to the humanity defined by Jesus. As such, it is clear enough that "spirit" doesn't designate some part of an organism, which is why arguments about whether Paul was thinking of a twofold or threefold human constitution are so frustratingly inconclusive: spirit is the life of the organism lived in Christ. Thus to grow in the life of the spirit is the process of having Christ formed in us (Galatians 4:19). And if "spirituality" designates growing in the life of the spirit, it must be first and foremost about this process; it must be an *education in the new humanity*. As such, it has to do with the whole range of our human experience, our art and our politics, our sexuality and our economics, and the prayerful looking to God that must pervade them all; it is not a subdivision of our humanity (or our theology), any more than "spirit" is an item in the list of things that make up a human being. Relating to what was said in the first address, we could say that spiritual formation was the business of making our lives, our identities, mean what Christ's life means: the presence of gift, promise, commitment, new relation. A spirituality uninterested in this would indeed be divorced from mission—and thus divorced from God.

We have already seen how we Christians are capable of turning our mission (God's mission) into a travesty by behaving as if we were the proprietors of a system that we alone were licensed to manage or administer. We constantly try to use the action of God for the sake of the manageable plans and ideologies of an unregenerate humanity, to make it serve some kind of exclusive interest, national or sectional, liberal or conservative, or whatever. We become *anxious* about the gospel entrusted to us, about how easily it might be corrupted by error or fashion, and so we corrupt it by trying to put up fences around it. Confidence triumphs over iconoclasm, though it is a confidence paradoxically rooted in anxiety, confidence in our capacity to overcome the threat of insecurity. At such a moment, what we must rediscover is the discipline of silence—not an absolute, unbroken inarticulacy, but the discipline of letting go our own easy chattering about the gospel so that our words may come again with a new and different depth or force from something beyond our fantasies.

This is what Bonhoeffer talks about in his prison letters, above all in that luminous text written for his godson's baptism in May 1944. We have used our religious words as if we had no idea what they meant, used them in a project of self-protection, as if they didn't judge us or alarm us; and now we must let go, prepare for the silence of "prayer and righteous action among [human beings]," hoping that words will again be given us that might change the world.[1] But it is not, of course, primarily a twentieth-century perception we are talking about. The idiom is of our own day, but the recognition of the possible corruptions of talk about God is common to the Jewish refusal to pronounce or even write the sacred name, to the theology of the Cappadocians and Dionysius, to the contemplative discipline of John of the Cross and the poetic theory of George Herbert, and so on. In what follows, I want to look briefly at two very different writers within the catholic spiritual tradition to see how their profound unease with "easy" words about God can relate to the issues we have been discussing so far.

I turn first to one of the more difficult and teasing writers in the tradition, the fourteenth-century German, Meister Eckhart.[2] Eckhart's Latin writings ascribe to God the simultaneous descriptions *esse innominabile* and *esse omninominabile*, being-without-name and being-named-by-every-name. Nothing tells us what God is, yet everything speaks to us of God, and the specific thisness and thatness of all things can be traced to the fecund life of the one source that—in another well-known image—"boils over" into the manifold life of this world. These two perceptions are not, however, simply given side by side: the latter would not make sense if we didn't understand the former. Nothing tells us what God is: well then, think nothing and you will think God! Ridiculous, a play on words, a dangerous nihilism perhaps, but what exactly does Eckhart do with this?

First of all, we get rid of all that we assume gives us a purchase on God: pious actions and words, church and sacraments, Jesus, the Trinity. This is where hasty readers of Eckhart assume—whether with shock or delight—that he can't really be a *Christian* at all. But the point is simply one about the way we see our words and actions: fluency and familiarity with the "busi-

---

1 Dietrich Bonhoeffer, *Letters and Papers from Prison: The Enlarged Edition* (London, 1971), pp. 294-300.

2 Among recent books, Oliver Davies' *Meister Eckhart: Mystical Theologian* (London, 1991), deserves special mention as a full and clear guide.

ness" of religious life can make us overlook entirely the fact that what we are talking about is not an item in any list of objects. This, I think, is what Eckhart is after when he exhorts us to look beyond "God" to "Godness": to look beyond what sounds like a nice ordinary proper name like yours or mine to the more troubling question of the *kind of life* we are speaking of. (Incidentally, the idea that "God" designates a kind of life rather than being the name of an individual is a good medieval scholastic doctrine: Eckhart is just using the less technical vernacular to shock us into thinking harder.)

So we stop thinking about any thises or thats, and in this process our minds become "simplified." They are no longer shaped by one concept or another, but turn into a kind of sheer expectancy, a wanting without any image of the gratification that might satisfy us. It is this level of sheer expectancy that Eckhart often calls the *fünkelein* (the little spark) of the soul, and his habit of talking about this as eternal or uncreated was to guarantee great trouble for him. But it is reasonably clear what he means; this empty longing is not a particular thing, does not have a history or a physiognomy, and so the language we ordinarily use about *things* (the language of time and creation) is irrelevant here. It is perhaps not completely out of the question to connect this with what Paul means by "spirit"—the desire to live in what is not simply a world of jostling essences-in-competition; but this comparison may become clearer later on.

Our thinking about God becomes more and more indefinite, and in this process our own mental identity becomes more and more undetermined. The culmination of Eckhart's scheme is when the point is reached of pure receptivity to the unnameable "Godness," which is the point at which the Word is born in the soul. This latter image, which was to become the common currency of the next generation of Rhineland mystics and is echoed by the early Luther, is perhaps too familiar for us to feel its proper weight. In its context in Eckhart's thought, it is in fact making a theological claim of immense significance for the understanding of "spiritual life." The point is simply that when we have thought away all the specific determinations by which we domesticate God, we arrive not at a featureless absolute but at the source of eternal generativity or fecundity. In something more like Eckhart's own idiom, we can say that when we reach the silence of God, we reach the moment in which God speaks.

Only by getting away from the *language* of God's action can we be properly open to that action. We can talk about the Trinity until the cows come home, but we can only "know" what we are talking about by letting the Word be generated in us—being sufficiently silent to know the simplicity of what sustains our Christian identity, the act of God that generates relation and communion, as it *happens* in us.

It is difficult to compress the rich implications of Eckhart's model into a brief space, but we could characterize the main themes as these. First, God is never without the Word, the act of self-sharing; we cannot arrive at a "pure" divine life before the outpouring of the Word. Second, our struggle to purify our minds in the simplicity of expectant contemplation is not directed to some sort of escape from the world of multiplicity and interaction. Like Augustine, Eckhart uses the rhetoric of Neo-Platonism to overturn it. We open ourselves to silence *so that* we may be brought into the stream of God's active self-imparting, God's "boiling over," as he sometimes puts it. This is not to say that contemplation is a means to action or "better" action: authentic opening of the mind to God only happens when we desire truth for its own sake, not a reinforcement of what we are doing or should like to do. The point was put epigrammatically by the twelfth-century monastic writer William of Saint Thierry: the love of truth drives us from the human world to God; the truth of love sends us from God back to the human world.[3]

If contemplation leads us to the reality of God, it leads us to the God whose being is in self-communicating—not to a monadic stillness but to the mission which is Jesus, the Word now coming to be in us. But here's the catch: to enter this mission requires us first to put aside our projections of how it will be. In other words, it is entirely right to say that the contemplative path, especially in its most drastically negative forms, is undertaken for its own sake, out of disinterested longing for the truthfulness of God to overcome our self-deceptions. Yet to undertake it at all presupposes the motion toward us of God, presupposes that my falsehood can be purged by something other than my ideas, that

---

3 See, for example, his *On Contemplating God*, 1, and *Meditation* 11:13 in vol. 3 of the Cistercian Fathers Series (Spencer, Mass., 1971).

the truth of God is in some sense active. This means that to receive that truth is to be taken into that action, into generation, incarnation, and the work of the kingdom. An unlikely conclusion to emerge from a reading of Eckhart? Only, I think, if we ignore the "dramatic" nature of Eckhart's rhetoric and the full implication of the image of the Word's birth in us. And if I read correctly, the link with Paul's conception of spirit should now be clearer: spirit is what wants the kingdom, and so desires to realize the humanity of Jesus in its own act and being. And the goal that, in Eckhart, the contemplating subject desires without definition is the divine act which is Christ, and so the communion of the kingdom.

The idea that what we (unhelpfully) call "mysticism" is, in the Christian framework, necessarily oriented toward incarnation and can be amply documented in a good many writers, notably Teresa of Avila. As I've recently tried to show, the structure of her *Interior Castle* is very much presupposed by William of Saint Thierry: a journey "inwards" to the hidden God at the soul's center, a journey that concludes in union with the *incarnating* God.[4] Union is a fusion of the gifts of Mary and Martha and entails an acceptance of the conditions of mortal life instead of a rebellion against them (Paul's account of spirit and "mortal flesh" comes to mind again). Teresa provides an exceptionally vivid and consistent picture, but for all her pithy skepticism in *Interior Castle* about religious fluency, she is seldom seen as a figure in the apophatic tradition. However, if we turn to John of the Cross, unquestionably the most rigorous exponent of spiritual iconoclasm at every level, we can find at least some elements of the same structure, the same refusal of a static or monistic conclusion to the spirit's struggle for the truth.

The clues are to be found in the *Ascent of Mount Carmel*. John here invokes the traditional threefold division of the subject into memory, understanding, and will, and explains, in good Augustinian style, that our problem is that these are attached to inadequate objects. They are made for God, and so must be firmly pried away from created objects. In John's scheme, this involves both the "active" darkness of our self-dispossession and a

---

4 Rowan Williams, *Teresa of Avila* (London, 1991), chp. 4.

"passive" darkness, a letting-go of control at a very deep and disturbing level, so that we are left with no clear image of ourselves, let alone God. Beyond this lies the state in which God is the object of our mental life: memory is transformed into hope, understanding into faith, and will into love.

We can already see here that the goal to which we move is not—as some seem to think—an objectless and timeless bliss for the solitary subject, but the state of a self engaged (in communion). This state is described very tellingly here and elsewhere, in the language of St. Paul. It seems at first as though it is a self simply engaged with God rather than with creation. And it is indeed hard to shake off the impression in reading John that he is a stranger to Teresa's very clearly delineated picture of an incarnational "trajectory" in which we are taken up. I don't think John can be wholly acquitted: he is both more systematic and less integrated than Teresa in his account of the spirit's growth, and he is less worried than Teresa by the rhetoric of dissatisfaction with bodiliness and earthly finitude.

Two bits of his writing stand out, however, as pointing us in the same direction as Eckhart and Teresa. In the *Ascent* he urges the soul on to the path of dispossession as a necessary element in imitating Christ. We are told that Christ's dereliction on the cross, the point when he is "brought to nothing" in body and in spirit, is the moment at which he is most supremely *active* in the salvation of the world. It seems clear here that the utter dispossession of Jesus' death, his own reaching the point of emptiness, is the occasion for God's mission to come to its final fullness. In the void of Calvary, the world is remade or, at least, its concrete remaking begins.

What exactly is God's work here? What is the remaking of the world? We can turn to the second of our texts for illumination: this is the sequence of lyrics, usually called the *Romanzas,* dealing with the purpose of creation and the incarnation of the Word; they are poetically very simple, almost naive in style, but extraordinarily subtle in theology. In the *Romanzas,* creation exists primarily to receive the overflowing of the eternal relation of Father and Son: it is the Son's designated bride. By the world's *bridal* communion with the Son, it enters the *filial* relation of the Word to the Word's Source—an original and striking nuancing of the fundamental idea of communion.[5]

Surprisingly, there is no explicit reference to sin and the fall: creation suffers, not so much because of sin but because of its unfulfilled longing for the bridal relation to be consummated. Thus the incarnation is above all the crown of the creation: when the Word is united with a human identity, creation enters into its heritage, becomes what it was made to be—the partner of the Word, united to the Word's relationship of joy and intimacy with the Father. It is perhaps worth noticing that the imagery of incarnation as a "bridal" union is also found in Teresa's *Meditations on the Song of Songs*. As in the cradle at Bethlehem, humanity and divinity are bound together: the Word weeps for the pain and grief of human beings, human beings are granted a share in the joy and fruition of the divinity.

God's saving work, then, is this exchange and this perfection of shared bliss; this is the work completed on Calvary, where the human vulnerability of the Word is brought to its mortal climax. In the emptiness and stripping of Jesus' death, we understand and are touched by the love that keeps nothing back, that does not claim and defend a place over against us in the world but is unequivocally *for* us. We are encountered by the perfect being-for-the-other that is God's life, and which, while we can only meet it in what seems appalling destitution, is nonetheless the fullness of God. The themes are tightly interwoven. The joyful mutual gift of Source and Word can only appear in the mortal world as "obedience unto death"; Christ's destitution calls forth our setting out on the path of risk and loss, our journey into darkness; only in the heart of the darkness is the union consummated that brings us into the active life of God. What is generated in that darkness is not only faith, hope and charity, but a world newly related to God—that is, a world seen afresh and loved properly (something at which John hints in his commentary on the *Spiritual Canticle* stanzas).

John's picture of what it is that "spirituality" moves toward can be seen, then, as complementing Eckhart's and adding a further dimension to the definition of "spirit" as that in us which is oriented to the communion of the kingdom. What spirit desires

---

5 I am greatly indebted here to the insights of my former student Fr. Iain Mathew, OCD.

is what the incarnation realizes, the marriage of heaven and earth. We might also pick up John's hints about new ways of seeing the created order to fill this out further. The soul that is passing through the "dark night," the soul being changed into faith, hope and charity, is letting go of its attachment to the objects of this world. Initially this means—as in the early sections of his *Spiritual Canticle*—that we come to see all things speaking to us of a single absence: God has "passed by," leaving the traces of beauty behind in the path. We see a fundamental *lack* in the world while we are still seeking to let go; as long as we are still wrestling with the problems of desire and gratification, the world will be perceived as not meeting our desire, and so pointing beyond. But the more our desire becomes (as in Eckhart) sheer expectancy without the fantasy of a satisfying object, the more free we are to find the material world a gift. It doesn't *have* to "satisfy" us: the more our desire is for God, the more we can allow the stuff of the world to be what it is, not to be only the raw material for the ego and fulfillment. In this sense, the "negative way" leads directly to the acceptance of the otherness and density of a world we do not and cannot master. Communion is possible with our material environment as well as with God and the human other; this too belongs with our reflection on mission. God's purpose for community is undermined if reconciliation with the human other has nothing to do with the material life around—corporate human egotism is no better than individual.

This is what I meant by saying that I hoped to challenge the dichotomy between "negative" and "positive" in spirituality. John, like others, suggests that the true apprehension of the world as gift, letting it be itself, presupposes the disciplines of silence and destitution. For the creative Word to be born in our relation with our environment, we have to confront the same journey, the same stripping and questioning, as in our relation with God and each other. This is why, incidentally, I am not sympathetic to the glib affirmativeness of some of what we call "creation spirituality." If the truthful seeing and loving of the created order requires of us a radical self-displacement, a "night" of sense and spirit, there is no single dissolution possible of the tension between affirmation and denial, no paradisiacal and undialectical access to "original blessing." Creation spirituality has done much to remind us of the scope of full reconciliation with body and matter so often ignored or distorted, and the significance of Eckhart for Matthew Fox in particular guarantees that elements of dialectic and negation are not completely swept aside. The overall rhetoric, however, remains too optimistic and indulgent.

Let me try to sum up the direction of these lectures and draw a moral or two for what we might want to say about evangelism. What the church has to communicate is the reality of new humanity and new creation, a reality only communicated in the facts of corporate life and the invitation they carry (or fail to carry). How exactly the communion of the church can enter into and transform the situations in which Christians live is not something the church can project or control. The action is God's, since God alone can radically overcome our servitude to fear and rivalry. In order to sustain our refusal to become enslaved afresh by anxieties and fantasies about success, we need to give the fullest possible weight to the disciplines of silence, in which the profoundly expectant movement toward the central truth of God's generative and generous act, beyond our organized words, begins.

This implies *first* that evangelism is not identical with techniques and programs of church growth; it is important not to confuse mission with adding recruits to the institution. There may well be a certain mystique of failure that we need to combat, a romantic feeling for the idea of a tiny, faithful remnant, which is clearly a rationalizing of the perception that a church is not making a difference. Against this, we can properly argue that a church that produces no visible sign in its inner life or its vicinity of the extending of communion or the challenging or breaking of competitive and destructive patterns of life is a church that ought to ask itself whether it is really in love with the kingdom. But such work may or may not mean "success" by conventional ecclesiastical criteria.

Let me refer here to Vincent Donovan's second book, *The Church in the Midst of Creation,* and above all to its vivid conclusion: a fictionalized account of how an inner-city black Catholic parish becomes a radically different kind of community. Out of new levels of shared worship and reflection, that parish becomes a focus for patient commitments to change, both local and global, vulnerable commitments with small chance of triumphing, but indispensable points of promise. No dramatic revivalist successes occur, and the issue of membership in one or another Christian institution comes to be seen as irrelevant. But there is a firmly anchored practice of eucharist and meditation, an implied theology of where God's act is directed, and so a difference made. Communities like this exist, and they (along with those other expressions of communion mentioned earlier, the L'Arche group, the hospice, and so on) tell us most of what we really ought to know about mission.

Second, this should make us look very hard at what our anxieties are in the church. The quite widespread suspicion, not least in the Anglican churches, that numerical decline just might be arrested if we could guarantee firmer and clearer teaching on faith and morals is understandable but is, at best, a seductive half-truth. On the one hand, a church that has no conception of the rationale of its existence, of what kind of difference it is or might be making, is a depressing spectacle: without the conviction of gift and judgment, and the vision of a humanity converging on Christ, there is no *excuse* for the church. If it doesn't exist for the sake of something other than itself, if it is not to be held answerable for what it is and does, we are simply faced with an institution whose corruption and folly has cost the human race more than it can afford. On the other hand, grasping that rationale is itself to see why clarion calls to traditional faithfulness for the sake of success are faithless. A theology of the cross or the dark night carries with it a good many doctrinal implications, and to live within such a theology needs disciplines of thought and imagination; it is not merely a vague religious sensibility. Yet living within it prohibits or should prohibit the mentality of ideological uniformity and insistent statements of conviction. If the theology of the cross cannot be shown in lives of dispossession and expectancy, there is no use talking about it; where it is shown, it enforces humility in what we say.

The nexus between mission and spirituality I am trying to delineate is a place where our categories of liberalism and traditionalism should be brought seriously into question. Deploying those categories confidently and uncritically leaves little room either for proper theology or for what is perhaps the most central and disturbing and genuinely *theological* question we could ask, "How do I know it's *God* I'm talking about?"

The Welsh philosopher and pupil of Wittgenstein, Rush Rhees, observed a good many years ago that there was no object you could point to that would settle that question. The burden of this second lecture has been to suggest that there are practices and styles of life that at least make some sense of the question, for in the very act of *asking* that question radically and persistently, we show something of what the word "God" means that cannot be shown by conceptual refinement or pious enthusiasm. The challenge for the theologian, pastor, or preacher, indeed for every even faintly articulate Christian, is to find a speech that allows this question to be heard—not as a moment of corrosive doubt or comfortable uncertainty, but as a kind of confessional pointing to the truth that can reconstitute our words and our human bonds.

Cowley Publications is a ministry of the Society of Saint John the Evangelist, a religious community of men in the Episcopal Church. Emerging from the Society's tradition of prayer, theological reflection, and diversity of mission, the press is centered in the rich heritage of the Anglican Communion.

Cowley Publications seeks to provide books, audio cassettes, CDs, and other resources for the ongoing theological exploration and spiritual development of the Episcopal Church and others in the body of Christ. To this end, it is dedicated to developing a new generation of theological writers, encouraging them to produce timely, creative, and stimulating publications of excellence, and making these publications available widely, reaching both clergy and lay persons.